The

NORTON MIX

W · W · NORTON & COMPANY · *New York · London*

The
NORTON MIX

A CUSTOM PUBLICATION

A-B TECH

W. W. Norton & Company has been independent since its founding in 1923, when William Warder Norton and Mary D. Herter Norton first published lectures delivered at the People's Institute, the adult education division of New York City's Cooper Union. The firm soon expanded its program beyond the Institute, publishing books by celebrated academics from America and abroad. By mid-century, the two major pillars of Norton's publishing program— trade books and college texts—were firmly established. In the 1950s, the Norton family transferred control of the company to its employees, and today—with a staff of four hundred and a comparable number of trade, college, and professional titles published each year— W. W. Norton & Company stands as the largest and oldest publishing house owned wholly by its employees.

Printed in the United States of America

Editor: Katie Hannah
Developmental editors: Mike Fleming and Erin Granville
Managing editor: Marian Johnson
Project editor: Melissa Atkin
Editorial assistant: Sophie Hagen
Production managers: Eric Pier-Hocking and Ashley Horna
Permissions editor: Nancy Rodwan
Photo permissions editor: Trish Marx, Stephanie Romeo
Designer: Toni Krass
Cover designs: Debra Morton-Hoyt
Emedia editor: Eileen Connell
Marketing manager: Scott Berzon
Proofreaders: Paulette McGee, Ben Reynolds
Composition: RR Donnelley
Manufacturing: RR Donnelley

ISBN-13 978-0-393-27827-9

W. W. Norton & Company, Inc., 500 Fifth Avenue, New York, N.Y. 10110
www.wwnorton.com
W. W. Norton & Company Ltd., Castle House, 75/76 Wells Street, London W1T 3QT

GENERAL EDITORS

ELIZABETH RODRIGUEZ KESSLER
COORDINATING EDITOR
University of Houston

JEFFREY ANDELORA
Mesa Community College

MELISSA GOLDTHWAITE
St. Joseph's University

CHARLES HOOD
Antelope Valley College

KATHARINE N. INGS
Manchester College

ANGELA L. JONES
Western Kentucky University

CHRISTOPHER KELLER
University of Texas–Pan American

WITH CONTRIBUTIONS FROM

CEDRIC BURROWS
University of Kansas

LORI CHASTAINE
Boise State University

MICHELLE L. CHESTER
Towson University

DENNIS McGLOTHIN
University of North Carolina at Pembroke

WANDA FRIES
Somerset Community College

HOLLY HASSEL
University of Wisconsin–Marathon County

BETH DINATALE JOHNSON
Ursuline College

Contents

KAREN ARMSTRONG { *Is a Holy War Inevitable?*

KAREN ARMSTRONG (b. 1944) grew up in Bromsgrove and Birmingham, England. At seventeen, she became a nun in a teaching order, which eventually sent her to study English at St. Anne's College, Oxford University. While an undergraduate there, Armstrong left the order after seven years of service. Since then Armstrong has written many books and articles on comparative religion, including *The Battle for God: Fundamentalism in Judaism, Christianity and Islam* (2000). She has also written memoirs: *Through the Narrow Gate* (1982) is an account of her difficult years as a nun; *The Spiral Staircase: My Climb Out of Darkness* (2004) documents her struggle with epilepsy. She has advised the television host Bill Moyers on his PBS series on religion and has addressed both the United States Congress and the UN's inaugural session on religion.

In this essay from 2002, Armstrong examines the roots of Islamic fundamentalism and challenges her readers to reconsider fundamentalism and the Muslim world's path to modernity. She argues that Muslim extremism results not from hatred of America but from hatred of American policy. As you read, consider how Armstrong's definitions of *fundamentalism*, *jihad*, and the *Great Satan* help explain the tensions between the Muslim and Western worlds.

ALTHOUGH UNCERTAINTIES REMAIN ABOUT THE causes and effects of the terror that has gripped the Western world since September 11, one fact is clear: We are feeling the onslaught of a nihilistic Muslim rage. How deep are its roots, and how far might it go? Many Western leaders and thinkers, struggling to distinguish between "good" and "bad" Muslims, see the rage rooted in Islamic cultures. Some feel a civilizational inevitability: that Islam is entirely incompatible with Western culture and that the West has long been heading for a major confrontation with the Islamic world.

The roots, first, are not as ancient as some of the pundits imagine. But they are substantive. Since the late 1960s, the Islamic world has been convulsed by a fundamentalism that seems to fill Muslims with an atavistic rage against the West in general and the United States in particular. During the Islamic Revolution in Iran (1978–79), we saw mass crowds clutching copies of the Koran[1] and yelling "Death to America!" We heard the United States denounced as "the Great Satan." Though the level of enmity toward the West has decreased in Iran, in other circles it has become more intense, as the attacks of September 11 painfully show. Still, in the aftermath of that tragedy, the word *fundamentalism* has frequently been used imprecisely and in ways that are misleading. It is often equated with extremism and terror, but in fact only a tiny proportion of religious fundamentalists resort to violence. The vast majority are simply struggling to live truly religious lives in a world that seems increasingly inimical to faith.

Fundamentalism is often described as a Muslim phenomenon, but during the twentieth century this militant type of piety erupted in every major faith worldwide, so that we have not only Christian fundamentalism but also Jewish, Sikh, Hindu, Buddhist and even Confucian forms. The first fundamentalist movement developed in Christian circles in the United States at the turn of the twentieth century, whereas fundamentalism did not appear in the Muslim world until the late 1960s. This is not surprising, since fundamentalism is essentially a revolt against modern secular civilization. In almost every region where a Western-style society has established itself, a religious counterculture has grown alongside in conscious reaction. That is why fundamentalism appeared first in North America, the showcase of modernity, and could develop in the Middle East only after a degree of modernization had been achieved.

[1]The principal religious text of Islam.

Fundamentalists seek to drag God and religion from the sidelines to which they have been relegated in a secular polity and pull them back to center stage. Every fundamentalist movement I have studied, in Judaism, Christianity and Islam, is rooted in a profound fear of annihilation—a conviction that the liberal, secularist establishment wants to wipe out religion. This is as true of militant Christian groups in the United States as it is of Muslim extremists in Egypt and Iran. Fundamentalists believe they are fighting for survival, and when people feel that their backs are to the wall, they can lash out violently like a wounded animal.

One thing we in the West have to learn to appreciate is that disenchantment with modern society is fairly widespread. Those of us who enjoy modern society and value its freedoms and privileges need to realize that not everybody shares our enthusiasm. We must reflect seriously on the ubiquity of this fundamentalist disaffection. In Britain, where there is little interest in traditional faith, there is virtually no fundamentalism, because people do not express their discontent in a religious manner. But British soccer hooliganism reveals the same brew of emotions that fuels many fundamentalist movements: pent-up rage, frustration, a desire to belong to a clearly defined group, burning humiliation and a sense of lost prestige that on occasion can erupt into shameful violence. 5

These fears may seem irrational, but the history of fundamentalism shows that this aggressive new religiosity is not going to go away. Attempts to suppress fundamentalism simply make it more extreme. September 11 showed that the people who feel compelled to take part in this battle for God are moved by a level of distress, anxiety and, sometimes, fury that no society, no government, can safely ignore.

• ○ •

It wasn't always like this. When Muslims first became fully aware of Western modernity, they seemed to "recognize" it at a profound level. During the nineteenth and early twentieth centuries, almost every single Muslim intellectual was full of admiration for the new West. Islamic thinkers of the day wanted their countries to be just like Britain and France. In 1906 many of the leading ulama (religious scholars) in Iran joined secularists in a revolution demanding a constitution and parliamentary rule modeled on those of Europe. Any system that could reduce the tyranny of the shahs was clearly compatible with Shiite Islam. The nineteenth-century Egyptian writer Rifa'ah al-Tahtawi was enthralled by the ideas of the European Enlightenment, which reminded him of the teachings of the great Muslim philosophers. He loved the way everything worked properly in Paris, was impressed by the systematic education of French children and the literacy of the common people. In India, Sayyid Ahmad Khan (1817–1898) tried to adapt the ideals of Islam to modern Western liberalism. He founded a college at Aligarh,[2] where Muslims could study science and English alongside their traditional Islamic subjects. This would help Muslims live in a modernized society without becoming inferior copies of the British, since they would retain a sense of their own cultural identity.

In the Islamic world, however, disenchantment with the West and its accelerating form of modernity became more widespread during the twentieth century. What is it about modernity that fills so many people all over the world with visceral dread? Modernization, we are apt to forget, is a traumatic process. In Europe and the United States, it took us some 300 years to develop our secular and democratic institutions. Starting in the sixteenth century, we began creating a new form of civilization. Economically, it was based not on a surplus of agricultural produce, as all premodern civilizations had been, but on technology and the constant reinvestment of capital. This enabled us to reproduce our resources indefinitely and thus freed us from the constraints of the more vulnerable traditional agrarian cultures. But because this was such a major social undertaking, it required change in almost every sphere of life—political, social, economic, intellectual and religious—which was often accompanied by pain and bloodshed. Political institutions had to be altered to accommodate these new conditions. In the West, it was found, by trial and error, that a modern state had to be democratic, secular and tolerant—but this trial and error had grave costs. Europe and America both witnessed revolutions, which were sometimes succeeded by reigns of terror. As we made the painful rite of passage to modernity—which did

[2]A city in India about ninety miles southeast of New Delhi; it is known as a university town.

not come into its own until the nineteenth century—we experienced fearful wars of religion, genocide, persecution of minorities, exploitation of workers in factories, despoliation of the countryside and anomie and spiritual disorientation in the slums of the newly industrialized cities. Today we are witnessing similar distress in developing countries that are now in the throes of this transformation.

In Europe and America, the emerging modern spirit had two main characteristics. The first was independence. Modernization was accompanied by declarations of independence on all fronts: political, religious, scientific and intellectual. People could no longer be constrained by coercive governments or churches; they had to have the freedom to follow their ideas and projects wherever they might lead, a luxury no previous society could afford. The second characteristic was innovation. The West also came to accept—even value—institutionalized change. In the more vulnerable premodern economies, it had always been more important to conserve what had been achieved. But now the people of the West came to find a virtue in the pace of change—we were always creating something fresh and breaking into uncharted realms, and despite the inherent difficulties, this gave our lives a wholly new excitement. Instead of looking back at past achievements, we were continually thrusting forward into the future.

The modernization process has been very different in the Muslim world. Modernity came not with independence but with political and economic subjection. Muslim countries were colonized by the European powers, organized into mandates or protectorates and reduced to a dependent bloc. Instead of innovation, their modern experience was one of imitation, since Western countries were so far ahead that Muslim modernizers could only copy us. Lagging behind and endlessly trying to play catch-up, Muslim countries found their own way to modernity. Because the process has been so different, so too has been the end product. Democratic, liberal, secular societies could not automatically emerge in these more problematic circumstances. 10

Modernization has also been too rapid in the Muslim world, and inevitably, the new ideas have not been able to filter down gradually to all sectors of the population as they did in the West. Muslim countries have been split unhealthily into two camps: an elite, who have received a Western-style education and can understand the new norms and institutions, and the vast majority who have not. Because the process has been so accelerated, the secularization of society, the separation of religion and politics, has been experienced by religious people as a deadly assault. Thus when Atatürk (1881–1938), the founder of the Turkish republic, was creating modern secular Turkey, he closed all the madrasahs, the colleges of Islamic education, abolished the orders of Sufi mystics, which had played a crucial role in the social and spiritual lives of the people, and forced the Sufis underground. Men and women were compelled to wear Western dress, because Atatürk wanted the country to look modern. In Iran the shahs had their soldiers go through the streets, taking off Muslim women's veils with their bayonets and tearing them to pieces. In 1935, Reza Shah Pahlavi gave his soldiers orders to shoot at hundreds of unarmed demonstrators at the holy shrine of Mashhad who were peacefully protesting against obligatory Western dress. His son Muhammad Reza shot down hundreds of madrasah students who dared to protest against his dictatorship, and leading clerics were tortured to death, imprisoned or exiled. In such forceful circumstances, secularism is not the liberating polity we have experienced in the West. It is invasive and frightening, an attack on one's way of life.

This has been keenly felt in Egypt. The Egyptian ideologue Sayyid Qutb (1906–1966)[3] founded the most influential form of fundamentalism in Sunni Islam (the version of the faith followed by the majority of Muslims). Qutb had once greatly admired Western culture and secular politics, had been a moderate, eager to reform Egypt. In 1953 he joined the Muslim Brotherhood, a welfare society intent on religious and social reform, only to watch President Gamal Abdel Nasser imprison, torture and execute thousands of Brothers, often without trial and for doing nothing more incriminating than attending a meeting or handing out leaflets. Spending years in vile concentration camps made him a radical, determined to fight against the corrupt secularism of Nasser and his

[3]Egyptian author and leading intellectual of the Egyptian Muslim Brotherhood; regarded as a martyr, his writings, mainly extensive commentaries on the Koran, became the theoretical base for Al Qaeda, a Sunni Muslim extremist movement.

counterparts in the Muslim world. He was executed by Nasser in 1966, but his ideology has shaped most Sunni fundamentalists, including Osama bin Laden.

The case of Qutb shows us the path fundamentalism invariably takes. Fundamentalism always begins as an internal struggle. It is an intrareligious conflict, in that fundamentalists start by attacking their own coreligionists and fellow countrymen. Qutb was sickened by the colonial activities of the French and the British in North Africa and the Middle East, and he had been disillusioned by a visit to the United States, whose culture seemed to him trivial, decadent and materialistic. But Qutb did not become a fundamentalist until he saw his country overtaken by an ethos that seemed cruel, tyrannical and corrupt. Similarly, bin Laden's original targets were the so-called Muslim regimes of Saudi Arabia, Egypt, Jordan and Iran, which he regarded as defecting from the Islamic norm. It was only at a later stage that bin Laden turned his attention to the United States, which supports many of these regimes and which he now regards as the root of the problem.

So Muslim fundamentalism was not originally inspired by a hatred of America per se, but it has become increasingly disturbed by the role of the United States in Islamic countries. This was certainly the case in Iran. Americans were understandably shocked to hear their nation described as "the Great Satan." But Westerners—particularly Christian Westerners—misread that phrase. In Christianity, Satan is a figure of absolute, towering evil, and though the policy of the United States was often shortsighted, exploitative and self-interested, it did not deserve to be stigmatized in this way. But in popular Shiism, the Shaitan is a rather pathetic creature, incapable of appreciating spirituality. In one folk legend, he complains to God that humans are acquiring gifts that he wants for himself. He would like to have a scripture and beautifully illuminated manuscripts; God tells him to get himself a few tattoos. He wants to have a mosque, so God tells him to go to the bazaar. He wants prophets, and God fobs him off with fortune-tellers. And the Shaitan is quite happy with these inferior gifts. He is incurably trivial, trapped forever in the realm of the exterior and unable to see that there is a deeper and more important dimension to life. For many Iranians, America, the Great Shaitan, was "the Great Trivializer." The bars, casinos and the secularist ethos of north Tehran, the Americanized zone, seemed to be the abode of the superficial and materialistic Shaitan. The Great Satan was a joke, and its icons were often ridiculous: a giant figure of Ronald Reagan in an Uncle Sam outfit.

Furthermore, the word *Shaitan* means "tempter." America, it was thought, had tempted the shah away from the true values of Islam to a life of unspiritual secularism. Rightly or wrongly, Iranians believed that the shah would not have behaved so tyrannically toward his people had he not been assured of the unconditional support of the United States. The image of the Great Satan, therefore, did not reflect a hatred of American culture in itself; Iranians simply did not want to see this materialism in their own country. Nor did they want their destinies to be controlled by the Great Tempter of the shah. 15

The same kind of precise symbolism underlay the capture of the American hostages in the United States embassy in Tehran. Since an embassy is considered native soil, the siege amounted to an invasion of American sovereignty. Yet to some Iranians, it seemed appropriate that American citizens should be held captive in their own embassy, because for decades, under the Pahlavi shahs,[4] Iranians felt they had been held prisoner in their own country, with the connivance of the United States.

But this is revenge, not religion. Hostage taking is repugnant to Western values, and not unnaturally many Americans assumed Islam condones such behavior and must, therefore, be an immoral creed. But when he refused to return the hostages, Ayatollah Khomeini[5] was violating clear legislation in the Koran. The Koran demands that Muslims treat their opponents humanely. It is unlawful to take prisoners, except during the fighting of a regular war. Prisoners must not be ill-treated and should be released after hostilities have come to an end. If no ransom is forthcoming, the prisoner must be allowed to earn money to pay the sum himself, and his captor is urged to help him out of his own pocket (Koran 8:68, 47:5, 24:34, 2:178). A tradition has preserved the

[4]Rulers of Iran from the Pahlavi family dynasty.

[5]Ruholla Khomeini (1900–89), Shia Muslim leader (Ayatollah) and Iranian head of state; in 1979, following the deposition of the shah, Khomeini returned from exile to lead the Iranian revolution and impose strict Islamic rule.

Prophet's directions about the treatment of captives: "You must feed them as you feed yourselves, and clothe them as you clothe yourselves, and if you should set them a hard task, you must help them in it yourselves." This is the true teaching of Islam, and it is clearly close to the Western ideal.

This example reminds us that fundamentalism very often distorts the tradition it is trying to defend. Because fundamentalists believe they are facing a massive threat to their faith, they can accentuate the more intransigent elements of their scriptures and downplay those that speak of compassion and benevolence. It would be a great mistake to assume that fundamentalist discourse represents the rich and complex traditions of Islam or to imagine that the Muslim faith is adamantly opposed to our values. In fact, it shares most of the central tenets of the Judeo-Christian traditions that have shaped our culture. We are not speaking here about a clash of civilizations that are essentially opposed. We are much closer to Muslims than we imagine.

There are passages in the Koran that seem to give license to unfettered violence, and we have all heard bin Laden quoting these. But in the Koran, these verses are in almost every case followed by exhortations to peace and mercy. The Koran teaches that the only valid war is one of self-defense, which is clearly in line with the Western notion of the just war. War is always abhorrent and evil, but it is sometimes necessary to fight in order to preserve decent values or to defend oneself against persecution.

20

Nor would it be fair to say Muslims are incapable of separating religion and politics. For much of their history, Muslims effected a de facto separation of what we would call church and state. During the Abbasid caliphate (750–1258)—when Baghdad was the capital of the Islamic world—the court was ruled by an aristocratic ethos, which had little to do with Islam. Indeed the shari'a, the system of Islamic holy law, initially developed as a countercultural revolt against this ethos. The clerics and the ruling class thus operated according to entirely different norms. Though secularism as practiced in the West has since acquired sinister connotations, Islam is a realistic faith; it understands that politics is a messy business that can corrupt religion. In Shiite Islam, religion and politics were separated as a matter of sacred principle.

Nor is Islam inherently opposed to the democratic ideal. It is true that fundamentalists, be they Jewish, Christian or Muslim, have little time for democracy, since their militant beliefs are not typical of any of these faiths' traditions. It is also true that Muslims would have difficulty with the classic definition of democracy, as "government of the people, by the people and for the people." In Islam, God, not the people, gives a government legitimacy, and this elevation of humanity could seem a usurpation of God's sovereignty. But Muslim countries could well introduce representative governments without relying on this Western slogan. This is what is beginning to happen in Iran, which had never been permitted to have a fully functioning parliament before the Islamic Revolution. In fact, Muslim thinkers have pointed out that Islamic laws have principles that are eminently compatible with democracy. The notion of *shura,* for example, which decrees that there must be some form of "consultation" with the people before new legislation can be passed, is clearly congenial to the democratic ideal, as is ijma, the "consensus" of the people, which gives legitimacy to a legal decision.

Even today, when so many Muslims feel alienated by American foreign policy, important and influential thinkers emphasize the kinship that exists between Islam and Western thought. President Mohammad Khatami of Iran is an obvious example; immediately after his landslide election victory in 1997, he made it clear that he wanted to build stronger links to the West, and that he represented a platform that stood for greater pluralism, more democracy and improved rights for women. The leading Iranian intellectual, Abdolkarim Sorush, who held office under Khomeini, argues that Iranians have a Western as well as an Iranian identity. He rejects the secularism of the West and insists that Iranians hold on to their Shiite identity. But he also believes that traditional Islamic law must evolve to embrace a philosophy of civil rights.

In the Sunni world, the Tunisian thinker Rashid al-Ghannouchi describes himself as a "democratic Islamist." Muslims, he believes, want modernity, but not one that has been imposed upon them by America, Britain or France. They admire the efficiency and technology of the West but want to hold on to their own religious and moral traditions while incorporating some of the best aspects of Western civilization. Similarly, Yusuf al-Qaradawi, currently at the University of

Qatar, preaches moderation and is adamantly opposed to the extremism that has recently appeared in the Muslim world. This fundamentalist intolerance will impoverish the Muslim people, by depriving them of the insights and visions of other human beings.

Qaradawi argues, "It is better for the West that Muslims should be religious, hold to their religion and try to be moral." He makes an important point. Like any other great world religion, Islam has helped Muslims to cultivate decent values. The religion does not preach bigotry and hatred but justice, compassion and peace. The Koran has a pluralistic vision and respects other faiths. Constantly, it insists that Muhammad has not come to cancel out the revelations of such earlier prophets as Abraham, Moses and Jesus. God commands Muslims to "speak courteously" to Jews and Christians, "the People of the Book," and to tell them: "We believe what you believe; your God and our God is one" (Koran 29:46). Alongside the more intransigent and fundamentalist voices that fill us all with fear have always been Muslims such as Tahtawi, Sorush, Ghannouchi and Qaradawi, who recognize this relationship, even in these difficult days. Unlike the fundamentalists, these moderate Muslim thinkers, who are every bit as influential, if not more so, than bin Laden and his like, have not become repelled by our modern Western society but still see it as deeply compatible with the Islamic ideal.

25 The bedrock message of the Koran is that it is wrong for Muslims to stockpile their wealth selfishly and good to share their resources equally. Since the time of the Prophet Muhammad, Islamic piety and spirituality have been inspired by the ideal of a just society, in which the poor and vulnerable are treated with respect. Such a goal is obviously close to Western aspirations, and the search for a more just and, therefore, safer world could bring us closer to Muslims today.

Both Qaradawi and Ghannouchi assume, however, that there is no religion in the secular West. As Ghannouchi said, Muslims see no light, no heart and no spirituality when they look at Western culture. But they are wrong. Many Europeans may have little interest in conventional faith, but the United States is a deeply religious country. Every time I land on American soil, I am struck anew by this fact. But the Muslim world sees the West at its worst. It sees the bars, nightclubs and materialism of "the Great Satan," which are alien to its culture. It has also experienced the West, led by the United States, as coercive and exploitative. Muslims find American policy difficult to square with true faith, which, according to the Koran, must go hand in hand with the pursuit of justice. At the time of the Iranian Revolution, the clerics were astonished that President Jimmy Carter, a religious man who was so passionate about human rights, supported the shah, who denied his people rights that most Americans take for granted.

All over the world, Muslims have been outraged by the carnage of September 11, which violates the essential principles of Islam. But many feel bitter about American policy in their region, and as we have seen, it is this, rather than a dislike for Western modernity and democracy, that fuels fundamentalist rage.

In all three monotheistic religions, fundamentalism is becoming more extreme. In the United States, the movements known as Reconstructionism and Christian Identity have left Jerry Falwell's[6] Moral Majority far behind. They both, in different ways, look forward to the destruction of the democratic federal government and would not be too unhappy about the burning towers of the World Trade Center. As September 11 showed, Islamic fundamentalism has also entered a more radical phase, which has outstripped Sayyid Qutb and Ayatollah Khomeini and embraced a totally nihilistic vision.

This is a dangerous moment. It is crucial that we convince those millions of Muslims who abhor the September atrocities but have been alienated from the United States that Americans are indeed religious, because they share this monotheistic passion for a just world. The word *jihad* does not primarily mean "holy war." It means "struggle, effort." Muslims have to make a strenuous effort to implement God's will in a flawed and tragic world. It is a jihad that must be conducted on all fronts: political, spiritual, moral, intellectual and social. The Prophet Muhammad once said on returning from a battle: "We are returning from the lesser jihad [the battle] to the greater jihad," the far

[6]American televangelist and conservative political commentator (1933–2007); in 1979 he cofounded the Moral Majority, a Christian lobbyist organization that was influential in the Republican Party throughout the 1980s.

more difficult and crucial effort to reform our own hearts, our own attitudes and our own societies. In our present crisis, we have begun the lesser jihad in Afghanistan,[7] but we must make sure we conduct a greater jihad and scrutinize our own conduct and our own policies, in the interests of peace.

[7]The American military invaded Afghanistan and overthrew the Islamist Taliban regime in 2001, shortly before this article was first published.

ISAAC ASIMOV { *Thinking About Thinking*

ISAAC ASIMOV (1920–1992) was born in Russia and immigrated to New York City with his family at age three. A self-taught reader who read science fiction as a youth, he earned a PhD in biochemistry from Columbia in 1949, then joined the faculty at Boston University's School of Medicine. While a faculty member, he turned increasingly toward his lifelong passion for writing imaginative fiction. Best known for the seven novels in his *Foundation* series, Asimov was one of the most acclaimed science fiction writers of the twentieth century. However, his interests were broad and he also wrote extensively on history, religion, literature, and many other topics. He is credited with authoring or editing more than five hundred books in his lifetime.

In this selection from *The Planet That Wasn't* (1976), a collection of his nonfiction writing, Asimov attacks the popular notion that intelligence can be measured by a universal test. He asserts that intelligence tests measure only the skills that those who make the tests consider relevant—skills, he says that reflect the values and prejudices of the test designers' culture. Asimov argues that these IQ tests therefore define intelligence subjectively, and he explores the implications of this subjectivity for African Americans and other marginalized groups. As you read, consider how Asimov uses personal experience to support his argument.

NOW, THEN, WE COME TO the matter of intelligence-testing, the determination of the "intelligence quotient" or "IQ."

If, as I maintain and firmly believe, there is no objective definition of intelligence, and what we call intelligence is only a creation of cultural fashion and subjective prejudice, what the devil is it we test when we make use of an intelligence test?

I hate to knock the intelligence test, because I am a beneficiary of it. I routinely end up on the far side of 160 when I am tested and even then I am invariably underestimated because it almost always takes me less time to do a test than the time allotted.

In fact, out of curiosity, I got a paperback book containing a sizable number of different tests designed to measure one's IQ. Each test had a half-hour time limit. I worked on each one as honestly as I could, answering some questions instantly, some after a bit of thought, some by guesswork, and some not at all.—And naturally, I got some answers wrong.

5 When I was done, I worked out the results according to directions and it turned out I had an IQ of 135.—But wait! I had not accepted the half-hour limit offered me, but broke off each section of the test at the fifteen-minute mark and went on to the rest. I therefore doubled the score and decided I have an IQ of 270. (I'm sure that the doubling is unjustified, but the figure of 270 pleases my sense of cheerful self-appreciation, so I intend to insist on it.)

But however much all this soothes my vanity, and however much I appreciate being vice-president of Mensa, an organization which bases admission to its membership on IQ, I must, in all honesty, maintain that it means nothing.

What, after all, does such an intelligence test measure but those skills that are associated with intelligence by the individuals designing the test? And those individuals are subject to the cultural pressures and prejudices that force a subjective definition of intelligence.

Thus, important parts of any intelligence test measure the size of one's vocabulary, but the words one must define are just those words one is apt to find in reading approved works of literature. No one asks for the definition of "two-bagger" or "snake eyes" or "riff," for the simple reason that those who design the tests don't know these terms or are rather ashamed of themselves if they do.

This is similarly true of tests of mathematical knowledge, of logic, of shape-visualization, and of all the rest. You are tested in what is culturally fashionable—in what educated men consider to be the criteria of intelligence—i.e., of minds like their own.

The whole thing is a self-perpetuating device. Men in intellectual control of a dominating section of society define themselves as intelligent, then design tests that are a series of clever little doors that can let through only minds like their own, thus giving them more evidence of "intelligence" and more examples of "intelligent people" and therefore more reason to devise additional tests of the same kind. More circular reasoning! 10

And once someone is stamped with the label "Intelligent" on the basis of such tests and such criteria, any demonstration of stupidity no longer counts. It is the label that matters, not the fact. I don't like to label others, so I will merely give you two examples of clear stupidity which I myself perpetrated (though I can give you two hundred, if you like)—

1) On a certain Sunday, something went wrong with my car and I was helpless. Fortunately, my younger brother, Stan, lived nearby and since he is notoriously goodhearted, I called him. He came out at once, absorbed the situation, and began to use the yellow pages and the telephone to try to reach a service station, while I stood by with my lower jaw hanging loose. Finally, after a period of strenuous futility, Stan said to me with just a touch of annoyance, 'With all your intelligence, Isaac, how is it you lack the brains to join the AAA?" Whereupon, I said, "Oh, I belong to the AAA," and produced the card. He gave me a long, strange look and called the AAA. I was on my wheels in half an hour.

2) Sitting in Ben Bova's room (he's editor of *Analog*) at a recent science fiction convention, I was waiting, rather impatiently, for my wife to join us. Finally, there was a ring at the door. I sprang to my feet with an excited "Here's Janet!" flung open a door, and dashed into the closet—when Ben opened the room door and let her in.

Stan and Ben love to tell these stories about me and they're harmless. Because I have the label "intelligent," what would surely be evidence of stupidity is converted into lovable eccentricity.

This brings us to a serious point. There has been talk in recent years of racial differences in IQ. Men like William B. Shockley, who has a Nobel Prize (in physics), point out that measurements show the average IQ of Blacks to be substantially lower than that of Whites, and this has created quite a stir. 15

Many people who, for one reason or another, have already concluded that Blacks are "inferior" are delighted to have "scientific" reason to suppose that the undesirable position in which Blacks find themselves is their own fault after all.

Shockley, of course, denies racial prejudice (sincerely, I'm sure) and points out that we can't deal intelligently with racial problems if, out of political motives, we ignore an undoubted scientific finding; that we ought to investigate the matter carefully and study the intellectual inequality of man. Nor is it just a matter of Blacks versus Whites; apparently some groups of Whites score less well than do other groups of Whites, and so on.

Yet to my mind the whole hip-hurrah is a colossal fraud. Since intelligence is (as I believe) a matter of subjective definition and since the dominant intellectuals of the dominant sector of society have naturally defined it in a self-serving manner, what is it we say when we say that Blacks have a lower average IQ than Whites have? What we are saying is that the Black subculture is substantially different from the dominant White subculture and that the Black values are sufficiently different from dominant White values to make Blacks do less well on the carefully designed intelligence tests produced by the Whites.

In order for Blacks, on the whole, to do as well as Whites, they must abandon their own subculture for the White and produce a closer fit to the IQ-testing situation. This they may not want to do; and even if they want to, conditions are such that it is not made easy for them to fulfill that desire.

To put it as succinctly as possible: Blacks in America have had a subculture created for them, chiefly by White action, and have been kept in it chiefly by White action. The values of that subculture are defined as inferior to those of the dominant culture, so that the Black IQ is arranged to be lower; and the lower IQ is then used as an excuse 20 for the continuation of the very conditions that produced it. Circular reasoning? Of course.

But then, I don't want to be an intellectual tyrant and insist that what I speak must be the truth.

Let us say that I am wrong; that there *is* an objective definition of intelligence, that it *can* be measured accurately, and that Blacks *do* have lower IQ ratings than Whites do, on the average, not because of any cultural differences but because of some innate, biologically based intellectual inferiority. Now what? How should Whites treat Blacks?

That's a hard question to answer, but perhaps we can get some good out of supposing the reverse. What if we test Blacks and find out, more or less to our astonishment, that they end up showing a *higher* IQ than do Whites, on the average?

How should we *then* treat them? Should we give them a double vote? Give them preferential treatment in jobs, particularly in the government? Let them have the best seats in the bus and theater? Give them cleaner restrooms than Whites have, and a higher average pay scale?

25 I am *quite* certain that the answer would be a decided, forceful, and profane negative for each of these propositions and any like them. I suspect that if it were reported that Blacks had higher IQ ratings than Whites do, most Whites would at once maintain, with considerable heat, that IQ could not be measured accurately and that it was of no significance if it could be, that a person was a person regardless of book learning, fancy education, big words, and fol-de-rol, that plain ordinary horsesense was all anyone needed, that all men were equal in the good old United States, and those damned pinko professors and their IQ tests could just shove it—

Well, if we're going to ignore IQ when *we* are on the low end of the scale, why should we pay such pious attention to it when *they* are?

But hold on. I may be wrong again. How do I know how the dominants would react to a high-IQ minority? After all, we *do* respect intellectuals and professors to a certain extent, don't we? Then, too, we're talking about oppressed minorities, and a high-IQ minority wouldn't be oppressed in the first place, so the artificial situation I set up by pretending the Blacks scored high is just a straw man, and knocking it down has no value.

Really? Let's consider the Jews, who, for some two millennia, have been kicked around whenever Gentiles found life growing dull. Is this because Jews, as a group, are low-IQ?—You know, I *never* heard that maintained by anyone, however anti-Semitic.

I do not, myself, consider Jews, as a group, to be markedly high-IQ. The number of stupid Jews I have met in the course of a lifetime is enormous. That, however, is not the opinion of the anti-Semite, whose stereotype of the Jews involves their possession of a gigantic and dangerous intelligence. Although they may make up less than half a percent of a nation's population, they are forever on the point of "taking over."

30 But then, shouldn't they, if they are high-IQ? Oh, no, for that intelligence is merely "shrewdness," or "low cunning," or "devious slyness," and what really counts is that they lack the Christian, or the Nordic, or the Teutonic, or the what-have-you virtues of other sorts.

In short, if you are on the receiving end of the game-of-power, any excuse will do to keep you there. If you are seen as low-IQ, you are despised and kept there because of that. If you are seen as high-IQ, you are feared and kept there because of that.

Whatever significance IQ may have, then, it is, at present, being made a game for bigots.

Let me end, then, by giving you my own view. Each of us is part of any number of groups corresponding to any number of ways of subdividing mankind. In each of these ways, a given individual may be superior to others in the group, or inferior, or either, or both, depending on definition and on circumstance.

Because of this, "superior" and "inferior" have no useful meaning. What *does* exist, objectively, is "different." Each of us is different. I am different, and you are different, and you, and you, and you—

35 It is this difference that is the glory of *Homo sapiens* and the best possible salvation, because what some cannot do, others can, and where some cannot flourish, others can, through a wide range of conditions. I think we should value these differences as mankind's chief asset, as a species, and try never to use them to make our lives miserable, as individuals.

RICK BASS { *The Value of a Place*

RICK BASS (b. 1958), a native of Fort Worth, Texas, earned a BS in petroleum geology from Utah State University in 1979. A committed environmentalist, he has worked to protect the Yaak Valley of Troy, Montana, from loggers, and he continues his environmental work through his collections of short stories and essays, his novels and nonfiction nature writing. Bass has received both a Pushcart Prize and an O. Henry Award, and his autobiography *Why I Came West* (2008) was a finalist for a National Book Critics Circle Award. He is the author of more than twenty works, including the short-story collection *The Watch: Stories* (1989), the novel *Where the Sea Used to Be* (1998), and the nonfiction work *The Book of Yaak* (1996).

This selection from *The Book of Yaak* reveals the depth of Bass's attachment to his adopted home, the Yaak Valley in Montana. He analyzes the process of how he and his wife learned to "fit" a place, how they both take from and give back to the land. As you read, keep Bass's title—"The Value of a Place"—in mind, and ask yourself how Bass understands the value of the valley where he lives.

ALMOST AS BAD AS A writer asking for something, rather than giving, is the sin of repeating one's self, like some tired spit-dribbling codger at Christmas dinner telling that same damn story.

I wrote a book, *Winter*, which was about falling in love with this valley. I long for that innocence and suppleness of heart. Forgive me for repeating this one story, of how I stumbled into this place, but what was part of that old story—falling in love with, and learning to fit a place—is also part of this new story, which is about, I suppose, the second part of my cycle: the moon that must always answer to the sun—the giving back, after so much taking.

We wanted to be artists—my wife and I. Or rather, she was an artist, and I was a geologist and wanted to become instead a writer. I knew it would be hard to do both—geology and writing, science and art.

We left Mississippi when we were twenty-nine—in my old truck with our two hounds, who were only puppies then, and headed west, were pulled west, as seems to be the genetic predisposition in our country's blood—the handwriting of it telling us to move across the country from right to left, always farther from some echo of England, perhaps, or farther from everything—something in our blood and perhaps in the country beneath us that whispers for us always to rebel, even if only mildly—and that was what we did; we ran, for both the thrill of flight and for the searching-for-a-place.

5

All over the west we drove—we knew we loved mountains, loved rocks and ice and forests and creeks, loved sky and smoke—and we traveled through July thunderstorms and August snowstorms until one day we came over a pass and a valley appeared beneath us, a blue-green valley hidden beneath heavy clouds, with smoke rising from a couple of chimneys far below, and a lazy river snaking its way through the valley's narrow center, and a power, an immensity, that stopped us in our tracks. It was perhaps like the feeling of traveling a deep ocean while dragging an anchor, the anchor catching on something far below. It was the gravity of the place that caught my heart—that caught our hearts.

It took us a long time to settle in, to fit in, but not as long as it would have taken had we moved to yet another city, I don't believe. The move wasn't seamless, to say the least—I didn't even own a coat, or long underwear, for instance (Mississippi!)—but there was a match, right from the very start. I was starving for a thing but until then I had not realized what it was—and still, even as I discovered it, did not know the name of it, *peace*—though I knew that this valley had it, and would offer it to me, would let me feast upon it as if it were a meal: as if it were the sum of some strange combination of rock and forest and river that spoke only to our hearts—though I think it is safe to say that it speaks to the hearts of all those who have committed to living here: the whole hundred or so of us.

Is it too much to imagine that the pulsings of our blood, and our emotions, follow the rough profile of the days of light in this valley? the short summers of long days followed by the long winters of short days? the play of light in these strange forests, and even the sound of its creeks, somehow a place and sound that has almost always existed, which mirrors the sounds and rhythms inside us? Not a direct overlay, but a predisposition, so that our settling in was not so much work and effort as it was relief, pleasure and peace.

Does such a place exist for everyone?

How many places are left in the world—what diversity of them still exists—and for that diversity, what tolerance, and what affinity?

If a place is peaceful, can it impart that peace to its inhabitants—and if so, then how far—like a stone dropped into a pond—can that peace be spread? 10

What is the value of a place?

I wrote, and Elizabeth painted. I wrote in a place that was half-greenhouse, half-root-cellar—half submerged in the rich black earth, like a bear in hibernation, dreaming, yet also half immersed in light and surrounded by the scent and flavor of growing things—and Elizabeth painted out in the bright sun and wind, after that first winter had passed: painted scarves of bright colors, and bright landscapes.

We took, and took, and took. We feasted.

I can't tell you when the blinders of art, only art, first lifted: at what precise point I looked beyond the immediate visual reaction of what was being done to the country—the surgical incisions of the clearcuts, the scalpings—and felt the unease, or dis-ease, deeply enough to begin acting, or trying to act, against it. I'm not sure at which point I allowed the pain of it to be absorbed by me deeply enough so that I had no choice but to react against it. The clearcuts were never attractive, but for at least a year or two they did not touch me or harm me, nor my belief in peace, the way they do now—as does the threat of those clearcuts yet to come: those in the planning stages, and those that will come still later.

There had to be some point, though—some moment, some place, where something in me reached saturation—where I could not accept the sight of it anymore, and the knowledge of what the roads and clearcuts were doing to the ecology of the valley as well as to the economy of man. Undoubtedly this feeling of pain, of saturation, came at some point after I had gone through a full cycle of the four seasons; perhaps after I had gone through them a couple of times. I moved through the woods on hikes and hunts, open-minded—I had heard that the clearcuts were sometimes beneficial for the production of summer browse for deer (never mind that the deer populations might then rise beyond the limitations of their winter range). There still seemed to be plenty of diversity in the forest types I saw, and the roadless cores—the sanctuaries—still seemed intact. 15

That was just over a decade ago. I'm not sure when I began to realize that they—the timber industry—wanted it all: or if not all of it immediately, then access to all of it, forever. Or as the occasional bumper sticker declared, "Wilderness = Land of No Use."

Each season, I picked up the feel and taste of cycles. My blood began to learn new rhythms. My body became increasingly fluent in the language of cycles: splitting wood on cold mornings, cleaning a grouse in the evening—the solace, and ceremony, of plucking the feathers. Noticing where elk foraged in summer and where they foraged in winter. Noticing where the bears fed and what they ate. Watching the pulse of different creeks and the Yaak River itself—skinny in autumn, icy but poised in winter—wild, joyful and enormous in spring, then steady and clear on into summer, with caddis flies and mayflies rising from it every evening, and the giant spruce and fir trees shadowing it, keeping it cool and alive. . . .

Small cycles radiated into larger ones. I kept following them—noticing different ones each day—and continue to. I became more comfortable moving through the woods—slipping between alder, climbing under and over the lattice-work of lodgepole blowdown, crossing streams on slippery cedar logs, climbing the rock cliffs, descending the avalanche chutes into the parklike stands of old-growth larch, their needles brilliant gold in the autumn, and brilliant gold underfoot, as if moving across a land padded with gold, and an inch of black soil atop the rocky rubble-traces of glaciers; sometimes two inches of soil, sometimes three, but then rock, with the soil so thin underfoot that you did not have to be a scientist to understand that one shot was all most of this place was ever going to have at grace—that it had taken some of these trees, these forests, five hundred years to achieve climax, five hundred years and three inches, and that once you swept them clean, the soil would go with them, and for a long time there would be only emptiness, rather than grace—that then there would be only the echo of grace.

I hiked around, just watching and listening. Making up my own mind. Noticing the differences between logged and unlogged areas. Not all logged areas had that confusion of spirit or loss of grace; some of them retained, or reshaped, the grace of the woods (or rather, the grace of the woods altered itself and still flowed around and through those areas that had been logged with care and respect).

20 But even those areas compared in no way with the untouched areas—the incredible vitality of cycles still ongoing in the deep places of the valley—the last untouched corners.

I realize that the point at which what was being done to the valley began to hurt me deeply was the time I first began to feel that I was starting to fit: that the landscape and I were engaged in a relationship. That I was being reshaped and refashioned, to better fit it in spirit and desire. That I was neither fighting this nor resisting it. As it became my home, the wounds that were being inflicted upon it—the insults—became my own.

No one can say for sure when a place becomes your home, or when a fit is achieved, or peace, any more than one can say when a river best fits the valley through which it cuts. It flows and changes, shifts—cuts deep in some places, fills in in others. It transports sediment, logs and lives. It makes music in the day and in the night. Animals come down out of the mountains at dusk to stand at the river's edge and drink. In the dimness, as light fails, the animals sometimes cross the river, wading or swimming.

Even the valley itself is moving—shifting slightly, the mountains like the slowest yet most powerful pistons in the world, some rising and others falling—the valley sinking and tilting toward the ocean—and as it sinks, it carries within it, as if in a bowl or a nest, all the surprises, secrets and cycles—all the miracles—anyone could ever ask for: more miracles than even the most uncompromising glutton could desire. We are all born with an appreciation of, a love and a need for beauty and grace.

But as if frightened of it, we carve, prod and poke at it. We view mystery as the enemy of knowledge, and in trying to find knowledge we end up attempting to harm the sheath of mystery which encases that knowledge—cutting or attacking that mystery, in either fear or anger—and in so doing, harming or altering the knowledge that lies beneath that mystery.

We take in a manner that does not replenish. We search out the last corners to do injury to them as if we have become confused—as if forgetting that we cannot live, cannot survive, without grace and magic. 25

What I was hungry for when we first wandered into the valley, early in the fall—snow flurries already sifting through the high country—was wood. I needed firewood by the ton—more wood, it felt like, than the most ravenous timber beast. I desired wood, dreamed of wood—we had none and needed cords and cords of it, to heat the hunting lodge where we'd be staying. We'd fallen in love with the valley around one o'clock in the afternoon, that first afternoon that we saw it, and by two-thirty we had been asked to caretake this massive old hunting lodge in the valley's center—there were no phones or electricity in it, and for heat the forty-room lodge—all the rooms were empty—had just two wood stoves. We never could keep the pipes from freezing.

Forty rooms. A room for each story we intended to tell; a room for each painting.

Our old raggedy Mississippi truck broke. Then my chainsaw broke. For some now-unremembered reason, I still had the moving van in which we'd moved West, so we prowled the back roads, going from clearcut to clearcut, walking up into those steep savaged lands to pick up stove-sized pieces of wood, scraps and chips and residues. Sometimes, we'd drag whole trees out of the slash piles, where they had been bulldozed and abandoned—and we attempted to fill the moving van with these odds and ends—carrying whole logs down the steep muddy hills like crucifixes before shoving them into the maw of the van, like lunatic, lost tourists searching for some kind of authentic souvenir. Our big yellow top-heavy moving van swayed along the back roads, moving slowly through the autumn rains and mist. There is a certain undeniable raggedness of spirit—a newness, a roughness—to the place. It is not a place for anything slick and smooth. It is not a place filled with easy certainties.

After we got the moving van unloaded and swept out the wood chips and turned it in, I raced down to Mississippi and got my old Ford Falcon, which I knew was too old for the trip, but which was all I had. The radiator was clogged in some places and leaky in others, so I patched the leaks with duct tape and, as per the advice of a mechanic at a truck stop in Louisiana—such a long second journey home!—I bought a box of Tide laundry detergent and dumped it into the radiator. The mechanic had said that the detergent would slosh around in the hot waters of the radiator as if it were inside a washing machine, and would get all sudsy, which would cleanse the rust-clods; and that was in fact how it worked, and I made it back across the plains and up over the mountains a second time, driving days and nights without stopping: except that some of my duct tape patches began to leak, and soap bubbles then filtered through those leaks, so that a steady, wistful stream of bubbles trailed me the last several hundred miles. And that was how I rode back into the valley, the car looking like some renegade escapee from *The Lawrence Welk Show.*

30

I took the back seat out of the Falcon and used it in that manner as a mini-pickup. I got the saw fixed and was back in business, cruising those back roads in the low rider, muffler and frame sometimes dragging in the back, such was the weight of the wood. Our friend Nancy, who has an eye for the woods, says that that was when she first made the guess that we would stay—that we would find a fit with this place—when she saw us driving back and forth with a sedan stuffed full of firewood, sparks roostertailing behind us in the dusk, hurrying to get our wood in before winter. Before the world disappeared beneath snow, before Canada slipped down over us like an avalanche; like the curve of a breaking wave, a typhoon of snow.

Those first couple of years were days of heaven—wandering around taking from the grace of the woods, and just watching things and listening: not yet sensing or understanding that the wildness that nourished this place—and us—was slipping away.

Two years—maybe a little longer—of free grace. It was as though those days were days of harvest: art. Paintings and drawings stacked everywhere. And stories, too, all of them fiction—all of them trying to give something to the reader. (It was as if the stories came from the woods and flowed through me out to the reader, rather than the contrary, which I would later attempt, wherein I would try to take from the reader: reversing that electrical current in an effort to get the reader to give something, which would then pass through me and back out into the woods. The kind of charge-reversal that happens sometimes when lightning strikes a transformer and sends the power surging back in the direction from which it came—often frying the transformer. . . .)

Slowly fitting myself to the new cycles I was learning—deeper cycles, more subtle cycles. Fiction, nonfiction; literature, advocacy. Letters to friends, letters to Congress. Adjusting the mix of them gradually, and hopefully in concert with all the other rhythms around. Slowly waking up to the rudeness and quickness of what was going on around me—the carving away into the last corners of untouched country.

Sometimes panic would spike up deep within me—electrical charges of fear registering off the scale—and I would want to abandon all art and spend all my time in advocacy. I still believed in art, but art seemed utterly extravagant in the face of what was happening. If your home were burning, for instance, would you grab a bucket of water to pour on it, or would you step back and write a poem about it?

35 A great work of fiction can become a cornerstone in the literature of a place, and a cornerstone or foundation for all manners of ideas, such as the importance of wildness and wilderness, or concepts of grace, freedom, liberty. A great novel can reach thirty, fifty, even a hundred years into the future, across history, with such an idea, whereas a magazine article or newspaper editorial might have a shelf life of about two or three weeks.

And yet, what good does it do that great novel to extend so far into the future—forty years, say—if the place about which it was written vanished, oh, thirty-five, thirty-six, thirty-seven years ago?

Art is incredibly important to me—fiction, especially. But there are thousands of fiction writers in the world, and only one Yaak. It would certainly not cause the earth to pause on its axis if I never wrote another story again. I don't think there was ever any writer about whom that could be said.

On the other hand, if a thing like the wilderness of Yaak were to be lost—I do believe that would cause a hesitation on the axis, an imbalance—a friction and an injury whose loss—like the cumulative effect of so many others which have already occurred—we would be hard-pressed to recover from. It's possible art could protect the last roadless areas of Yaak Valley. But I just don't think there's time for it.

Cycles and rhythms—an extravagance of cycles still operating in the Yaak's roadless areas, a wildness of cycles, still connected to one another and weaving together to make grace—still making order, every day and every season, out of disorder. This is of course what art does—takes characters' actions and emotions, in fiction, or colors and shapes, in painting, and weaves them to make order, as nature selects carbon and hydrogen to braid and weave the magic of life. And as order and logic become increasingly lost to our societies, I'm certain that these things—art, and the wilderness—are critical to stabilizing the troubling tilt, the world's uneasiness, that we can all feel with every nerve of our senses, but which we still cannot name.

The cycle of dying trees giving birth to living ones—we're all familiar with this, familiar with the necessity of rot, and diversity, in an ecosystem: the way that the richness, or tithing, of rot, and the flexibility, the suppleness, of diversity, guarantees that an ecosystem, or any other kind of system, will have a future. I like to walk—and sometimes crawl—through the jungle up here, examining the world on my hands and knees—watching the pistonlike rise and fall of individual trees—noticing the ways they block light from some places and funnel or focus light into other places—watching the way, when the weaker trees 40 fall, that they sometimes help prop up and brace those around them. Other times the fallen trees crash all the way to the ground to become fern-beds, soil-mulch, lichen-pads. It's not a thing we can measure yet, but I like to imagine that each different tree, after it has fallen, gives off a different quality of rot—a diversity even in the manner in which nutrients are released to the soil. The slow rot of a giant larch having a taste to the soil, perhaps, of bread; the faster disintegration of ice-snapped saplings tasting like sugar, or honey. The forest *feasting* on its own diversity, with grace and mystery lying thick everywhere.

Like the manner in which nutrients are recycled through the forest, so too are the movements of the animals through it like a cycle, or a pulse—a rhythm of blood, chlorophyll and magic: especially the migratory patterns. There are a lot of deer in the valley—an overabundance, or sign of imbalance, some would say—against which, of course, a correction will always occur, as long as the earth corrects itself to the sun; for as long as there is gravity. It—the rhythm of the increasing deer herds—becomes more pronounced, more visible—more strongly felt—each winter.

In spring, summer and fall, the deer occupy nearly every square foot of the valley; it would be difficult for you to go anywhere here during those seasons where you could not find deer, or the signs of deer. But then as winter's snows cover most of their available forage, and as thermal regulation—south slopes, and heavy overstories and canopies—become critical, as temperatures drop, the places where the valley will allow deer to survive become extremely narrow. As the winter deepens, you can see almost all of the deer in the valley, and the elk too, being squeezed into a small fraction of the whole: the parameters tightening daily, so that each day, if you are deep into the rhythm of your place, you can feel the deer coming down off the mountains in the night, moving lower and lower into the valley and rotating toward those south slopes—crowding into spaces one-tenth, or one one-hundredth, of that which they previously occupied. You can feel the energy shifts, the lone deer and does with fawns combining and joining into huge herds, which then move like braids or ribbons, weaving their way along the same few ice trails, cutting paths deeper and deeper, browsing the limited winter food, and waiting for the release of spring. . . .

It becomes a pulse, winter like the contraction of a heart squeezing blood through the vessels of an organism—and you can feel the waiting for backwash, the waiting for the moment between beats, when the blood can wash back into the heart's chambers and take a brief rest—six months' worth—before being constricted, squeezed tight again: the deer flowing up and then down the mountains, focusing and then spreading, concentrating then sprawling, and it too is like art, like breathing.

For so long, the story of the West has been that blood-scribing, that heartbeat of lighting out for "the territory"—the continental drift, westward toward freedom and liberty, as if some great magnetic store of it lies somewhere west of the Great Plains. But I sense that pulse may be—of necessity—finally changing and slowing, even reversing itself. I see more and more the human stories in the West becoming those not of passing through and drifting on, but of settling in and making a stand; and I think that there is a hunger for this kind of rhythm in towns, neighborhoods and cities throughout the country—not just in rural areas, and not just in the West, but all over: that the blood-rhythms of wilderness which remain in us (as the old seas and oceans remain in us) are declaring, in response to the increasing instability of the outside forces that are working against us, the need for reconnection to rhythms that are stable and natural. And no matter whether those rhythms are found in a city, or in a garden, or in a relationship, or in the wilderness—it is the need and desire for them that we are recognizing and searching for, and I can feel it, the notion that settling-in and stand-making is the way to achieve or rediscover these rhythms. I can sense a turning-away from the idea, once pulsing in our own blood, that drifting or running is the answer, perhaps because the rhythms we need are becoming so hard to find, out in the fragmented worlds of both nature and man.

We can find these rhythms within ourselves. 45

I know we can all sense this blood turning; this incredible, increasing uncertainty in the world, and the instability of things—whether in the city or in the woods. What holds things together, and what tears them apart?

What is the value of art?

What is the value of a place?

WENDELL BERRY { *The Pleasures of Eating*

WENDELL BERRY (b. 1934) is a farmer and prolific writer of fiction, poetry, and essays, having written more than fifty books. He often writes about sustainability and the importance of a connection to one's local community. Berry has demonstrated such a connection to place not only in his writing but also by living and working on the same farm in Kentucky for more than forty years.

"The Pleasures of Eating" appeared in Berry's 1990 essay collection *What Are People For?* In this essay, Berry provides guidelines for eating responsibly, including trying to participate in food production by growing at least some of one's own food; preparing one's own meals; buying locally produced food; dealing directly with local food producers; and learning about farming, gardening, industrial food production, and the life histories of what one eats. Berry links such awareness and practices not only to health, environmental, and economic concerns, but also to pleasure—to eating with gratitude, understanding, and enjoyment. As you read Berry's essay consider how much you know about where your food comes from and whether you can not only learn more about food production but also take more pleasure in eating.

MANY TIMES, AFTER I HAVE finished a lecture on the decline of American farming and rural life, someone in the audience has asked, "What can city people do?"

"Eat responsibly," I have usually answered. Of course, I have tried to explain what I meant by that, but afterwards I have invariably felt that there was more to be said than I had been able to say. Now I would like to attempt a better explanation.

I begin with the proposition that eating is an agricultural act. Eating ends the annual drama of the food economy that begins with planting and birth. Most eaters, however, are no longer aware that this is true. They think of food as an agricultural product, perhaps, but they do not think of themselves as participants in agriculture. They think of themselves as "consumers." If they think beyond that, they recognize that they are passive consumers. They buy what they want—or what they have been persuaded to want—within the limits of what they can get. They pay, mostly without protest, what they are charged. And they mostly ignore certain critical questions about the quality and the cost of what they are sold: How fresh is it? How pure or clean is it, how free of dangerous chemicals? How far was it transported, and what did transportation add to the cost? How much did manufacturing or packaging or advertising add to the cost? When the food product has been manufactured or "processed" or "precooked," how has that affected its quality or price or nutritional value?

Most urban shoppers would tell you that food is produced on farms. But most of them do not know what farms, or what kinds of farms, or where the farms are, or what knowledge or skills are involved in farming. They apparently have little doubt that farms will continue to produce, but they do not know how or over what obstacles. For them, then, food is pretty much an abstract idea—something they do not know or imagine—until it appears on the grocery shelf or on the table.

5 The specialization of production induces specialization of consumption. Patrons of the entertainment industry, for example, entertain themselves less and less and have become more and more passively dependent on commercial suppliers. This is certainly true also of patrons of the food industry, who have tended more and more to be *mere* consumers—passive, uncritical, and dependent. Indeed, this sort of consumption may be said to be one of the chief goals of industrial production. The food industrialists have by now persuaded millions of consumers to prefer food that is already prepared. They will grow, deliver, and cook your food for you and (just like your mother) beg you to eat it. That they do not yet offer to insert it, prechewed, into

your mouth is only because they have found no profitable way to do so. We may rest assured that they would be glad to find such a way. The ideal industrial food consumer would be strapped to a table with a tube running from the food factory directly into his or her stomach.

Perhaps I exaggerate, but not by much. The industrial eater is, in fact, one who does not know that eating is an agricultural act, who no longer knows or imagines the connections between eating and the land, and who is therefore necessarily passive and uncritical—in short, a victim. When food, in the minds of eaters, is no longer associated with farming and with the land, then the eaters are suffering a kind of cultural amnesia that is misleading and dangerous. The current version of the "dream home" of the future involves "effortless" shopping from a list of available goods on a television monitor and heating precooked food by remote control. Of course, this implies and depends on, a perfect ignorance of the history of the food that is consumed. It requires that the citizenry should give up their hereditary and sensible aversion to buying a pig in a poke. It wishes to make the selling of pigs in pokes an honorable and glamorous activity. The dreamer in this dream home will perforce know nothing about the kind or quality of this food, or where it came from, or how it was produced and prepared, or what ingredients, additives, and residues it contains—unless, that is, the dreamer undertakes a close and constant study of the food industry, in which case he or she might as well wake up and play an active and responsible part in the economy of food.

There is, then, a politics of food that, like any politics, involves our freedom. We still (sometimes) remember that we cannot be free if our minds and voices are controlled by someone else. But we have neglected to understand that we cannot be free if our food and its sources are controlled by someone else. The condition of the passive consumer of food is not a democratic condition. One reason to eat responsibly is to live free.

But if there is a food politics, there are also a food esthetics and a food ethics, neither of which is dissociated from politics. Like industrial sex, industrial eating has become a degraded, poor, and paltry thing. Our kitchens and other eating places more and more resemble filling stations, as our homes more and more resemble motels. "Life is not very interesting," we seem to have decided. "Let its satisfactions be minimal, perfunctory, and fast." We hurry through our meals to go to work and hurry through our work in order to "recreate" ourselves in the evenings and on weekends and vacations. And then we hurry, with the greatest possible speed and noise and violence, through our recreation—for what? To eat the billionth hamburger at some fast-food joint hellbent on increasing the "quality" of our life? And all this is carried out in a remarkable obliviousness to the causes and effects, the possibilities and the purposes, of the life of the body in this world.

One will find this obliviousness represented in virgin purity in the advertisements of the food industry, in which food wears as much makeup as the actors. If one gained one's whole knowledge of food from these advertisements (as some presumably do), one would not know that the various edibles were ever living creatures, or that they all come from the soil, or that they were produced by work. The passive American consumer, sitting down to a meal of pre-prepared or fast food, confronts a platter covered with inert, anonymous substances that have been processed, dyed, breaded, sauced, gravied, ground, pulped, strained, blended, prettified, and sanitized beyond resemblance to any part of any creature that ever lived. The products of nature and agriculture have been made, to all appearances, the products of industry. Both eater and eaten are thus in exile from biological reality. And the result is a kind of solitude, unprecedented in human experience, in which the eater may think of eating as, first, a purely commercial transaction between him and a supplier and then as a purely appetitive transaction between him and his food.

And this peculiar specialization of the act of eating is, again, of obvious benefit to the food industry, which has good reasons to obscure the connection between food and farming. It would not do for the consumer to know that the hamburger she is eating came from a steer who spent much of his life standing deep in his own excrement in a feedlot, helping to pollute the local streams, or that the calf that yielded the veal cutlet on her plate spent its life in a box in which it did not have room to turn around. And, though her sympathy for the slaw might be less tender, she should not be encouraged to meditate on the hygienic and biological implications of mile-square fields of cabbage, 10 for vegetables grown in huge monocultures are dependent on toxic chemicals—just as animals in close confinement are dependent on antibiotics and other drugs.

The consumer, that is to say, must be kept from discovering that, in the food industry—as in any other industry—the overriding concerns are not quality and health, but volume and price. For decades now the entire industrial food economy, from the large farms and feedlots to the chains of supermarkets and fast-food restaurants, has been obsessed with volume. It has relentlessly increased scale in order to increase volume in order (presumably) to reduce costs. But as scale increases, diversity declines; as diversity declines, so does health; as health declines, the dependence on drugs and chemicals necessarily increases. As capital replaces labor, it does so by substituting machines, drugs, and chemicals for human workers and for the natural health and fertility of the soil. The food is produced by any means or any shortcut that will increase profits. And the business of the cosmeticians of advertising is to persuade the consumer that food so produced is good, tasty, healthful, and a guarantee of marital fidelity and long life.

It is possible, then, to be liberated from the husbandry and wifery of the old household food economy. But one can be thus liberated only by entering a trap (unless one sees ignorance and helplessness as the signs of privilege, as many people apparently do). The trap is the ideal of industrialism: a walled city surrounded by valves that let merchandise in but no consciousness out. How does one escape this trap? Only voluntarily, the same way that one went in: by restoring one's consciousness of what is involved in eating; by reclaiming responsibility for one's own part in the food economy. One might begin with the illuminating principle of Sir Albert Howard's *The Soil and Health*, that we should understand "the whole problem of health in soil, plant, animal, and man as one great subject." Eaters, that is, must understand that eating takes place inescapably in the world, that it is inescapably an agricultural act, and that how we eat determines, to a considerable extent, how the world is used. This is a simple way of describing a relationship that is inexpressibly complex. To eat responsibly is to understand and enact, so far as one can, this complex relationship. What can one do? Here is a list, probably not definitive:

1. Participate in food production to the extent that you can. If you have a yard or even just a porch box or a pot in a sunny window, grow something to eat in it. Make a little compost of your kitchen scraps and use it for fertilizer. Only by growing some food for yourself can you become acquainted with the beautiful energy cycle that revolves from soil to seed to flower to fruit to food to offal to decay, and around again. You will be fully responsible for any food that you grow for yourself, and you will know all about it. You will appreciate it fully, having known it all its life.

2. Prepare your own food. This means reviving in your own mind and life the arts of kitchen and household. This should enable you to eat more cheaply, and it will give you a measure of "quality control": you will have some reliable knowledge of what has been added to the food you eat.

3. Learn the origins of the food you buy, and buy the food that is produced closest to your home. The idea that every locality should be, as much as possible, the source of its own food makes several kinds of sense. The locally produced food supply is the most secure, the freshest, and the easiest for local consumers to know about and to influence.

4. Whenever possible, deal directly with a local farmer, gardener, or orchardist. All the reasons listed for the previous suggestion apply here. In addition, by such dealing you eliminate the whole pack of merchants, transporters, processors, packagers, and advertisers who thrive at the expense of both producers and consumers.

5. Learn, in self-defense, as much as you can of the economy and technology of industrial food production. What is added to food that is not food, and what do you pay for these additions?

6. Learn what is involved in the *best* farming and gardening.

7. Learn as much as you can, by direct observation and experience if possible, of the life histories of the food species.

The last suggestion seems particularly important to me. Many people are now as much estranged from the lives of domestic plants and animals (except for flowers and dogs and cats) as they are from the lives of the wild ones. This is regrettable, for these domestic creatures are in diverse ways attractive; there is much pleasure in knowing them. And farming, animal husbandry, horticulture, and gardening, at their best, are complex and comely arts; there is much pleasure in knowing them, too.

It follows that there is great *dis*pleasure in knowing about a food economy that degrades and abuses those arts and those plants and animals and the soil from which they come. For anyone who does know something of the modern history of food, eating away from home can be a chore. My own inclination is to eat seafood instead of red meat or poultry when I am traveling. Though I am by no means a vegetarian, I dislike the thought that some animal has been made miserable in order to feed me. If I am going to eat meat, I want it to be from an animal that has lived a pleasant, uncrowded life outdoors, on bountiful pasture, with good water nearby and trees for shade. And I am getting almost as fussy about food plants. I like to eat vegetables and fruits that I know have lived happily and healthy in good soil, not the products of the huge, bechemicaled factory-fields that I have seen, for example, in the Central Valley of California. The industrial farm is said to have been patterned on the factory production line. In practice, it looks more like a concentration camp.

The pleasure of eating should be an *extensive* pleasure, not that of the mere gourmet. People who know the garden in which their vegetables have grown and know that the garden is healthy will remember the beauty of the growing plants, perhaps in the dewy first light of morning when gardens are at their best. Such a memory involves itself with the food and is one of the pleasures of eating. The knowledge of the good health of the garden relieves and frees and comforts the eater. The same goes for eating meat. The thought of the good pasture and of the calf contentedly grazing flavors the steak. Some, I know, will think it bloodthirsty or worse to eat a fellow creature you have known all its life. On the contrary, I think it means that you eat with understanding and with gratitude. A significant part of the pleasure of eating is in one's accurate consciousness of the lives and the world from which food comes. The pleasure of eating, then, may be the best available standard of our health. And this pleasure, I think, is pretty fully available to the urban consumer who will make the necessary effort.

I mentioned earlier the politics, esthetics, and ethics of food. But to speak of the pleasure of eating is to go beyond those categories. Eating with the fullest pleasure—pleasure, that is, that does not depend on ignorance—is perhaps the profoundest enactment of our connection with the world. In this pleasure we experience and celebrate our dependence and our gratitude, for we are living from mystery, from creatures we did not make and powers we cannot comprehend. When I think of the meaning of food, I always remember these lines by the poet William Carlos Williams, which seem to me merely honest:

> There is nothing to eat,
> seek it where you will,
> but the body of the Lord.
> The blessed plants
> and the sea, yield it
> to the imagination
> intact.

JOAN DIDION { *On Going Home*

JOAN DIDION (b. 1934), a native of California and graduate of the University of California at Berkeley, wrote for *Vogue* magazine until she published her first novel, *River Run* (1963). Didion is probably best known for her essays, many of which are haunting reflections on the changes that overtook her home state in the middle of the twentieth century. Her essay collections include *Slouching Towards Bethlehem* (1969), from which "On Going Home" is taken, *The White Album* (1979), and *The Year of Magical Thinking* (2005).

Didion frames this memoir with her daughter's first birthday, focusing on her visit to the home where she grew up. The essay probes her feelings about her family and about her husband's presence in her family's home, revealing Didion's inner conflicts. As you read, notice how Didion uses specific objects to help paint a picture of her family.

I AM HOME FOR MY daughter's first birthday. By "home" I do not mean the house in Los Angeles where my husband and I and the baby live, but the place where my family is, in the Central Valley of California. It is a vital although troublesome distinction. My husband likes my family but is uneasy in their house, because once there I fall into their ways, which are difficult, oblique, deliberately inarticulate, not my husband's ways. We live in dusty houses ("D-U-S-T," he once wrote with his finger on surfaces all over the house, but no one noticed it) filled with mementos quite without value to him (what could the Canton dessert plates mean to him? how could he have known about the assay scales,[1] why should he care if he did know?), and we appear to talk exclusively about people we know who have been committed to mental hospitals, about people we know who have been booked on drunk-driving charges, and about property, particularly about property, land, price per acre and C-2 zoning and assessments and freeway access. My brother does not understand my husband's inability to perceive the advantage in the rather common real-estate transaction known as "sale-leaseback," and my husband in turn does not understand why so many of the people he hears about in my father's house have recently been committed to mental hospitals or booked on drunk-driving charges. Nor does he understand that when we talk about sale-leasebacks and right-of-way condemnations we are talking in code about things we like best, the yellow fields and the cottonwoods and the rivers rising and falling and the mountain roads closing when the heavy snow comes in. We miss each other's points, have another drink and regard the fire. My brother refers to my husband, in his presence, as "Joan's husband." Marriage is the classic betrayal.

Or perhaps it is not anymore. Sometimes I think that those of us who are now in our thirties were born into the last generation to carry the burden of "home," to find in family life the source of all tension and drama. I had by all objective accounts a "normal" and a "happy" family situation, and yet I was almost thirty years old before I could talk to my family on the telephone without crying after I had hung up. We did not fight. Nothing was wrong. And yet some nameless anxiety colored the emotional charges between me and the place that I came from. The question of whether or not you could go home again was a very real part of the sentimental and largely literary baggage with which we left home in the fifties; I suspect that it is irrelevant to the children born of the fragmentation after World War II. A few weeks ago in a San Francisco bar I saw a pretty young girl on crystal[2] take off her clothes and dance for the cash prize in an "amateur-topless" contest. There was no particular sense of moment about this, none of the effect of

[1]Scales such as those used during the California Gold Rush (1848–55) to determine the weight and purity of mineral ore.

[2]Common name for methamphetamine, a psychoactive stimulant.

romantic degradation, of "dark journey," for which my generation strived so assiduously. What sense could that girl possibly make of, say, *Long Day's Journey into Night?*[3] Who is beside the point?

That I am trapped in this particular irrelevancy is never more apparent to me than when I am home. Paralyzed by the neurotic lassitude engendered by meeting one's past at every turn, around every corner, inside every cupboard, I go aimlessly from room to room. I decide to meet it head-on and clean out a drawer, and I spread the contents on the bed. A bathing suit I wore the summer I was seventeen. A letter of rejection from *The Nation,* an aerial photograph of the site for a shopping center my father did not build in 1954. Three teacups hand-painted with cabbage roses and signed "E.M.," my grandmother's initials. There is no final solution for letters of rejection from *The Nation* and teacups hand-painted in 1900. Nor is there any answer to snapshots of one's grandfather as a young man on skis, surveying around Donner Pass[4] in the year 1910. I smooth out the snapshot and look into his face, and do and do not see my own. I close the drawer, and have another cup of coffee with my mother. We get along very well, veterans of a guerrilla war we never understood.

Days pass. I see no one. I come to dread my husband's evening call, not only because he is full of news of what by now seems to me our remote life in Los Angeles, people he has seen, letters which require attention, but because he asks what I have been doing, suggests uneasily that I get out, drive to San Francisco or Berkeley. Instead I drive across the river to a family graveyard. It has been vandalized since my last visit and the monuments are broken, overturned in the dry grass. Because I once saw a rattlesnake in the grass I stay in the car and listen to a country-and-Western station. Later I drive with my father to a ranch he has in the foothills. The man who runs his cattle on it asks us to the round-up, a week from Sunday, and although I know that I will be in Los Angeles I say, in the oblique way my family talks, that I will come. Once home I mention the broken monuments in the graveyard. My mother shrugs.

[3]Play by Eugene O'Neill (1888–1952), a tragedy about family relationships and addiction.
[4]High mountain pass in California's northern Sierra Nevada.

I go to visit my great-aunts. A few of them think now that I am my cousin, or their daughter who died young. We recall an anecdote about a relative last seen in 1948, and they ask if I still like living in New York City. I have lived in Los Angeles for three years, but I say that I do. The baby is offered a horehound drop, and I am slipped a dollar bill "to buy a treat." Questions trail off, answers are abandoned, the baby plays with the dust motes in a shaft of afternoon sun. 5

It is time for the baby's birthday party: a white cake, strawberry-marshmallow ice cream, a bottle of champagne saved from another party. In the evening, after she has gone to sleep, I kneel beside the crib and touch her face, where it is pressed against the slats, with mine. She is an open and trusting child, unprepared for and unaccustomed to the ambushes of family life, and perhaps it is just as well that I can offer her little of that life. I would like to give her more. I would like to promise her that she will grow up with a sense of her cousins and of rivers and of her great-grandmother's teacups, would like to pledge her a picnic on a river with fried chicken and her hair uncombed, would like to give her *home* for her birthday, but we live differently now and I can promise her nothing like that. I give her a xylophone and a sundress from Madeira,[5] and promise to tell her a funny story.

[5]Small group of Portuguese islands in the Atlantic Ocean.

THE ECONOMIST

Higher Education: Not What It Used to Be

ON THE FACE OF IT, American higher education is still in rude health. In worldwide rankings more than half of the top 100 universities, and eight of the top ten, are American. The scientific output of American institutions is unparalleled. They produce most of the world's Nobel laureates and scientific papers. Moreover college graduates, on average, still earn far more and receive better benefits than those who do not have a degree.

Nonetheless, there is growing anxiety in America about higher education. A degree has always been considered the key to a good job. But rising fees and increasing student debt, combined with shrinking financial and educational returns, are undermining at least the perception that university is a good investment.

Concern springs from a number of things: steep rises in fees, increases in the levels of debt of both students and universities, and the declining quality of graduates. Start with the fees. The cost of university per student has risen by almost five times the rate of inflation since 1983 (see chart 1), making it less affordable and increasing the amount of debt a student must take on. Between 2001 and 2010 the cost of a university education soared from 23% of median annual earnings to 38%; in consequence, debt per student has doubled in the past 15 years. Two-thirds of graduates now take out loans. Those who earned bachelor's degrees in 2011 graduated with an average of $26,000 in debt, according to the Project on Student Debt, a non-profit group.

More debt means more risk, and graduation is far from certain; the chances of an American student completing a four-year degree within

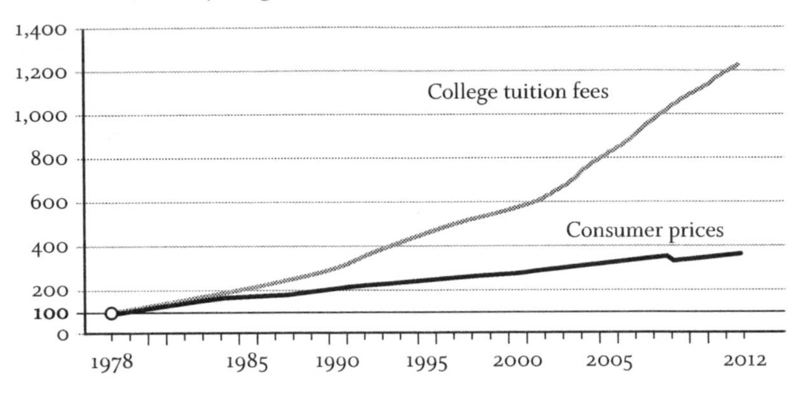

Figure 1: *Still worth it?*
January 1978=100
Source: Bureau of Labour Statistics

six years stand at only around 57%. This is poor by international standards: Australia and Britain, for instance, both do much better.

At the same time, universities have been spending beyond their means. Many have taken on too much debt and have seen a decline in the health of their balance-sheets. Moreover, the securitisation of student loans led to a rush of unwise private lending. This, at least, has now been curbed by regulation. In 2008 private lenders disbursed $20 billion; last year they shelled out only $6 billion.

Despite so many fat years, universities have done little until recently to improve the courses they offer. University spending is driven by the need to compete in university league tables that tend to rank almost everything about a university except the (hard-to-measure) quality of the graduates it produces. Roger Geiger of Pennsylvania State University and Donald Heller of Michigan State University say that since 1990, in both public and private colleges, expenditures on instruction have risen more slowly than in any other category of spending, even as student numbers have risen. Universities are, however, spending plenty more on administration and support services (see chart 2).

Universities cannot look to government to come to the rescue. States have already cut back dramatically on the amount of financial aid they give universities. Barack Obama has made it clear that he is unhappy about rising tuition fees, and threatens universities with aid cuts if they

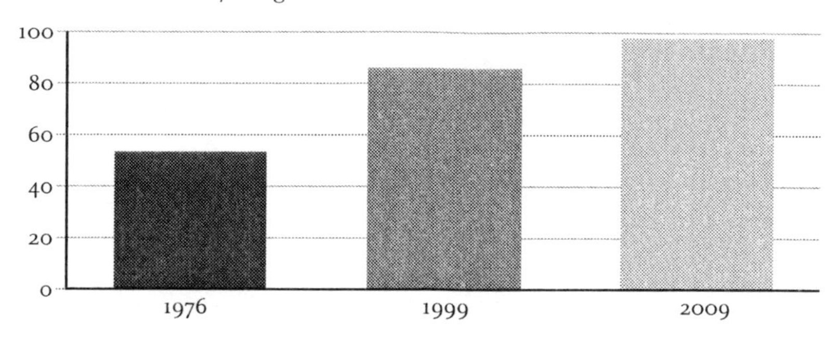

Figure 2: *Plenty of padding*
Non-faculty professional employees per 100 faculty members
Sources: Department of Education; National Centre for Education Statistics

rise any further. Roger Brinner from the Parthenon Group, a consultancy, predicts that enrollment rates will stay flat for the next five to seven years even as the economy picks up. The party may be well and truly over.

BALLOON DEBATE

In 1962 one cent of every dollar spent in America went on higher education; today this figure has tripled. Yet despite spending a greater proportion of its GDP on universities than any other country, America has only the 15th-largest proportion of young people with a university education. Wherever the money is coming from, and however it is being spent, the root of the crisis in higher education (and the evidence that investment in universities may amount to a bubble) comes down to the fact that additional value has not been created to match this extra spending. Indeed, evidence from declines in the quality of students and graduates suggests that a degree may now mean less than it once did.

For example, a federal survey showed that the literacy of college-educated citizens declined between 1992 and 2003. Only a quarter were deemed proficient, defined as "using printed and written information to function in society, to achieve one's goals and to develop one's knowledge and potential". Almost a third of students these days do not take any courses that involve more than 40 pages of reading over an entire term. Moreover, students are spending measurably less time studying and more on recreation. "Workload management", however, is studied with enthusiasm — students share online tips about "blow off" classes (those which can be avoided with no damage to grades) and which teachers are the easiest-going.

Yet neither the lack of investment in teaching nor the deficit of attention appears to have had a negative impact on grades. A remarkable 43% of all grades at four-year universities are As, an increase of 28 percentage points since 1960. Grade point averages rose from about 2.52 in the 1950s to 3.11 in 2006. 10

At this point a sceptic could argue that none of this matters much, since students are paid a handsome premium for their degree and on the whole earn back their investment over a lifetime. While this is still broadly true, there are a number of important caveats. One is that it is easily possible to overspend on one's education: just ask the hundreds of thousands of law graduates who have not found work as lawyers. And this premium is of little comfort to the 9.1% of borrowers who in 2011 had defaulted on their federal student loans within two years of graduating. There are 200 colleges and universities where the three-year default rate is 30% or more.

Another issue is that the salary gap between those with only a high-school diploma and those with a university degree is created by the plummeting value of the diploma, rather than by soaring graduate salaries. After adjusting for inflation, graduates earned no more in 2007 than they did in 1979. Young graduates facing a decline in earnings over the past decade (16% for women, 19% for men), and a lot more debt, are unlikely to feel particularly cheered by the argument that, over a lifetime, they would be even worse off without a degree than with one.

Moreover, the promise that an expensive degree at a traditional university will pay off rests on some questionable assumptions; for example, that no cheaper way of attaining this educational premium will emerge. Yet there is a tornado of change in education that might challenge this, either through technology or through attempts to improve the two-year community college degree and render it more economically valuable. Another assumption, which is proved wrong in the case of 40% of students, is that they will graduate at all. Indeed, nearly 30% of college students who took out loans eventually dropped out (up from 25% a decade ago). These students are saddled with a debt they have no realistic means of paying off.

Some argue that universities are clinging to a medieval concept of education in an age of mass enrolment. In a recent book, "Reinventing Higher Education," Ben Wildavsky and his colleagues at the Kauffman Foundation, which focuses on entrepreneurship, add that there has been a failure to innovate. Declining productivity and stiff economic headwinds mean that change is coming in a trickle of online learning inside universities, and a rush of "massive open online courses" (MOOCs) outside them. Some universities see online learning as a way of continuing to grow while facing harsh budget cuts. The University of California borrowed $6.9m to do this in the midst of a budget crisis. In 2011 about 6m American students took at least one online course in the autumn term. Around 30% of all college students are learning online—up from less than 10% in 2002.

DIGITAL DILEMMAS

To see how efficient higher education can be, look at the new online Western Governors University (WGU). Tuition costs less than $6,000 a year, compared with around $54,000 at Harvard. Students can study and take their exams when they want, not when the sabbaticals, holidays and scheduling of teaching staff allow. The average time to completion is just two-and-a-half years. 15

MOOCs have also now arrived with great fanfare. These offer free college-level classes taught by renowned lecturers to all-comers. Two companies, Coursera and Udacity, and one non-profit enterprise, edX, are leading the charge. At some point these outfits will need to generate some revenue, probably through certification.

The broader significance of MOOCs is that they are part of a trend towards the unbundling of higher education. This will shake many institutions whose business model is based on a set fee for a four-year campus-based degree course. As online education spreads, universities will come under pressure to move to something more like a "buffet" arrangement, under which they will accept credits from each other —

and from students who take courses at home or even at high school, spending much less time on campus. StraighterLine, a start-up based in Baltimore, is already selling courses that gain students credits for a few hundred dollars.

Some signs suggest that universities are facing up to their inefficiencies. Indiana University has just announced innovations aimed at lowering the cost and reducing the time it takes to earn a degree. More of this is needed. Universities owe it to the students who have racked up $1 trillion in debt, and to the graduate students who are taking second degrees because their first one was so worthless. They also bear some responsibility for the 17m who are overqualified for their jobs, and for the 3m unfilled positions for which skilled workers cannot be found. They even owe it to the 37m who went to college, dropped out and ended up with nothing: many left for economic reasons.

Universities may counter that the value of a degree cannot be reduced to a simple economic number. That, though, sounds increasingly cynical, when the main reason universities have been able to increase their revenue so much is because of loans given to students on the basis of what they are told they will one day earn.

BARBARA EHRENREICH

Bonfire of the Princesses

CONTRARY TO THE RUMORS I have been trying to spread for some time, Disney Princess products are not contaminated with lead. More careful analysis shows that the entire product line—books, DVD's, ball gowns, necklaces, toy cell phones, toothbrush holders, t-shirts, lunch boxes, backpacks, wallpaper, sheets, stickers, etc.—is saturated with a particularly potent time-release form of the date rape drug.

We cannot blame China this time, because the drug is in the concept, which was spawned in the Disney studios. Before 2000, the Princesses were just the separate, disunited, heroines of Disney animated films—Snow White, Cinderella, Ariel, Aurora, Pocahontas, Jasmine, Belle, and Mulan. Then Disney's Andy Mooney got the idea of bringing the gals together in a team. With a wave of the wand ($10.99 at Target, tiara included) they were all elevated to royal status and set loose on the world as an imperial cabal, and have since have busied themselves achieving global domination. Today, there is no little girl in the wired, industrial world who does not seek to display her allegiance to the pink- and-purple clad Disney dynasty.

Disney likes to think of the Princesses as role models, but what a sorry bunch of wusses they are. Typically, they spend much of their time in captivity or a coma, waking up only when a Prince comes along and kisses them. The most striking exception is Mulan, who dresses as a boy to fight in the army, but—like the other Princess of color, Pocahontas—she lacks full Princess status and does not warrant a line of tiaras and gowns. Otherwise the Princesses have no ambitions and no marketable skills, although both Snow White and Cinderella are good at housecleaning.

And what could they aspire to, beyond landing a Prince? In Princessland, the only career ladder leads from baby-faced adolescence to a position as an evil enchantress, stepmother or witch. Snow White's wicked stepmother is consumed with envy for her stepdaughter's beauty; the sea witch, Ursula, covets Ariel's lovely voice; Cinderella's stepmother exploits the girl's cheap, uncomplaining, labor. No need for complicated witch-hunting techniques—pin-prickings and dunkings—in Princessland. All you have to look for is wrinkles.

5 Feminist parents gnash their teeth. For this their little girls gave up Dora, who bounds through the jungle saving baby jaguars, whose mother is an archeologist and whose adventures don't involve smoochy rescues by Diego? There was drama in Dora's life too, and the occasional bad actor like Swiper the fox. Even Barbie looks like a suffragette compared to Disney's Belle. So what's the appeal of the pink tulle Princess cult?

Seen from the witchy end of the female life cycle, the Princesses exert their pull through a dark and undeniable eroticism. They're sexy little wenches, for one thing. Snow White has gotten slimmer and bustier over the years; Ariel wears nothing but a bikini top (though, admittedly, she is half fish.) In faithful imitation, the three-year old in my life flounces around with her tiara askew and her Princess gown sliding off her shoulder, looking for all the world like a London socialite after a hard night of cocaine and booze. Then she demands a poison apple and falls to the floor in a beautiful swoon. Pass the Rohypnol-laced margarita, please.

It may be old-fashioned to say so, but sex—and especially some middle-aged man's twisted version thereof—doesn't belong in the pre-K playroom. Children are going to discover it soon enough, but they're got to do so on their own.

There's a reason, after all, why we're generally more disgusted by sexual abusers than adults who inflict mere violence on children: We sense that sexual abuse more deeply messes with a child's mind. One's sexual inclinations—straightforward or kinky, active or passive, heterosexual or homosexual—should be free to develop without adult intervention or manipulation. Hence our harshness toward the kind of sexual predators who leer at kids and offer candy. But Disney, which also owns ABC, Lifetime, ESPN, A&E and Miramax, is rewarded with $4 billion a year for marketing the masochistic Princess cult and its endlessly proliferating paraphernalia.

Let's face it, no parent can stand up against this alone. Try to ban the Princesses from your home, and you might as well turn yourself in to Child Protective Services before the little girls get on their Princess cell phones. No, the only way to topple royalty is through a mass uprising of the long-suffering serfs. Assemble with your neighbors and make a holiday bonfire out of all that plastic and tulle! March on Disney World with pitchforks held high!

BARBARA EHRENREICH { *Cultural Baggage*

BARBARA EHRENREICH (b. 1941), a native of Butte, Montana, earned a PhD in biology from Rockefeller University in New York City. She turned to writing later in her professional life, and she now wears many hats: journalist, feminist, social critic, and political activist. She has written almost twenty books, two of which became *New York Times* best sellers: *Nickel and Dimed: On (Not) Getting By in America* (2001), a record of her experiment trying to live only on what she earned at minimum-wage jobs, and *Bait and Switch: The (Futile) Pursuit of the American Dream* (2006), in which she examines the growing trend of white-collar unemployment. Her articles have appeared in *Harper's*, *Time*, *Mother Jones*, *Ms.*, *The Atlantic Monthly*, and many other periodicals.

In "Cultural Baggage," originally published in the *New York Times* in 1992, Ehrenreich explains the difficulty she has had identifying with a particular ethnic heritage, even as she claims an intellectual heritage: she belongs among those who think for themselves and try new things. She argues that "skepticism, curiosity, and wide-eyed ecumenical tolerance" are as worthy a heritage as any other. As you read, notice how Ehrenreich uses narrative and dialogue to trace her intellectual lineage.

AN ACQUAINTANCE WAS TELLING ME about the joys of rediscovering her ethnic and religious heritage. "I know exactly what my ancestors were doing 2,000 years ago," she said, eyes gleaming with enthusiasm,

"HERS; Cultural Baggage" by Barbara Ehrenreich. Originally published in the *New York Times Magazine*, April 5, 1992. Used by permission of the New York Times Syndication.

"and *I can do the same things now.*" Then she leaned forward and inquired politely, "And what is your ethnic background, if I may ask?"

"None," I said, that being the first word in line to get out of my mouth. Well, not "none," I backtracked. Scottish, English, Irish—that was something, I supposed. Too much Irish to qualify as a WASP; too much of the hated English to warrant a "Kiss Me, I'm Irish" button; plus there are a number of dead ends in the family tree due to adoptions, missing records, failing memories and the like. I was blushing by this time. Did "none" mean I was rejecting my heritage out of Anglo-Celtic self-hate? Or was I revealing a hidden ethnic chauvinism in which the Britannically derived serve as a kind of neutral standard compared with the ethnic "others"?

Throughout the 1960's and 70's I watched one group after another—African Americans, Latinos, Native Americans—stand up and proudly reclaim their roots while I just sank back ever deeper into my seat. All this excitement over ethnicity stemmed, I uneasily sensed, from a past in which *their* ancestors had been trampled upon by *my* ancestors, or at least by people who looked very much like them. In addition, it had begun to seem almost un-American not to have some sort of hyphen at hand, linking one to more venerable times and locales.

But the truth is I was raised with none. We'd eaten ethnic foods in my childhood home, but these were all borrowed, like the pastries, or Cornish meat pies, my father had picked up from his fellow miners in Butte, Montana. If my mother had one rule, it was militant ecumenism in all matters of food and experience. "Try new things," she would say, meaning anything from sweetbreads to clams, with an emphasis on the "new."

As a child, I briefly nourished a craving for tradition and roots. I immersed myself in the works of Sir Walter Scott. I pretended to believe that the bagpipe was a musical instrument. I was fascinated to learn from my grandmother that we were descended from certain Highland clans and longed for a pleated skirt in one of their distinctive tartans. 5

But in *Ivanhoe,* it was the dark-eyed "Jewess" Rebecca I identified with, not the flaxen-haired bimbo Rowena. As for clans: Why not call them "tribes," those bands of half-clad peasants and warriors whose idea of cuisine was stuffed sheep gut washed down with whisky? And then in my early teens I was stung by Disraeli's[1] remark to the effect that his ancestors had been leading orderly, literate lives when my ancestors were still rampaging through the highlands daubing themselves with blue paint.

Motherhood put the screws on me, ethnicity-wise. I had hoped that by marrying a man of Eastern European-Jewish ancestry I would acquire for my descendants the ethnic genes that my own forebears so sadly lacked. At one point, I even subjected the children to a Passover seder[2] of my own design, which included a little talk about the flight from Egypt and its relevance to modern social issues. But the kids insisted on buttering their matzohs and snickering through my talk. "Give me a break, Mom," the older one said. "You don't even believe in God."

After the tiny pagans had been put to bed, I sat down to brood over Elijah's wine.[3] What had I been thinking? The kids knew that their Jewish grandparents were secular folks who didn't hold seders themselves. And if ethnicity eluded me, how could I expect it to take root in my children, who are not only Scottish-English-Irish, but Hungarian-Polish-Russian to boot?

But, then, on the fumes of Manischewitz,[4] a great insight took form in my mind. It was true, as the kids said, that I didn't "believe in God." But this could be taken as something very different from an accusation—a reminder of a genuine heritage. My parents had not believed in God either, nor had my grandparents or any other progenitors going back to the great-great level. They had become disillusioned with Christianity generations ago—just as, on the in-law side, my children's other ancestors had shaken off their Orthodox Judaism. This

[1]Benjamin Disraeli (1804–81), British prime minister in 1868 and from 1874 to 1880 and the only Jew to hold that office.

[2]A ceremonial dinner held to commemorate the exodus of the Jews from Egypt.

[3]At a seder, a portion of wine set aside as "Elijah's cup."

[4]A kosher brand of sweet red wine, common at seders.

insight did not exactly furnish me with an "identity," but it was at least something to work with: we are the kind of people, I realized—whatever our distant ancestors' religions—who do *not* believe, who do not carry on traditions, who do not do things just because someone has done them before.

10 The epiphany went on: I recalled that my mother never introduced a procedure for cooking or cleaning by telling me, "Grandma did it this way." What did Grandma know, living in the days before vacuum cleaners and disposable toilet mops? In my parents' general view, new things were better than old, and the very fact that some ritual had been performed in the past was a good reason for abandoning it now. Because what was the past, as our forebears knew it? Nothing but poverty, superstition, and grief. "Think for yourself," Dad used to say. "Always ask why."

In fact, this may have been the ideal cultural heritage for my particular ethnic strain—bounced as it was from the Highlands of Scotland across the sea, out to the Rockies, down into the mines and finally spewed out into high-tech, suburban America. What better philosophy, for a race of migrants, than "think for yourself"? What better maxim, for a people whose whole world was rudely inverted every thirty years or so, than "try new things"?

The more tradition minded, the newly enthusiastic celebrants of Purim and Kwanzaa and Solstice,[5] may see little point to survival if the survivors carry no cultural freight—religion, for example, or ethnic tradition. To which I would say that skepticism, curiosity, and wide-eyed ecumenical tolerance are also worthy elements of the human tradition and are at least as old as such notions as "Serbian" or "Croatian," "Scottish," or "Jewish." I make no claims for my personal line of progenitors except that they remained loyal to the values that may have induced all of our ancestors, long, long ago, to climb down from the trees and make their way into the open plains.

A few weeks ago, I cleared my throat and asked the children, now mostly grown and fearsomely smart, whether they felt any stirrings of

[5]Holidays celebrated by, respectively, Jewish groups, African American groups, and so-called "Neopagans."

ethnic or religious identity, etc., which might have been, ahem, insufficiently nourished at home. "None," they said, adding firmly, "and the world would be a better place if nobody else did, either." My chest swelled with pride, as would my mother's, to know that the race of "none" marches on.

STEPHANIE ERICSSON { *The Ways We Lie*

STEPHANIE ERICSSON (b. 1953), born and raised in San Francisco, studied filmmaking in college and has worked as a screenwriter, advertising copywriter, and freelance writer. She is the author of *Companion Through the Darkness: Inner Dialogues on Grief* (1993) and *Companion into the Dawn: Inner Dialogues on Loving* (1994), both responses to the unexpected death of her husband when she was two months pregnant with their only child. Ericsson is also the author of *Shamefaced: The Road to Recovery* (1985) and *Women of AA: Recovering Together* (1985), which document her struggles with substance abuse.

"The Ways We Lie," taken from her notes on *Companion into the Dawn,* originally appeared in the *Utne Reader,* a progressive magazine that focuses on politics, the environment, and pop culture. In this essay, Ericsson classifies the kinds of lies we tell. Like many of us, she regularly tells lies but thinks of herself as an honest person. As you read, pay attention to how she provides an anecdote to illustrate each kind of lie, then shows why lying is morally and ethically questionable, no matter the context in which it is told.

THE BANK CALLED TODAY AND I told them my deposit was in the mail, even though I hadn't written a check yet. It'd been a rough day. The baby I'm pregnant with decided to do aerobics on my lungs for two hours, our three-year-old daughter painted the living-room couch with lipstick, the IRS put me on hold for an hour, and I was late to a business meeting because I was tired.

I told my client the traffic had been bad. When my partner came home, his haggard face told me his day hadn't gone any better than mine, so when he asked, "How was your day?" I said, "Oh, fine," knowing that one more straw might break his back. A friend called and wanted to take me to lunch. I said I was busy. Four lies in the course of a day, none of which I felt the least bit guilty about.

We lie. We all do. We exaggerate, we minimize, we avoid confrontation, we spare people's feelings, we conveniently forget, we keep secrets, we justify lying to the big-guy institutions. Like most people, I indulge in small falsehoods and still think of myself as an honest person. Sure I lie, but it doesn't hurt anything. Or does it?

I once tried going a whole week without telling a lie, and it was paralyzing. I discovered that telling the truth all the time is nearly impossible. It means living with some serious consequences: The bank charges me $60 in overdraft fees, my partner keels over when I tell him about my travails, my client fires me for telling her I didn't feel like being on time, and my friend takes it personally when I say I'm not hungry. There must be some merit to lying.

5 But if I justify lying, what makes me any different from slick politicians or the corporate robbers who raided the S&L industry?[1] Saying it's okay to lie one way and not another is hedging. I cannot seem to escape the voice deep inside me that tells me: When someone lies, someone loses.

What far-reaching consequences will I, or others, pay as a result of my lie? Will someone's trust be destroyed? Will someone else pay *my* penance because I ducked out? We must consider the *meaning of our actions.* Deception, lies, capital crimes, and misdemeanors all carry meanings. *Webster's* definition of *lie* is specific:

> *1: a false statement or action especially made with the intent to deceive; 2: anything that gives or is meant to give a false impression.*

[1]The so-called "Savings and Loan crisis" of the 1980s and 1990s was brought about in part by fraud and insider-trading abuses.

A definition like this implies that there are many, many ways to tell a lie. Here are just a few.

THE WHITE LIE

A man who won't lie to a woman has very little consideration for her feelings.

—Bergen Evans

The white lie assumes that the truth will cause more damage than a simple, harmless untruth. Telling a friend he looks great when he looks like hell can be based on a decision that the friend needs a compliment more than a frank opinion. But, in effect, it is the liar deciding what is best for the lied to. Ultimately, it is a vote of no confidence. It is an act of subtle arrogance for anyone to decide what is best for someone else.

Yet not all circumstances are quite so cut-and-dried. Take, for instance, the sergeant in Vietnam who knew one of his men was killed in action but listed him as missing so that the man's family would receive indefinite compensation instead of the lump-sum pittance the military gives widows and children. His intent was honorable. Yet for twenty years this family kept their hopes alive, unable to move on to a new life.

FACADES

Et tu, Brute?

—Caesar

We all put up facades to one degree or another. When I put on a suit to go to see a client, I feel as though I am putting on another face, obeying the expectation that serious businesspeople wear suits rather than sweatpants. But I'm a writer. Normally, I get up, get the kid off to school, and sit at my computer in my pajamas until four in the afternoon. When I answer the phone, the caller thinks I'm wearing a suit (though the UPS man knows better). 10

But facades can be destructive because they are used to seduce others into an illusion. For instance, I recently realized that a former friend was a liar. He presented himself with all the right looks and the right words and offered lots of new consciousness theories, fabulous books to read, and fascinating insights. Then I did some business with him, and the time came for him to pay me. He turned out to be all talk and no walk. I heard a plethora of reasonable excuses, including in-depth descriptions of the big break around the corner. In six months of work, I saw less than a hundred bucks. When I confronted him, he raised both eyebrows and tried to convince me that I'd heard him wrong, that he'd made no commitment to me. A simple investigation into his past revealed a crowded graveyard of disenchanted former friends.

IGNORING THE PLAIN FACTS

Well, you must understand that Father Porter is only human . . .

—A MASSACHUSETTS PRIEST

In the '60s, the Catholic Church in Massachusetts began hearing complaints that Father James Porter was sexually molesting children. Rather than relieving him of his duties, the ecclesiastical authorities simply moved him from one parish to another between 1960 and 1967, actually providing him with a fresh supply of unsuspecting families and innocent children to abuse. After treatment in 1967 for pedophilia, he went back to work, this time in Minnesota. The new diocese was aware of Father Porter's obsession with children, but they needed priests and recklessly believed treatment had cured him. More children were abused until he was relieved of his duties a year later. By his own admission, Porter may have abused as many as a hundred children.

Ignoring the facts may not in and of itself be a form of lying, but consider the context of this situation. If a lie is *a false action done with the intent to deceive,* then the Catholic Church's conscious covering for Porter created irreparable consequences. The church became a co-perpetrator with Porter.

DEFLECTING

When you have no basis for an argument, abuse the plaintiff.
—Cicero

I've discovered that I can keep anyone from seeing the true me by being selectively blatant. I set a precedent of being up-front about intimate issues, but I never bring up the things I truly want to hide; I just let people assume I'm revealing everything. It's an effective way of hiding.

Any good liar knows that the way to perpetuate an untruth is to deflect attention from it. When Clarence Thomas exploded with accusations that the Senate hearings were a "high-tech lynching," he simply switched the focus from a highly charged subject to a radioactive subject.[2] Rather than defending himself, he took the offensive and accused the country of racism. It was a brilliant maneuver. Racism is now politically incorrect in official circles—unlike sexual harassment, which still rewards those who can get away with it. 15

Some of the most skillful deflectors are passive-aggressive people who, when accused of inappropriate behavior, refuse to respond to the accusations. This you-don't-exist stance infuriates the accuser, who, understandably, screams something obscene out of frustration. The trap is sprung and the act of deflection successful, because now the passive-aggressive person can indignantly say, "Who can talk to someone as unreasonable as you?" The real issue is forgotten and the sins of the original victim become the focus. Feeling guilty of name-calling, the victim is fully tamed and crawls into a hole, ashamed. I have watched this fighting technique work thousands of times in disputes between men and women, and what I've learned is that the real culprit is not necessarily the one who swears the loudest.

[2]The 1991 Senate hearings that led to the confirmation of Clarence Thomas's appointment to the U.S. Supreme Court were marked with allegations of sexual harassment and countercharges of racism.

OMISSION

The cruelest lies are often told in silence.

—R. L. Stevenson

Omission involves telling most of the truth minus one or two key facts whose absence changes the story completely. You break a pair of glasses that are guaranteed under normal use and get a new pair, without mentioning that the first pair broke during a rowdy game of basketball. Who hasn't tried something like that? But what about omission of information that could make a difference in how a person lives his or her life?

For instance, one day I found out that rabbinical legends tell of another woman in the Garden of Eden before Eve. I was stunned. The omission of the Sumerian goddess Lilith from Genesis—as well as her demonization by ancient misogynists as an embodiment of female evil—felt like spiritual robbery. I felt like I'd just found out my mother was really my stepmother. To take seriously the tradition that Adam was created out of the same mud as his equal counterpart, Lilith, redefines all of Judeo-Christian history.

Some renegade Catholic feminists introduced me to a view of Lilith that had been suppressed during the many centuries when this strong goddess was seen only as a spirit of evil. Lilith was a proud goddess who defied Adam's need to control her, attempted negotiations, and when this failed, said adios and left the Garden of Eden.

This omission of Lilith from the Bible was a patriarchal strategy to keep women weak. Omitting the strong-woman archetype of Lilith from Western religions and starting the story with Eve the Rib has helped keep Christian and Jewish women believing they were the lesser sex for thousands of years. 20

STEREOTYPES AND CLICHÉS

Where opinion does not exist, the status quo becomes stereotyped and all originality is discouraged.

—Bertrand Russell

Stereotype and cliché serve a purpose as a form of shorthand. Our need for vast amounts of information in nanoseconds has made the stereotype vital to modern communication. Unfortunately, it often shuts down original thinking, giving those hungry for the truth a candy bar of misinformation instead of a balanced meal. The stereotype explains a situation with just enough truth to seem unquestionable.

All the "isms"—racism, sexism, ageism, et al.—are founded on and fueled by the stereotype and the cliché, which are lies of exaggeration, omission, and ignorance. They are always dangerous. They take a single tree and make it a landscape. They destroy curiosity. They close minds and separate people. The single mother on welfare is assumed to be cheating. Any black male could tell you how much of his identity is obliterated daily by stereotypes. Fat people, ugly people, beautiful people, old people, large-breasted women, short men, the mentally ill, and the homeless all could tell you how much more they are like us than we want to think. I once admitted to a group of people that I had a mouth like a truck driver. Much to my surprise, a man stood up and said, "I'm a truck driver, and I never cuss." Needless to say, I was humbled.

GROUPTHINK

Who is more foolish, the child afraid of the dark, or the man afraid of the light?

—Maurice Freehill

Irving Janis, in *Victims of Group Think,* defines this sort of lie as a psychological phenomenon within decision-making groups in which loyalty to the group has become more important than any other value, with the result that dissent and the appraisal of alternatives are suppressed. If you've ever worked on a committee or in a corporation, you've encountered groupthink. It requires a combination of other forms of lying—ignoring facts, selective memory, omission, and denial, to name a few.

The textbook example of groupthink came on December 7, 1941. From as early as the fall of 1941, the warnings came in, one after another, that Japan was preparing for a massive military operation. The Navy command in Hawaii assumed Pearl Harbor was invulnerable—the Japanese weren't stupid enough to attack the United States' most important base. On the other hand, racist stereotypes said the Japanese weren't smart enough to invent a torpedo effective in less than 60 feet of water (the fleet was docked in 30 feet); after all, the U.S. technology hadn't been able to do it.

25 On Friday, December 5, normal weekend leave was granted to all the commanders at Pearl Harbor, even though the Japanese consulate in Hawaii was busy burning papers. Within the tight, good-ole-boy cohesiveness of the U.S. command in Hawaii, the myth of invulnerability stayed well entrenched. No one in the group considered the alternatives. The rest is history.[3]

OUT-AND-OUT LIES

> *The only form of lying that is beyond reproach is lying for its own sake.*
>
> —OSCAR WILDE

Of all the ways to lie, I like this one the best, probably because I get tired of trying to figure out the real meanings behind things. At least I can trust the bald-faced lie. I once asked my five-year-old nephew, "Who broke the fence?" (I had seen him do it.) He answered, "The murderers." Who could argue?

At least when this sort of lie is told it can be easily confronted. As the person who is lied to, I know where I stand. The bald-faced lie doesn't toy with my perceptions—it argues with them. It doesn't try to refash-

[3]Japan's surprise attack on the U.S. naval base at Pearl Harbor, Hawaii, on December 7, 1941, resulted in the destruction of much of America's Pacific fleet and the immediate entry of the United States into World War II.

ion reality, it tries to refute it. Read my lips . . . [4] No sleight of hand. No guessing. If this were the only form of lying, there would be no such thing as floating anxiety or the adult-children of alcoholics movement.

DISMISSAL

Pay no attention to that man behind the curtain! I am the Great Oz!

—THE WIZARD OF OZ

Dismissal is perhaps the slipperiest of all lies. Dismissing feelings, perceptions, or even the raw facts of a situation ranks as a kind of lie that can do as much damage to a person as any other kind of lie.

The roots of many mental disorders can be traced back to the dismissal of reality. Imagine that a person is told from the time she is a tot that her perceptions are inaccurate. *"Mommy, I'm scared."* "No you're not, darling." *"I don't like that man next door, he makes me feel icky."* "Johnny, that's a terrible thing to say, of course you like him. You go over there right now and be nice to him."

I've often mused over the idea that madness is actually a sane reaction to an insane world. Psychologist R. D. Laing supports this hypothesis in *Sanity, Madness & The Family,* an account of his investigations into the families of schizophrenics. The common thread that ran through all of the families he studied was a deliberate, staunch dismissal of the patient's perceptions from a very early age. Each of the patients started out with an accurate grasp of reality, which, through meticulous and methodical dismissal, was demolished until the only reality the patient could trust was catatonia. 30

Dismissal runs the gamut. Mild dismissal can be quite handy for forgiving the foibles of others in our day-to-day lives. Toddlers who have just learned to manipulate their parents' attention sometimes are dismissed out of necessity. Absolute attention from the parents would require so much energy that no one would get to eat dinner. But we

[4]Upon receiving the Republican Party presidential nomination in 1988, George H. W. Bush famously pledged, "Read my lips: no new taxes"; as president, however, he signed the Omnibus Budget Reconciliation Act of 1990, which included numerous new taxes.

must be careful and attentive about how far we take our "necessary" dismissals. Dismissal is a dangerous tool, because it's nothing less than a lie.

DELUSION

We lie loudest when we lie to ourselves.

—Eric Hoffer

I could write the book on this one. Delusion, a cousin of dismissal, is the tendency to see excuses as facts. It's a powerful lying tool because it filters out information that contradicts what we want to believe. Alcoholics who believe that the problems in their lives are legitimate reasons for drinking rather than results of the drinking offer the classic example of deluded thinking. Delusion uses the mind's ability to see things in myriad ways to support what it wants to be the truth.

But delusion is also a survival mechanism we all use. If we were to fully contemplate the consequences of our stockpiles of nuclear weapons or global warming, we could hardly function on a day-to-day level. We don't want to incorporate that much reality into our lives because to do so would be paralyzing.

Delusion acts as an adhesive to keep the status quo intact. It shamelessly employs dismissal, omission, and amnesia, among other sorts of lies. Its most cunning defense is that it cannot see itself.

• ○ •

The liar's punishment . . . is that he cannot believe anyone else.

—George Bernard Shaw

These are only a few of the ways we lie. Or are lied to. As I said earlier, it's not easy to entirely eliminate lies from our lives. No matter how pious we may try to be, we will still embellish, hedge, and omit to lubricate the daily machinery of living. But there is a world of difference between telling functional lies and living a lie. Martin Buber once said, "The lie is the spirit committing treason against itself." Our acceptance of lies becomes a cultural cancer that eventually shrouds and reorders reality until moral garbage becomes as invisible to us as water is to a fish.

How much do we tolerate before we become sick and tired of being sick and tired? When will we stand up and declare our *right* to trust? When do we stop accepting that the real truth is in the fine print? Whose lips do we read this year when we vote for president? When will we stop being so reticent about making judgments? When do we stop turning over our personal power and responsibility to liars?

Maybe if I don't tell the bank the check's in the mail I'll be less tolerant of the lies told me every day. A country song I once heard said it all for me: "You've got to stand for something or you'll fall for anything."

JOHN TAYLOR GATTO

Against School: How Public Education Cripples Our Kids, and Why

I TAUGHT FOR THIRTY YEARS in some of the worst schools in Manhattan, and in some of the best, and during that time I became an expert in boredom. Boredom was everywhere in my world, and if you asked the kids, as I often did, why they felt so bored, they always gave the same answers: They said the work was stupid, that it made no sense, that they already knew it. They said they wanted to be doing something real, not just sitting around. They said teachers didn't seem to know much about their subjects and clearly weren't interested in learning more. And the kids were right: their teachers were every bit as bored as they were.

Boredom is the common condition of schoolteachers, and anyone who has spent time in a teachers' lounge can vouch for the low energy, the whining, the dispirited attitudes, to be found there. When asked why they feel bored, the teachers tend to blame the kids, as you might expect. Who wouldn't get bored teaching students who are rude and interested only in grades? If even that. Of course, teachers are themselves products of the same twelve-year compulsory school programs that so thoroughly bore their students, and as school personnel they are trapped inside structures even more rigid than those imposed upon the children. Who, then, is to blame?

We all are. My grandfather taught me that. One afternoon when I was seven I complained to him of boredom, and he batted me hard on the head. He told me that I was never to use that term in his presence again, that if I was bored it was my fault and no one else's. The obligation to amuse and instruct myself was entirely my own, and people who didn't know that were childish people, to be avoided if possible. Certainly not to be trusted. That episode cured me of boredom forever, and here and there over the years I was able to pass on the lesson to some remarkable student. For the most part, however, I found it futile to challenge the official notion that boredom and childishness were the natural state of affairs in the classroom. Often I had to defy custom, and even bend the law, to help kids break out of this trap.

The empire struck back, of course; childish adults regularly conflate opposition with disloyalty. I once returned from a medical leave to discover that all evidence of my having been granted the leave had been purposely destroyed, that my job had been terminated, and that I no longer possessed even a teaching license. After nine months of tormented effort I was able to retrieve the license when a school secretary testified to witnessing the plot unfold. In the meantime my family suffered more than I care to remember. By the time I finally retired in 1991, I had more than enough reason to think of our schools—with their long-term, cell-block-style, forced confinement of both students and teachers—as virtual factories of childishness. Yet I honestly could not see *why* they had to be that way. My own experience had revealed to me what many other teachers must learn along the way, too, yet keep to themselves for fear of reprisal: if we wanted to we could easily and inexpensively jettison the old, stupid structures and help kids take an education rather than merely receive a schooling. We could encourage the best qualities of youthfulness—curiosity, adventure, resilience, the capacity for surprising insight—simply by being more flexible about time, texts, and tests, by introducing kids to truly competent adults, and by giving each student what autonomy he or she needs in order to take a risk every now and then.

5 But we don't do that. And the more I asked why not, and persisted in thinking about the "problem" of schooling as an engineer might, the more I missed the point: What if there is no "problem" with our schools? What if they are the way they are, so expensively flying in the face of common sense and long experience in how children learn things, not because they are doing something wrong but because they are doing something right? Is it possible that George W. Bush accidentally spoke the truth when he said we would "leave no child behind"?

Could it be that our schools are designed to make sure not one of them ever really grows up?

Do we really need school? I don't mean education, just forced schooling: six classes a day, five days a week, nine months a year, for twelve years. Is this deadly routine really necessary? And if so, for what? Don't hide behind reading, writing, and arithmetic as a rationale, because 2 million happy homeschoolers have surely put that banal justification to rest. Even if they hadn't, a considerable number of well-known Americans never went through the twelve-year wringer our kids currently go through, and they turned out all right. George Washington, Benjamin Franklin, Thomas Jefferson, Abraham Lincoln? Someone taught them, to be sure, but they were not products of a school *system*, and not one of them was ever "graduated" from a secondary school. Throughout most of American history, kids generally didn't go to high school, yet the unschooled rose to be admirals, like Farragut; inventors, like Edison; captains of industry, like Carnegie and Rockefeller, writers, like Melville and Twain and Conrad; and even scholars, like Margaret Mead. In fact, until pretty recently people who reached the age of thirteen weren't looked upon as children at all. Ariel Durant, who co-wrote an enormous, and very good, multivolume history of the world with her husband. Will, was happily married at fifteen, and who could reasonably claim that Ariel Durant was an uneducated person? Unschooled, perhaps, but not uneducated.

We have been taught (that is, schooled) in this country to think of "success" as synonymous with, or at least dependent upon, "schooling," but historically that isn't true in either an intellectual or a financial sense. And plenty of people throughout the world today find a way to educate themselves without resorting to a system of compulsory secondary schools that all too often resemble prisons. Why, then, do Americans confuse education with just such a system? What exactly is the purpose of our public schools?

Mass schooling of a compulsory nature really got its teeth into the United States between 1905 and 1915, though it was conceived of much earlier and pushed for throughout most of the nineteenth century. The reason given for this enormous upheaval of family life and cultural traditions was, roughly speaking, threefold:

1) To make good people.

2) To make good citizens.

3) To make each person his or her personal best. 10

These goals are still trotted out today on a regular basis, and most of us accept them in one form or another as a decent definition of public education's mission, however short schools actually fall in achieving them. But we are dead wrong. Compounding our error is the fact that the national literature holds numerous and surprisingly consistent statements of compulsory schooling's true purpose. We have, for example, the great H. L. Mencken, who wrote in *The American Mercury* for April 1924 that the aim of public education is not

> to fill the young of the species with knowledge and awaken their intelligence. . . . Nothing could be further from the truth. The aim . . . is simply to reduce as many individuals as possible to the same safe level, to breed and train a standardized citizenry, to put down dissent and originality. That is its aim in the United States . . . and that is its aim everywhere else.

Because of Mencken's reputation as a satirist, we might be tempted to dismiss this passage as a bit of hyperbolic sarcasm. His article, however, goes on to trace the template for our own educational system back to the now vanished, though never to be forgotten, military state of Prussia. And although he was certainly aware of the irony that we had recently been at war with Germany, the heir to Prussian thought and culture, Mencken was being perfectly serious here. Our educational system really is Prussian in origin, and that really is cause for concern.

The odd fact of a Prussian provenance for our schools pops up again and again once you know to look for it. William James alluded to it many times at the turn of the century. Orestes Brownson, the hero of Christopher Lasch's 1991 book, *The True and Only Heaven*, was publicly denouncing the Prussianization of American schools back in the 1840s. Horace Mann's "Seventh Annual Report" to the Massachu- 15 setts State Board of Education in 1843 is essentially a paean to the land of Frederick the Great and a call for its schooling to be brought here. That Prussian culture loomed large in America is hardly surprising, given our early association with that utopian state. A Prussian served as Washington's aide during the Revolutionary War, and so many German-speaking people had settled here by 1795 that Congress considered publishing a German-language edition of the federal laws. But what shocks is that we should so eagerly have adopted one of the very worst aspects of Prussian culture: an educational system deliberately designed to produce mediocre intellects, to hamstring the inner life, to deny students appreciable leadership skills, and to ensure docile and incomplete citizens—all in order to render the populace "manageable."

It was from James Bryant Conant—president of Harvard for twenty years, WWI poison-gas specialist, WWII executive on the atomic-bomb project, high commissioner of the American zone in Germany after WWII, and truly one of the most influential figures of the twentieth century—that I first got wind of the real purposes of American schooling. Without Conant, we would probably not have the same style and degree of standardized testing that we enjoy today, nor would we be blessed with gargantuan high schools that warehouse 2,000 to 4,000 students at a time, like the famous Columbine High in Littleton, Colorado. Shortly after I retired from teaching I picked up Conant's 1959 book-length essay, *The Child the Parent and the State*, and was more than a little intrigued to see him mention in passing that the modern schools we attend were the result of a "revolution" engineered between 1905 and 1930. A revolution? He declines to elaborate, but he does direct the curious and the uninformed to Alexander Inglis's 1918 book, *Principles of Secondary Education*, in which "one saw this revolution through the eyes of a revolutionary."

Inglis, for whom a lecture in education at Harvard is named, makes it perfectly clear that compulsory schooling on this continent was intended to be just what it had been for Prussia in the 1820s: a fifth column into the burgeoning democratic movement that threatened to give the peasants and the proletarians a voice at the bargaining table. Modern, industrialized, compulsory schooling was to make a sort of surgical incision into the prospective unity of these underclasses. Divide children by subject, by age-grading, by constant rankings on tests, and by many other more subtle means, and it was unlikely that the ignorant mass of mankind, separated in childhood, would ever reintegrate into a dangerous whole.

Inglis breaks down the purpose—the *actual* purpose—of modern schooling into six basic functions, any one of which is enough to curl the hair of those innocent enough to believe the three traditional goals listed earlier:

1) The *adjustive* or *adaptive* function. Schools are to establish fixed habits of reaction to authority. This, of course, precludes critical judgment completely. It also pretty much destroys the idea that useful or interesting material should be taught, because you can't test for *reflexive* obedience until you know whether you can make kids learn, and do, foolish and boring things.

2) The *integrating* function. This might well be called "the conformity function," because its intention is to make children as alike as possible. People who conform are predictable, and this is of great use to those who wish to harness and manipulate a large labor force. 20

3) The *diagnostic and directive* function. School is meant to determine each student's proper social role. This is done by logging evidence mathematically and anecdotally on cumulative records. As in "your permanent record." Yes, you do have one.

4) The *differentiating* function. Once their social role has been "diagnosed," children are to be sorted by role and trained only so far as their destination in the social machine merits—and not one step further. So much for making kids their personal best.

5) The *selective* function. This refers not to human choice at all but to Darwin's theory of natural selection as applied to what he called "the favored races." In short, the idea is to help things along by consciously attempting to improve the breeding stock. Schools are meant to tag the unfit—with poor grades, remedial placement, and other punishments—clearly enough that their peers will accept them as inferior and effectively bar them from the reproductive sweepstakes. That's what all those little humiliations from first grade onward were intended to do: wash the dirt down the drain.

6) The *propaedeutic* function. The societal system implied by these rules will require an elite group of caretakers. To that end, a small fraction of the kids will quietly be taught how to manage this continuing project, how to watch over and control a population deliberately dumbed down and declawed in order that government might proceed unchallenged and corporations might never want for obedient labor.

That, unfortunately, is the purpose of mandatory public education in this country. And lest you take Inglis for an isolated crank with a rather too cynical take on the educational enterprise, you should know that he was hardly alone in championing these ideas. Conant himself, building on the ideas of Horace Mann and others, campaigned tirelessly for an American school system designed along the same lines. Men like George Peabody, who funded the cause of mandatory schooling throughout the South, surely understood that the Prussian system was useful in creating not only a harmless electorate and a servile labor force but also a virtual herd of mindless consumers. In time a great number of industrial titans came to recognize the enormous profits to be had by cultivating and tending just such a herd via public education, among them Andrew Carnegie and John D. Rockefeller. 25

There you have it. Now you know. We don't need Karl Marx's conception of a grand warfare between the classes to see that it is in the interest of complex management, economic or political, to dumb people down, to demoralize them, to divide them from one another, and to discard them if they don't conform. Class may frame the proposition, as when Woodrow Wilson, then president of Princeton University, said the following to the New York City School Teachers Association in 1909: "We want one class of persons to have a liberal education, and we want another class of persons, a very much larger class, of necessity, in every society, to forgo the privileges of a liberal education and fit themselves to perform specific difficult manual tasks." But the motives behind the disgusting decisions that bring about these ends need not be class-based at all. They can stem purely from fear, or from the by now familiar belief that "efficiency" is the paramount virtue, rather than love, liberty, laughter, or hope. Above all, they can stem from simple greed.

There were vast fortunes to be made, after all, in an economy based on mass production and organized to favor the large corporation rather than the small business or the family farm. But mass production required mass consumption, and at the turn of the twentieth century most Americans considered it both unnatural and unwise to buy things they didn't actually need. Mandatory schooling was a godsend on that count. School didn't have to train kids in any direct sense to think they should consume nonstop, because it did something even better: it encouraged them not to think at all. And that left them sitting ducks for another great invention of the modern era—marketing.

Now, you needn't have studied marketing to know that there are two groups of people who can always be convinced to consume more than they need to: addicts and children. School has done a pretty good job of turning our children into addicts, but it has done a spectacular job of turning our children into children. Again, this is no accident. Theorists from Plato to Rousseau to our own Dr. Inglis knew that if children could be cloistered with other children, stripped of responsibility and independence, encouraged to develop only the trivializing emotions of greed, envy, jealousy, and fear, they would grow older but never truly grow up. In the 1934 edition of his once well-known book *Public Education in the United States*, Ellwood P. Cubberley detailed and praised the way the strategy of successive school enlargements had extended childhood by two to six years, and forced schooling was at that point still quite new. This same Cubberley—who was dean of Stanford's School of Education, a textbook editor at Houghton Mifflin, and Conant's friend and correspondent at Harvard—had written the following in the 1922 edition of his book *Public School Administration*: "Our schools are . . . factories in which the raw products (children) are to be shaped and fashioned. . . . And it is the business of the school to build its pupils according to the specifications laid down."

It's perfectly obvious from our society today what those specifications were. Maturity has by now been banished from nearly every aspect of our lives. Easy divorce laws have removed the need to work at relationships; easy credit has removed the need for fiscal self-control; easy entertainment has removed the need to learn to entertain oneself; easy answers have removed the need to ask questions. We have become a nation of children, happy to surrender our judgments and our wills to political exhortations and commercial blandishments that would insult actual adults. We buy televisions, and then we buy the things we see on the television. We buy computers, and then we buy the things we see on the computer. We buy $150 sneakers whether we need them or not, and when they fall apart too soon we buy another pair. We drive SUVs and believe the lie that they constitute a kind of life insurance, even when we're upside-down in them. And, worst of all, we don't bat an eye when Art Fleischer tells us to "be careful what you say," even if we remember having been told somewhere back in school that America is the land of the free. We simply buy that one too. Our schooling, as intended, has seen to it.

Now for the good news. Once you understand the logic behind modern schooling, its tricks and traps are fairly easy to avoid. School trains children to be employees and consumers; teach your own to be leaders and adventurers. School trains children to obey reflexively; teach your own to think critically and independently. Well-schooled kids have a low threshold for boredom; help your own to develop an inner life so that they'll never be bored. Urge them to take on the serious material, the *grown-up* material, in history, literature, philosophy, music, art, economics, theology—all the stuff schoolteachers know well enough to avoid. Challenge your kids with plenty of solitude so that they can learn to enjoy their own company, to conduct inner dialogues. Well-schooled people are conditioned to dread being alone, and they seek constant companionship through the TV, the computer, the cell phone, and through shallow friendships quickly acquired and quickly abandoned. Your children should have a more meaningful life, and they can. 30

First, though, we must wake up to what our schools really are: laboratories of experimentation on young minds, drill centers for the habits and attitudes that corporate society demands. Mandatory education serves children only incidentally; its real purpose is to turn them into servants. Don't let your own have their childhoods extended, not even for a day. If David Farragut could take command of a captured British warship as a preteen, if Thomas Edison could publish a broadsheet at the age of twelve, if Ben Franklin could apprentice himself to a printer at the same age (then put himself through a course of study that would choke a Yale senior today), there's no telling what your own kids could do. After a long life, and thirty years in the public school trenches, I've concluded that genius is as common as dirt. We suppress our genius only because we haven't yet figured out how to manage a population of educated men and women. The solution, I think, is simple and glorious. Let them manage themselves.

LINDA HOGAN | *Hearing Voices*

LINDA HOGAN (b. 1947) is a Chickasaw writer whose work often addresses the connections between humans and the natural world. Hogan was born in Denver, Colorado; her father was in the army and the family moved frequently, but whenever possible they returned to her father's family home in Oklahoma. She earned her undergraduate degree at the University of Colorado at Colorado Springs and her MA at the University of Colorado at Boulder. She taught at several colleges and universities before joining the faculty at the University of Colorado at Boulder in 1989; she is now professor emerita there. Hogan has published several collections of short stories, poems, and essays, as well as many novels and plays. Her first novel, *Mean Spirit* (1990), describes life for the Osage Indians during the Oklahoma oil boom of the 1920s and was a finalist for the Pulitzer Prize in Fiction.

In "Hearing Voices," Hogan skillfully weaves several topics, including corn genetics, mythology, and politics, into her discussion of writing and writers' responsibilities. Notice how she emphasizes the importance of language and of using it strategically to accomplish worthwhile goals—and how her own essay is carefully arranged to accomplish its own goals.

WHEN BARBARA MCCLINTOCK WAS AWARDED a Nobel Prize for her work on gene transposition in corn plants, the most striking thing about her was that she made her discoveries by listening to what the corn spoke to her, by respecting the life of the corn and "letting it come."

McClintock says she learned "the stories" of the plants. She "heard"

"Hearing Voices" from *The Writer and her Work, Volume II.* Used by permission of Beth Vesel Literary Agency.

them. She watched the daily green journeys of growth from earth toward sky and sun. She knew her plants in the way a healer or mystic would have known them, from the inside, the inner voices of corn and woman speaking to one another.

As an Indian woman, I come from a long history of people who have listened to the language of this continent, people who have known that corn grows with the songs and prayers of the people, that it has a story to tell, that the world is alive. Both in oral traditions and in mythology—the true language of inner life—account after account tells of the stones giving guidance, the trees singing, the corn telling of inner earth, the dragonfly offering up a tongue. This is true in the European traditions as well: Psyche received direction from the reeds and the ants, Orpheus knew the languages of earth, animals, and birds.[1]

This intuitive and common language is what I seek for my writing, work in touch with the mystery and force of life, work that speaks a few of the many voices around us, and it is important to me that McClintock listened to the voices of corn. It is important to the continuance of life that she told the truth of her method and that it reminded us all of where our strength, our knowing, and our sustenance come from.

It is also poetry, this science, and I note how often scientific theories lead to the world of poetry and vision, theories telling us how atoms that were stars have been transformed into our living, breathing bodies. And in these theories, or maybe they should be called stories, we begin to understand how we are each many people, including the stars we once were, and how we are in essence the earth and the universe, how what we do travels clear around the earth and returns. In a single moment of our living, there is our ancestral and personal history, our future, even our deaths planted in us and already growing toward their fulfillment. The corn plants are there, and like all the rest we are forever merging our borders with theirs in the world collective. 5

Our very lives might depend on this listening. In the Chernobyl

[1]In Greek mythology, Psyche was a beautiful mortal woman who became the lover of Eros, the god of love, and was eventually made a goddess herself; Orpheus, "the father of song," was said to be able to charm animals, trees, and even rocks into dancing to his songs.

nuclear accident,[2] the wind told the story that was being suppressed by the people. It gave away the truth. It carried the story of danger to other countries. It was a poet, a prophet, a scientist.

Sometimes, like the wind, poetry has its own laws speaking for the life of the planet. It is a language that wants to bring back together what the other words have torn apart. It is the language of life speaking through us about the sacredness of life.

This life speaking life is what I find so compelling about the work of poets such as Ernesto Cardenal, who is also a priest and was the Nicaraguan Minister of Culture. He writes: "The armadilloes are very happy with this government. . . . Not only humans desired liberation/the whole ecology wanted it." Cardenal has also written "The Parrots," a poem about caged birds who were being sent to the United States as pets for the wealthy, how the cages were opened, the parrots allowed back into the mountains and jungles, freed like the people, "and sent back to the land we were pulled from."

How we have been pulled from the land! And how poetry has worked hard to set us free, uncage us, keep us from split tongues that mimic the voices of our captors. It returns us to our land. Poetry is a string of words that parades without a permit. It is a lockbox of words to put an ear to as we try to crack the safe of language, listening for the right combination, the treasure inside. It is life resonating. It is sometimes called Prayer, Soothsaying, Complaint, Invocation, Proclamation, Testimony, Witness. Writing is and does all these things. And like that parade, it is illegitimately insistent on going its own way, on being part of the miracle of life, telling the story about what happened when we were cosmic dust, what it means to be stars listening to our human atoms.

But don't misunderstand me. I am not just a dreamer. I am also the practical type. A friend's father, watching the United States stage another revolution in another Third World country, said, "Why doesn't the government just feed people and then let the political chips 10

[2]On April 26, 1986, an accident at the Chernobyl nuclear power plant in Ukraine resulted in a steam explosion and fire that released radioactive gases into the atmosphere, contaminating large areas of Belarus, Ukraine, and Russia.

fall where they may?" He was right. It was easy, obvious, even financially more reasonable to do that, to let democracy be chosen because it feeds hunger. I want my writing to be that simple, that clear and direct. Likewise, I feel it is not enough for me just to write, but I need to live it, to be informed by it. I have found over the years that my work has more courage than I do. It has more wisdom. It teaches me, leads me places I never knew I was heading. And it is about a new way of living, of being in the world.

I was on a panel recently where the question was raised whether we thought literature could save lives. The audience, book people, smiled expectantly with the thought. I wanted to say, Yes, it saves lives. But I couldn't speak those words. It saves spirits maybe, hearts. It changes minds, but for me writing is an incredible privilege. When I sit down at the desk, there are other women who are hungry, homeless. I don't want to forget that, that the world of matter is still there to be reckoned with. This writing is a form of freedom most other people do not have. So, when I write, I feel a responsibility, a commitment to other humans and to the animal and plant communities as well.

Still, writing has changed me. And there is the powerful need we all have to tell a story, each of us with a piece of the whole pattern to complete. As Alice Walker says, We are all telling part of the same story, and as Sharon Olds has said, Every writer is a cell on the body politic of America.[3]

Another Nobel Prize laureate is Betty William, a Northern Ireland co-winner of the 1977 Peace Prize. I heard her speak about how, after witnessing the death of children, she stepped outside in the middle of the night and began knocking on doors and yelling, behaviors that would have earned her a diagnosis of hysteria in our own medical circles. She knocked on doors that might have opened with weapons pointing in her face, and she cried out, "What kind of people have we become that we would allow children to be killed on our streets?" Within four hours the city was awake, and there were sixteen thousand names on petitions for peace. Now, that woman's work is a lesson to

[3]Alice Walker (b. 1944), American writer best known for her novel *The Color Purple*; Sharon Olds (b. 1942), American poet.

those of us who deal with language, and to those of us who are dealt into silence. She used language to begin the process of peace. This is the living, breathing power of the word. It is poetry. So are the names of those who signed the petitions. Maybe it is this kind of language that saves lives.

Writing begins for me with survival, with life and with freeing life, saving life, speaking life. It is work that speaks what can't be easily said. It originates from a compelling desire to live and be alive. For me, it is sometimes the need to speak for other forms of life, to take the side of human life, even our sometimes frivolous living, and our grief-filled living, our joyous living, our violent living, busy living, our peaceful living. It is about possibility. It is based in the world of matter. I am interested in how something small turns into an image that is large and strong with resonance, where the ordinary becomes beautiful. I believe the divine, the magic, is here in the weeds at our feet, unacknowledged. What a world this is. Where else could water rise up to the sky, turn into snow crystals, magnificently brought together, fall from the sky all around us, pile up billions deep, and catch the small sparks of sunlight as they return again to water?

15 These acts of magic happen all the time; in Chaco Canyon,[4] my sister has seen a kiva, a ceremonial room in the earth, that is in the center of the canyon. This place has been uninhabited for what seems like forever. It has been without water. In fact, there are theories that the ancient people disappeared when they journeyed after water. In the center of it a corn plant was growing. It was all alone and it had been there since the ancient ones, the old ones who came before us all, those people who wove dog hair into belts, who witnessed the painting of flute players on the seeping canyon walls, who knew the stories of corn. And there was one corn plant growing out of the holy place. It planted itself yearly. With no water, no person to care for it, no overturning of the soil, this corn plant rises up to tell its story, and that's what this poetry is.

[4]Onetime home of an ancient pueblo people and now a U.S. National Historical Park, located in northwestern New Mexico.

MARTIN LUTHER KING JR.

Letter from Birmingham Jail

MARTIN LUTHER KING JR. (1929–1968) was born in Atlanta, Georgia, and earned a BA from Morehouse College in 1948, a Bachelor of Divinity degree from Crozer Theological Seminary in 1951, and a PhD from Boston University in 1955. He led the Montgomery Bus Boycott in 1956, advocating nonviolent resistance to bring about social change. An outspoken and charismatic activist for civil rights, King delivered his well-known "I Have a Dream" speech during the 1963 March on Washington. In 1964 he became the youngest person to receive a Nobel Peace Prize, for his work to end racial discrimination and segregation. King was assassinated in 1968 in Memphis, Tennessee.

King wrote "Letter from Birmingham Jail" from his jail cell in Birmingham, Alabama, in April 1963, after being arrested for leading a nonviolent protest against discriminatory Jim Crow laws. The letter is a response to eight white Alabama clergymen who had issued a statement criticizing King's methods of protest and arguing that civil rights should be attained by "local Negro leadership"—not "outsiders" like King—through a slower process of negotiation and, if necessary, the courts, not through protests and direct action. Note how King addresses his critics directly throughout the letter and refers to them as "men of genuine good will." How might this approach be more effective than a more general, abstract response?

MY DEAR FELLOW CLERGYMEN:[1]

While confined here in the Birmingham city jail, I came across your recent statement calling my present activities "unwise and untimely." Seldom do I pause to answer criticism of my work and ideas. If I sought to answer all the criticisms that cross my desk, my secretaries would have little time for anything other than such correspondence in the course of the day, and I would have no time for constructive work. But since I feel that you are men of genuine good will and that your criticisms are sincerely set forth, I want to try to answer your statement in what I hope will be patient and reasonable terms.

I think I should indicate why I am here in Birmingham, since you have been influenced by the view which argues against "outsiders coming in." I have the honor of serving as president of the Southern Christian Leadership Conference, an organization operating in every southern state, with headquarters in Atlanta, Georgia. We have some eighty-five affiliated organizations across the South, and one of them is the Alabama Christian Movement for Human Rights. Frequently we share staff, educational, and financial resources with our affiliates. Several months ago the affiliate here in Birmingham asked us to be on call to engage in a nonviolent direct-action program if such were deemed necessary. We readily consented, and when the hour came we lived up to our promise. So I, along with several members of my staff, am here because I was invited here. I am here because I have organizational ties here.

But more basically, I am in Birmingham because injustice is here. Just as the prophets of the eighth century B.C. left their villages and carried their "thus saith the Lord" far beyond the boundaries of their

[1]This response to a published statement by eight fellow clergymen from Alabama (Bishop C. C. J. Carpenter, Bishop Joseph A. Durick, Rabbi Milton L. Grafman, Bishop Paul Hardin, Bishop Holan B. Harmon, the Reverend George M. Murray, the Reverend Edward V. Ramage and the Reverend Earl Stallings) was composed under somewhat constricting circumstances. Begun on the margins of the newspaper in which the statement appeared while I was in jail, the letter was continued on scraps of writing paper supplied by a friendly Negro trusty, and concluded on a pad my attorneys were eventually permitted to leave me. Although the text remains in substance unaltered, I have indulged in the author's prerogative of polishing it for publication. [Author's note. Unless otherwise indicated, as here, notes are those of the editor.]

home towns, and just as the Apostle Paul left his village of Tarsus and carried the gospel of Jesus Christ to the far corners of the Greco-Roman world, so am I compelled to carry the gospel of freedom beyond my own home town. Like Paul, I must constantly respond to the Macedonian call for aid.

Moreover, I am cognizant of the interrelatedness of all communities and states. I cannot sit idly by in Atlanta and not be concerned about what happens in Birmingham. Injustice anywhere is a threat to justice everywhere. We are caught in an inescapable network of mutuality, tied in a single garment of destiny. Whatever affects one directly, affects all indirectly. Never again can we afford to live with the narrow, provincial "outside agitator" idea. Anyone who lives inside the United States can never be considered an outsider anywhere within its bounds. 5

You deplore the demonstrations taking place in Birmingham. But your statement, I am sorry to say, fails to express a similar concern for the conditions that brought about the demonstrations. I am sure that none of you would want to rest content with the superficial kind of social analysis that deals merely with effects and does not grapple with underlying causes. It is unfortunate that demonstrations are taking place in Birmingham, but it is even more unfortunate that the city's white power structure left the Negro community with no alternative.

In any nonviolent campaign there are four basic steps: collection of the facts to determine whether injustices exist; negotiation; self-purification; and direct action. We have gone through all these steps in Birmingham. There can be no gainsaying the fact that racial injustice engulfs this community. Birmingham is probably the most thoroughly segregated city in the United States. Its ugly record of brutality is widely known. Negroes have experienced grossly unjust treatment in the courts. There have been more unsolved bombings of Negro homes and churches in Birmingham than in any other city in the nation. These are the hard, brutal facts of the case. On the basis of these conditions, Negro leaders sought to negotiate with the city fathers. But the latter consistently refused to engage in good-faith negotiation.

Then, last September, came the opportunity to talk with leaders of Birmingham's economic community. In the course of the negotiations, certain promises were made by the merchants—for example, to remove the stores' humiliating racial signs. On the basis of these promises, the Reverend Fred Shuttlesworth and the leaders of the Alabama Christian Movement for Human Rights agreed to a moratorium on all demonstrations. As the weeks and months went by, we realized that we were the victims of a broken promise. A few signs, briefly removed, returned; the others remained.

As in so many past experiences, our hopes had been blasted, and the shadow of deep disappointment settled upon us. We had no alternative except to prepare for direct action, whereby we would present our very bodies as a means of laying our case before the conscience of the local and the national community. Mindful of the difficulties involved, we decided to undertake a process of self-purification. We began a series of workshops on nonviolence, and we repeatedly asked ourselves: "Are you able to accept blows without retaliating?" "Are you able to endure the ordeal of jail?" We decided to schedule our direct-action program for the Easter season, realizing that except for Christmas, this is the main shopping period of the year. Knowing that a strong economic-withdrawal program would be the by-product of direct action, we felt that this would be the best time to bring pressure to bear on the merchants for the needed change.

10 Then it occurred to us that Birmingham's mayoral election was coming up in March, and we speedily decided to postpone action until after election day. When we discovered that the Commissioner of Public Safety, Eugene "Bull" Connor, had piled up enough votes to be in the run-off, we decided again to postpone action until the day after the run-off so that the demonstrations could not be used to cloud the issues. Like many others, we wanted to see Mr. Connor defeated, and to this end we endured postponement after postponement. Having aided in this community need, we felt that our direct-action program could be delayed no longer.

You may well ask, "Why direct action? Why sit-ins, marches, and so forth? Isn't negotiation a better path?" You are quite right in calling for negotiation. Indeed, this is the very purpose of direct action. Nonviolent direct action seeks to create such a crisis and foster such a tension that a community which has constantly refused to negotiate is forced to confront the issue. It seeks so to dramatize the issue that it can no longer be ignored. My citing the creation of tension as part of the work of the nonviolent-resister may sound rather shocking. But I must confess that I am not afraid of the word "tension." I have earnestly opposed violent tension, but there is a type of constructive, nonviolent tension which is necessary for growth. Just as Socrates felt that it was necessary to create a tension in the mind so that individuals could rise from the bondage of myths and half-truths to the unfettered realm of creative analysis and objective appraisal, so must we see the need for nonviolent gadflies to create the kind of tension in society that will help men rise from the dark depths of prejudice and racism to the majestic heights of understanding and brotherhood.

The purpose of our direct-action program is to create a situation so crisis-packed that it will inevitably open the door to negotiation. I therefore concur with you in your call for negotiation. Too long has our beloved Southland been bogged down in a tragic effort to live in monologue rather than dialogue.

One of the basic points in your statement is that the action that I and my associates have taken in Birmingham is untimely. Some have asked: "Why didn't you give the new city administration time to act?" The only answer that I can give to this query is that the new Birmingham administration must be prodded about as much as the outgoing one, before it will act. We are sadly mistaken if we feel that the election of Albert Boutwell as mayor will bring the millennium to Birmingham. While Mr. Boutwell is a much more gentle person than Mr. Connor, they are both segregationists, dedicated to maintenance of the status quo. I have hoped that Mr. Boutwell will be reasonable enough to see the futility of massive resistance to desegregation. But he will not see this without pressure from devotees of civil rights. My friends, I must say to you that we have not made a single gain in civil rights without determined legal and nonviolent pressure. Lamentably, it is an historical fact that privileged groups seldom give up their privileges voluntarily. Individuals may see the moral light and voluntarily give up their unjust posture; but, as Reinhold Niebuhr[2] has reminded us, groups tend to be more immoral than individuals.

[2]American theologian (1892–1971).

We know through painful experience that freedom is never voluntarily given by the oppressor; it must be demanded by the oppressed. Frankly, I have yet to engage in a direct-action campaign that was "well timed" in the view of those who have not suffered unduly from the disease of segregation. For years now I have heard the word "Wait!" It rings in the ear of every Negro with piercing familiarity. This "Wait" has almost always meant "Never." We must come to see, with one of our distinguished jurists, that "justice too long delayed is justice denied."[3]

We have waited for more than 340 years for our constitutional and God-given rights. The nations of Asia and Africa are moving with jet-like speed toward gaining political independence, but we still creep at horse-and-buggy pace toward gaining a cup of coffee at a lunch counter. Perhaps it is easy for those who have never felt the stinging darts of segregation to say, "Wait." But when you have seen vicious mobs lynch your mothers and fathers at will and drown your sisters and brothers at whim; when you have seen hate-filled policemen curse, kick, and even kill your black brothers and sisters; when you see the vast majority of your twenty million Negro brothers smothering in an airtight cage of poverty in the midst of an affluent society; when you suddenly find your tongue twisted and your speech stammering as you seek to explain to your six-year-old daughter why she can't go to the public amusement park that has just been advertised on television, and see tears welling up in her eyes when she is told that Funtown is closed to colored children, and see ominous clouds of inferiority beginning to form in her little mental sky, and see her beginning to distort her personality by developing an unconscious bitterness toward white people; when you have to concoct an answer for a five-year-old son who is asking, "Daddy, why do white people treat colored people so mean?"; when you take a cross-country drive and find it necessary to sleep night after night in the uncomfortable corners of your automobile because no motel will accept you; when you are humiliated day in and

15

[3]Variously attributed to British prime minister William Gladstone (1809–98), U.S. founding father William Penn (1644–1718), and the English legal document the Magna Carta (1215).

day out by nagging signs reading "white" and "colored"; when your first name becomes "nigger," your middle name becomes "boy" (however old you are) and your last name becomes "John," and your wife and mother are never given the respected title "Mrs."; when you are harried by day and haunted by night by the fact that you are a Negro, living constantly at tiptoe stance, never quite knowing what to expect next, and are plagued with inner fears and outer resentments; when you are forever fighting a degenerating sense of "nobodiness"—then you will understand why we find it difficult to wait. There comes a time when the cup of endurance runs over, and men are no longer willing to be plunged into the abyss of despair. I hope, sirs, you can understand our legitimate and unavoidable impatience.

You express a great deal of anxiety over our willingness to break laws. This is certainly a legitimate concern. Since we so diligently urge people to obey the Supreme Court's decision of 1954 outlawing segregation in the public schools, at first glance it may seem rather paradoxical for us consciously to break laws. One may well ask: "How can you advocate breaking some laws and obeying others?" The answer lies in the fact that there are two types of laws: just and unjust. I would be the first to advocate obeying just laws. One has not only a legal but a moral responsibility to obey just laws. Conversely, one has a moral responsibility to disobey unjust laws. I would agree with St. Augustine[4] that "an unjust law is no law at all."

Now, what is the difference between the two? How does one determine whether a law is just or unjust? A just law is a man-made code that squares with the moral law or the law of God. An unjust law is a code that is out of harmony with the moral law. To put it in the terms of St. Thomas Aquinas:[5] An unjust law is a human law that is not rooted in eternal law and natural law. Any law that uplifts human personality is just. Any law that degrades human personality is unjust. All segregation statutes are unjust because segregation distorts the soul and damages the personality. It gives the segregator a false sense of superiority and the segregated a false sense of inferiority. Segregation,

[4]Influential Christian church father (354–430).

[5]Medieval Christian theologian (1225–74).

to use the terminology of the Jewish philosopher Martin Buber,[6] substitutes an "I-it" relationship for an "I-thou" relationship and ends up relegating persons to the status of things. Hence segregation is not only politically, economically, and sociologically unsound, it is morally wrong and sinful. Paul Tillich[7] has said that sin is separation. Is not segregation an existential expression of man's tragic separation, his awful estrangement, his terrible sinfulness? Thus it is that I can urge men to obey the 1954 decision of the Supreme Court, for it is morally right; and I can urge them to disobey segregation ordinances, for they are morally wrong.

Let us consider a more concrete example of just and unjust laws. An unjust law is a code that a numerical or power majority group compels a minority group to obey but does not make binding on itself. This is *difference* made legal. By the same token, a just law is a code that a majority compels a minority to follow and that it is willing to follow itself. This is *sameness* made legal.

Let me give another explanation. A law is unjust if it is inflicted on a minority that, as a result of being denied the right to vote, had no part in enacting or devising the law. Who can say that the legislature of Alabama which set up that state's segregation laws was democratically elected? Throughout Alabama all sorts of devious methods are used to prevent Negroes from becoming registered voters, and there are some counties in which, even though Negroes constitute a majority of the population, not a single Negro is registered. Can any law enacted under such circumstances be considered democratically structured?

Sometimes a law is just on its face and unjust in its application. For instance, I have been arrested on a charge of parading without a permit. Now, there is nothing wrong in having an ordinance which requires a permit for a parade. But such an ordinance becomes unjust when it is used to maintain segregation and to deny citizens the First-Amendment privilege of peaceful assembly and protest. 20

[6]Austrian-born Jewish philosopher (1878–1965).

[7]Protestant theologian and philosopher (1886–1965).

I hope you are able to see the distinction I am trying to point out. In no sense do I advocate evading or defying the law, as would the rabid segregationist. That would lead to anarchy. One who breaks an unjust law must do so openly, lovingly, and with a willingness to accept the penalty. I submit that an individual who breaks a law that conscience tells him is unjust, and who willingly accepts the penalty of imprisonment in order to arouse the conscience of the community over its injustice, is in reality expressing the highest respect for law.

Of course, there is nothing new about this kind of civil disobedience. It was evidenced sublimely in the refusal of Shadrach, Meshach, and Abednego to obey the laws of Nebuchadnezzar,[8] on the ground that a higher moral law was at stake. It was practiced superbly by the early Christians, who were willing to face hungry lions and the excruciating pain of chopping blocks rather than submit to certain unjust laws of the Roman Empire. To a degree, academic freedom is a reality today because Socrates practiced civil disobedience.[9] In our own nation, the Boston Tea Party represented a massive act of civil disobedience.

We should never forget that everything Adolf Hitler did in Germany was "legal" and everything the Hungarian freedom fighters[1] did in Hungary was "illegal." It was "illegal" to aid and comfort a Jew in Hitler's Germany. Even so, I am sure that, had I lived in Germany at the time, I would have aided and comforted my Jewish brothers. If today I lived in a Communist country where certain principles dear to the Christian faith are suppressed, I would openly advocate disobeying that country's anti-religious laws.

I must make two honest confessions to you, my Christian and Jewish brothers. First, I must confess that over the past few years I have been gravely disappointed with the white moderate. I have almost reached the regrettable conclusion that the Negro's great stumbling block in his stride toward freedom is not the White Citizen's Counciler

[8]In Daniel 3 in the Hebrew Bible, the three men refused to worship a statue and were thrown into a furnace; God saved them from burning.

[9]Socrates, an ancient Greek philosopher, was tried and executed for corrupting the youth of Athens.

[1]In 1956, Hungary revolted against its Soviet-imposed government. Soviet forces moved to crush the revolution and installed a new government.

or the Ku Klux Klanner, but the white moderate, who is more devoted to "order" than to justice; who prefers a negative peace which is the absence of tension to a positive peace which is the presence of justice; who constantly says, "I agree with you in the goal you seek, but I cannot agree with your methods of direct action"; who paternalistically believes he can set the timetable for another man's freedom; who lives by a mythical concept of time and who constantly advises the Negro to wait for a "more convenient season." Shallow understanding from people of good will is more frustrating than absolute misunderstanding from people of ill will. Lukewarm acceptance is much more bewildering than outright rejection.

25 I had hoped that the white moderate would understand that law and order exist for the purpose of establishing justice and that when they fail in this purpose they become the dangerously structured dams that block the flow of social progress. I had hoped that the white moderate would understand that the present tension in the South is a necessary phase of the transition from an obnoxious negative peace, in which the Negro passively accepted his unjust plight, to a substantive and positive peace, in which all men will respect the dignity and worth of human personality. Actually, we who engage in nonviolent direct action are not the creators of tension. We merely bring to the surface the hidden tension that is already alive. We bring it out in the open, where it can be seen and dealt with. Like a boil that can never be cured so long as it is covered up but must be opened with all its ugliness to the natural medicines of air and light, injustice must be exposed, with all the tension its exposure creates, to the light of human conscience and the air of national opinion, before it can be cured.

In your statement you assert that our actions, even though peaceful, must be condemned because they precipitate violence. But is this a logical assertion? Isn't this like condemning a robbed man because his possession of money precipitated the evil act of robbery? Isn't this like condemning Socrates because his unswerving commitment to truth and his philosophical inquiries precipitated the act by the misguided populace in which they made him drink hemlock? Isn't this like condemning Jesus because his unique God-consciousness and never-ceasing devotion to God's will precipitated the evil act of crucifixion?

We must come to see that, as the federal courts have consistently affirmed, it is wrong to urge an individual to cease his efforts to gain his basic constitutional rights because the quest may precipitate violence. Society must protect the robbed and punish the robber.

I had also hoped that the white moderate would reject the myth concerning time in relation to the struggle for freedom. I have just received a letter from a white brother in Texas. He writes: "All Christians know that the colored people will receive equal rights eventually, but it is possible that you are in too great a religious hurry. It has taken Christianity almost two thousand years to accomplish what it has. The teachings of Christ take time to come to earth." Such an attitude stems from a tragic misconception of time, from the strangely irrational notion that there is something in the very flow of time that will inevitably cure all ills. Actually, time itself is neutral; it can be used either destructively or constructively. More and more I feel that the people of ill will have used time much more effectively than have the people of good will. We will have to repent in this generation not merely for the hateful words and actions of the bad people, but for the appalling silence of the good people. Human progress never rolls in on wheels of inevitability; it comes through the tireless efforts of men willing to be co-workers with God, and without this hard work, time itself becomes an ally of the forces of social stagnation. We must use time creatively, in the knowledge that the time is always ripe to do right. Now is the time to make real the promise of democracy and transform our pending national elegy into a creative psalm of brotherhood. Now is the time to lift our national policy from the quicksand of racial injustice to the solid rock of human dignity.

You speak of our activity in Birmingham as extreme. At first I was rather disappointed that fellow clergymen would see my nonviolent efforts as those of an extremist. I began thinking about the fact that I stand in the middle of two opposing forces in the Negro community. One is a force of complacency, made up in part of Negroes who, as a result of long years of oppression, are so drained of self-respect and a sense of "somebodiness" that they have adjusted to segregation; and in part of a few middle-class Negroes who, because of a degree of academic and economic security and because in some ways they profit by segregation, have become insensitive to the problems of the masses. The other force is one of bitterness and hatred, and it comes perilously close to advocating violence. It is expressed in the various black nationalist groups that are springing up across the nation, the largest and best-known being Elijah Muhammad's Muslim movement.[2] Nourished by the Negro's frustration over the continued existence of racial discrimination, this movement is made up of people who have lost faith in America, who have absolutely repudiated Christianity, and who have concluded that the white man is an incorrigible "devil."

I have tried to stand between these two forces, saying that we need emulate neither the "do-nothingism" of the complacent nor the hatred and despair of the black nationalist. For there is the more excellent way of love and nonviolent protest. I am grateful to God that, through the influence of the Negro church, the way of nonviolence became an integral part of our struggle.

30 If this philosophy had not emerged, by now many streets of the South would, I am convinced, be flowing with blood. And I am further convinced that if our white brothers dismiss as "rabblerousers" and "outside agitators" those of us who employ nonviolent direct action, and if they refuse to support our nonviolent efforts, millions of Negroes will, out of frustration and despair, seek solace and security in black-nationalist ideologies—a development that would inevitably lead to a frightening racial nightmare.

Oppressed people cannot remain oppressed forever. The yearning for freedom eventually manifests itself, and that is what has happened to the American Negro. Something within has reminded him of his birthright of freedom, and something without has reminded him that it can be gained. Consciously or unconsciously, he has been caught up by the *Zeitgeist*, and with his black brothers of Africa and his brown and yellow brothers of Asia, South America, and the Caribbean, the United States Negro is moving with a sense of great urgency toward the promised land of racial justice. If one recognizes this vital

[2]Elijah Muhammed (1897–1975) led the Nation of Islam from 1934 until his death; the religious organization's well-known leaders include Malcolm X (1925–65) and Louis Farrakhan (b. 1933).

urge that has engulfed the Negro community, one should readily understand why public demonstrations are taking place. The Negro has many pent-up resentments and latent frustrations, and he must release them. So let him march; let him make prayer pilgrimages to the city hall; let him go on freedom rides—and try to understand why he must do so. If his repressed emotions are not released in nonviolent ways, they will seek expression through violence; this is not a threat but a fact of history. So I have not said to my people, "Get rid of your discontent." Rather, I have tried to say that this normal and healthy discontent can be channeled into the creative outlet of nonviolent direct action. And now this approach is being termed extremist.

But though I was initially disappointed at being categorized as an extremist, as I continued to think about the matter I gradually gained a measure of satisfaction from the label. Was not Jesus an extremist for love: "Love your enemies, bless them that curse you, do good to them that hate you, and pray for them which despitefully use you, and persecute you." Was not Amos an extremist for justice: "Let justice roll down like waters and righteousness like an ever-flowing stream." Was not Paul an extremist for the Christian gospel: "I bear in my body the marks of the Lord Jesus." Was not Martin Luther an extremist: "Here I stand; I cannot do otherwise, so help me God." And John Bunyan:[3] "I will stay in jail to the end of my days before I make a butchery of my conscience." And Abraham Lincoln: "This nation cannot survive half slave and half free." And Thomas Jefferson: "We hold these truths to be self-evident, that all men are created equal. . . ." So the question is not whether we will be extremists, but what kind of extremists we will be. Will we be extremists for hate or for love? Will we be extremists for the preservation of injustice or for the extension of justice? In that dramatic scene on Calvary's hill three men were crucified. We must never forget that all three were crucified for the same crime—the crime of extremism. Two were extremists for immorality, and thus fell below their environment. The other, Jesus Christ, was an extremist for love,

[3]English preacher (1628–88). *Amos*: Prophet in the Hebrew Bible. *Paul*: St. Paul of Tarsus, early evangelist and author of much of the New Testament. *Martin Luther*: Monk (1483–1546) whose break with the Catholic Church led to the founding of Protestantism.

truth, and goodness, and thereby rose above his environment. Perhaps the South, the nation, and the world are in dire need of creative extremists.

I had hoped that the white moderate would see this need. Perhaps I was too optimistic; perhaps I expected too much. I suppose I should have realized that few members of the oppressor race can understand the deep groans and passionate yearnings of the oppressed race, and still fewer have the vision to see that injustice must be rooted out by strong, persistent, and determined action. I am thankful, however, that some of our white brothers in the South have grasped the meaning of this social revolution and committed themselves to it. They are still all too few in quantity, but they are big in quality. Some—such as Ralph McGill, Lillian Smith, Harry Golden, James McBridge Dabbs, Ann Braden, and Sarah Patton Boyle—have written about our struggle in eloquent and prophetic terms. Others have marched with us down nameless streets of the South. They have languished in filthy, roach-infested jails, suffering the abuse and brutality of policemen who view them as "dirty nigger-lovers." Unlike so many of their moderate brothers and sisters, they have recognized the urgency of the moment and sensed the need for powerful "action" antidotes to combat the disease of segregation.

Let me take note of my other major disappointment. I have been so greatly disappointed with the white church and its leadership. Of course, there are some notable exceptions. I am not unmindful of the fact that each of you has taken some significant stands on this issue. I commend you, Reverend Stallings, for your Christian stand on this past Sunday, in welcoming Negroes to your worship service on a nonsegregated basis. I commend the Catholic leaders of this state for integrating Spring Hill College several years ago.

35 But despite these notable exceptions, I must honestly reiterate that I have been disappointed with the church. I do not say this as one of those negative critics who can always find something wrong with the church. I say this as a minister of the gospel, who loves the church; who was nurtured in its bosom; who has been sustained by its spiritual blessings and who will remain true to it as long as the cord of life shall lengthen.

When I was suddenly catapulted into the leadership of the bus protest in Montgomery, Alabama, a few years ago,[4] I felt we would be supported by the white church. I felt that the white ministers, priests, and rabbis of the South would be among our strongest allies. Instead, some have been outright opponents, refusing to understand the freedom movement and misrepresenting its leaders; all too many others have been more cautious than courageous and have remained silent behind the anesthetizing security of stained-glass windows.

In spite of my shattered dreams, I came to Birmingham with the hope that the white religious leadership of this community would see the justice of our cause and, with deep moral concern, would serve as the channel through which our just grievances could reach the power structure. I had hoped that each of you would understand. But again I have been disappointed.

I have heard numerous southern religious leaders admonish their worshipers to comply with a desegregation decision because it is the law, but I have longed to hear white ministers declare: "Follow this decree because integration is morally right and because the Negro is your brother." In the midst of blatant injustices inflicted upon the Negro, I have watched white churchmen stand on the sideline and mouth pious irrelevancies and sanctimonious trivialities. In the midst of a mighty struggle to rid our nation of racial and economic injustice, I have heard many ministers say: "Those are social issues, with which the gospel has no real concern." And I have watched many churches commit themselves to a completely otherworldly religion which makes a strange, un-Biblical distinction between body and soul, between the sacred and the secular.

I have traveled the length and breadth of Alabama, Mississippi, and all the other southern states. On sweltering summer days and crisp autumn mornings I have looked at the South's beautiful churches with their lofty spires pointing heavenward. I have beheld the impressive outlines of her massive religious-education buildings. Over and over I have found myself asking: "What kind of people worship here?

[4]King led the 1955 bus boycott that was launched after Rosa Parks was arrested for refusing to give up her seat and move to the back of the bus.

Who is their God? Where were their voices when the lips of Governor Barnett[5] dripped with words of interposition and nullification? Where were they when Governor Wallace[6] gave a clarion call for defiance and hatred? Where were their voices of support when bruised and weary Negro men and women decided to rise from the dark dungeons of complacency to the bright hills of creative protest?"

Yes, these questions are still in my mind. In deep disappointment I have wept over the laxity of the church. But be assured that my tears have been tears of love. There can be no deep disappointment where there is not deep love. Yes, I love the church. How could I do otherwise? I am in the rather unique position of being the son, the grandson, and the great-grandson of preachers. Yes, I see the church as the body of Christ. But, oh! How we have blemished and scarred that body through social neglect and through fear of being nonconformists. 40

There was a time when the church was very powerful—in the time when the early Christians rejoiced at being deemed worthy to suffer for what they believed. In those days the church was not merely a thermometer that recorded the ideas and principles of popular opinion; it was a thermostat that transformed the mores of society. Whenever the early Christians entered a town, the people in power became disturbed and immediately sought to convict the Christians for being "disturbers of the peace" and "outside agitators." But the Christians pressed on, in the conviction that they were "a colony of heaven," called to obey God rather than man. Small in number, they were big in commitment. They were too God-intoxicated to be "astronomically intimidated." By their effort and example they brought an end to such ancient evils as infanticide and gladiatorial contests.

Things are different now. So often the contemporary church is a weak, ineffectual voice with an uncertain sound. So often it is an archdefender of the status quo. Far from being disturbed by the presence of the church, the power structure of the average community is con-

[5]Ross Barnett (1898–1987), governor of Mississippi (1960–64), who attempted to keep James Meredith from entering the University of Mississippi in 1963.

[6]George Wallace (1919–98), governor of Alabama (1963–67, 1971–79, 1983–87), whose "stand in the schoolhouse door" also sought to bar black students from the University of Alabama.

soled by the church's silent—and often even vocal—sanction of things as they are.

But the judgment of God is upon the church as never before. If today's church does not recapture the sacrificial spirit of the early church, it will lose its authenticity, forfeit the loyalty of millions, and be dismissed as an irrelevant social club with no meaning for the twentieth century. Every day I meet young people whose disappointment with the church has turned into outright disgust.

Perhaps I have once again been too optimistic. Is organized religion too inextricably bound to the status quo to save our nation and the world? Perhaps I must turn my faith to the inner spiritual church, the church within the church, as the true *ekklesia*[7] and the hope of the world. But again I am thankful to God that some noble souls from the ranks of organized religion have broken loose from the paralyzing chains of conformity and joined us as active partners in the struggle for freedom. They have left their secure congregations and walked the streets of Albany, Georgia, with us. They have gone down the highways of the South on tortuous rides for freedom. Yes, they have gone to jail with us. Some have been dismissed from their churches, have lost the support of their bishops and fellow ministers. But they have acted in the faith that right defeated is stronger than evil triumphant. Their witness has been the spiritual salt that has preserved the true meaning of the gospel in these troubled times. They have carved a tunnel of hope through the dark mountain of disappointment.

45 I hope the church as a whole will meet the challenge of this decisive hour. But even if the church does not come to the aid of justice, I have no despair about the future. I have no fear about the outcome of our struggle in Birmingham, even if our motives are at present misunderstood. We will reach the goal of freedom in Birmingham and all over the nation, because the goal of America is freedom. Abused and scorned though we may be, our destiny is tied up with America's destiny. Before the pilgrims landed at Plymouth, we were here. Before the pen of Jefferson etched the majestic words of the Declaration of Independence across the pages of history, we were here. For more than two centuries our

[7]Church (Greek).

forebears labored in this country without wages; they made cotton king; they built the homes of their masters while suffering gross injustice and shameful humiliation—and yet out of a bottomless vitality they continued to thrive and develop. If the inexpressible cruelties of slavery could not stop us, the opposition we now face will surely fail. We will win our freedom because the sacred heritage of our nation and the eternal will of God are embodied in our echoing demands.

Before closing I feel impelled to mention one other point in your statement that has troubled me profoundly. You warmly commended the Birmingham police force for keeping "order" and "preventing violence." I doubt that you would have so warmly commended the police force if you had seen its dogs sinking their teeth into unarmed, nonviolent Negroes. I doubt that you would so quickly commend the policemen if you were to observe their ugly and inhumane treatment of Negroes here in the city jail; if you were to watch them push and curse old Negro women and young Negro girls; if you were to see them slap and kick old Negro men and young boys; if you were to observe them, as they did on two occasions, refuse to give us food because we wanted to sing our grace together. I cannot join you in your praise of the Birmingham police department.

It is true that the police have exercised a degree of discipline in handling the demonstrators. In this sense they have conducted themselves rather "nonviolently" in public. But for what purpose? To preserve the evil system of segregation. Over the past few years I have consistently preached that nonviolence demands that the means we use must be as pure as the ends we seek. I have tried to make clear that it is wrong to use immoral means to attain moral ends. But now I must affirm that it is just as wrong, or perhaps even more so, to use moral means to preserve immoral ends. Perhaps Mr. Connor and his policemen have been rather nonviolent in public, as was Chief Pritchett in Albany, Georgia, but they have used the moral means of nonviolence to maintain the immoral end of racial injustice. As T. S. Eliot has said, "The last temptation is the greatest treason: To do the right deed for the wrong reason."[8]

[8]American-born English poet (1888–1965); the lines are from his play *Murder in the Cathedral.*

I wish you had commended the Negro sit-inners and demonstrators of Birmingham for their sublime courage, their willingness to suffer, and their amazing discipline in the midst of great provocation. One day the South will recognize its real heroes. They will be the James Merediths, with the noble sense of purpose that enables them to face jeering and hostile mobs, and with the agonizing loneliness that characterizes the life of the pioneer. They will be old, oppressed, battered Negro women, symbolized in a seventy-two-year-old woman in Montgomery, Alabama, who rose up with a sense of dignity and with her people decided not to ride segregated buses, and who responded with ungrammatical profundity to one who inquired about her weariness: "My feets is tired, but my soul is at rest." They will be the young high school and college students, the young ministers of the gospel and a host of their elders, courageously and nonviolently sitting in at lunch counters and willingly going to jail for conscience' sake. One day the South will know that when these disinherited children of God sat down at lunch counters, they were in reality standing up for what is best in the American dream and for the most sacred values in our Judaeo-Christian heritage, thereby bringing our nation back to those great wells of democracy which were dug deep by the founding fathers in their formulation of the Constitution and the Declaration of Independence.

Never before have I written so long a letter. I'm afraid it is much too long to take your precious time. I can assure you that it would have been much shorter if I had been writing from a comfortable desk, but what else can one do when he is alone in a narrow jail cell, other than write long letters, think long thoughts, and pray long prayers?

50

If I have said anything in this letter that overstates the truth and indicates an unreasonable impatience, I beg you to forgive me. If I have said anything that understates the truth and indicates my having a patience that allows me to settle for anything less than brotherhood, I beg God to forgive me.

I hope this letter finds you strong in the faith. I also hope that circumstances will soon make it possible for me to meet each of you, not as an integrationist or a civil-rights leader but as a fellow clergyman and a Christian brother. Let us all hope that the dark clouds of racial prejudice will soon pass away and the deep fog of misunderstanding will be lifted from our fear-drenched communities, and in some not too distant tomorrow the radiant stars of love and brotherhood will shine over our great nation with all their scintillating beauty.

Yours for the cause of Peace and Brotherhood,
Martin Luther King, Jr.

STEPHEN KING | *Why We Crave Horror Movies*

STEPHEN KING (b. 1947), prolific and popular author of psychological thrillers, horror, screenplays, and essays, earned a BA in English from the University of Maine at Orono in 1970. He sold his first short story in 1967, while still a student, and after graduation he continued selling stories to magazines to supplement his income. In 1973, while working as a teacher, he sold his first novel, *Carrie*; the proceeds from the sale of the paperback rights enabled him to write full-time. King has published such best-sellers as *Salem's Lot* (1975); *The Shining* (1977), which was made into a film starring Jack Nicholson; *Pet Sematary* (1983); and *Rose Madder* (1995). King is also the author of *On Writing* (2000), a well-received book about his craft. In 1996 his short story "The Man in the Black Suit" received an O. Henry award, and in 2003 the National Book Foundation cited King for his "Distinguished Contribution to American Letters." He plays rhythm guitar for the rock band the Rock Bottom Remainders.

In "Why We Crave Horror Movies," King explores what causes audience members to seek out frightening entertainment. Analyzing films from a historical and cultural perspective, King concludes that horror films directly respond to the social and political climate of the times, and that people watch them to feel better about their day-to-day lives. How might some horror movies that are currently popular respond to a particular cultural moment?

IF YOU'RE A GENUINE FAN of horror films, you develop the same sort of sophistication that a follower of the ballet develops; you get a feeling for the depth and the texture of the genre. Your ear develops with your eye, and the sound of quality always comes through to the keen ear. There is fine Waterford crystal that rings delicately when struck, no matter how thick and chunky it may look; and then there are Flintstone jelly glasses. You can drink your Dom Perignon out of either one, but, friends, there is a difference.

The difference here is between horror for horror's sake and art. There is art in a horror film when the audience gets more than it gives. Not when our fears are milked just to drive us crazy but when an actual liaison is found between our fantasy fears and our real fears. Few horror movies are conceived with art in mind; most are conceived for profit. The art is not consciously created but, rather, is thrown off, as an atomic pile throws off radiation. There are films that skate right up to the border where art ceases to be thrown off and exploitation begins, and those films are often the field's most striking successes. *The Texas Chainsaw Massacre* is one of those. I would happily testify to its redeeming social merit in any court in the country. I would not do so for *The Gory Ones*, a 1972 film in which we are treated to the charming sight of a woman being cut open with a two-handed bucksaw; the camera lingers as her intestines spew out onto the floor. The difference is more than the difference between a chain saw and a bucksaw; it is something like 70,000,000 light-years. The *Chainsaw Massacre* is done with taste and conscience. *The Gory Ones* is the work of morons with cameras.

If horror movies have redeeming social merit, it is because of that ability to form liaisons between the real and the unreal. In many cases—particularly in the Fifties and then again in the early Seventies—the fears expressed are sociopolitical in nature, a fact that gives such disparate pictures as Don Siegel's *Invasion of the Body Snatchers* and William Friedkin's *The Exorcist* a crazily convincing documentary feel. When the horror movies wear their various sociopolitical hats—the B picture as tabloid editorial—they often serve as an extraordinarily accurate barometer of those things that trouble the night thoughts of a whole society.

But horror movies don't always wear a hat that identifies them as disguised comments on the social or political scene (as David Cronenberg's *The Brood* comments on the disintegration of the generational family, or as his *They Came from Within* deals with the more cannibalistic side effects of Erica Jong's "zipless fuck"[1]). More often the horror movie points farther inward, looking for those deep-seated personal fears, those pressure points we all must cope with. This adds an element of universality to the proceedings and may produce an even truer sort of art.

5 This second kind of horror film has more in common with the Brothers Grimm[2] than with the op-ed pages of tabloid newspapers. It is the B picture as fairy tale. It doesn't want to score political points but, rather, to scare the hell out of us by crossing certain taboo lines. So if my idea about art is correct (it giveth more than it receiveth), this sort of film is of value to the audience by helping it to better understand what those taboos and fears are, and why it feels so uneasy about them.

• ○ •

I think we'd all agree that one of the great fears with which all of us must deal on a purely personal level is the fear of dying; without good old death to fall back on, the horror movies would be in bad shape.

A corollary to this is that there are "good" deaths and "bad" deaths; most of us would like to die peacefully in our beds at the age of 80 (preferably after a good meal, a bottle of really fine vino and a really super lay), but very few of us are interested in finding out how it might feel to get slowly crushed under an automobile lift while crankcase oil drips slowly onto our foreheads.

Lots of horror films derive their best effects from this fear of the bad death (as in *The Abominable Dr. Phibes*, in which Phibes dispatches his victims one at a time using the 12 plagues of Egypt,[3] slightly updated, a gimmick worthy of the *Batman* comics during their palmiest days). Who can forget the lethal binoculars in *The Black Zoo*, for instance? They came equipped with spring loaded six-inch prongs, so that when the victim put them to her eyes and then attempted to adjust the field of focus. . . .

[1]Jong (b. 1942) coined this phrase in her 1973 novel, *Fear of Flying*; it refers to casual sex with a stranger.

[2]Jacob (1785–1863) and Wilhelm (1786–1859) Grimm, German academics known for publishing fairy tales collected in Germany, such as Rapunzel and Hansel and Gretel.

[3]See Exodus, chapters 7–12. The number of plagues was ten.

Others derive their horror simply from the fact of death itself and the decay that follows death. In a society in which such a great store is placed in the fragile commodities of youth, health, and beauty, death and decay become inevitably horrible—and inevitably taboo. If you don't think so, ask yourself why the second grade doesn't get to tour the local mortuary along with the police department, the fire department and the nearest McDonald's. One can imagine—or I can in my more morbid moments—the mortuary and McDonald's combined; the highlight of the tour, of course, would be a viewing of the McCorpse.

No, the funeral parlor is taboo. Morticians are modern priests, working their arcane magic of cosmetics and preservation in rooms that are clearly marked off limits. Who washes the corpse's hair? Are the fingernails and toenails of the dear departed clipped one final time? Is it true that the dead are encoffined sans shoes? Who dresses them for their final star turn in the mortuary viewing room? How is a bullet hole plugged and concealed? How are strangulation bruises hidden? 10

The answers to all those questions are available, but they are not common knowledge. And if you try to make the answers part of your store of knowledge, people are going to think you a bit peculiar. I know: In the process of researching a forthcoming novel about a father who tries to bring his son back from the dead, I collected a stack of funeral literature a foot high—and any number of peculiar glances from folks who wondered why I was reading *The Funeral: Vestige or Value?*

But this is not to say that people don't have a certain occasional interest in what lies behind the locked door in the basement of the mortuary, or what may transpire in the local graveyard after the mourners have left . . . or at the dark of the moon. *The Body Snatcher*[4] is not really a tale of the supernatural, nor was it pitched that way to its audience; it was pitched as a film (as was that notorious Sixties documentary *Mondo Cane*[5]) that would take us beyond the pale, over that line that marks the edge of taboo ground:

[4]American film (1945) starring Boris Karloff and based on Scottish writer Robert Louis Stevenson's (1850–94) short story of the same name.

[5]Italian film (1962) intended to shock its audience with depraved human acts.

CEMETERIES RAIDED, CHILDREN SLAIN FOR BODIES TO DISSECT! the movie poster drooled. UNTHINKABLE REALITIES AND UNBELIEVABLE FACTS OF THE DARK DAYS OF EARLY SURGICAL RESEARCH EXPOSED IN THE MOST DARING SHRIEK-AND-SHUDDER SHOCK SENSATION EVER BROUGHT TO THE SCREEN! (All of this printed on a leaning tombstone.)

But the poster does not stop there; it goes on specifically to mark out the exact location of the taboo line and to suggest that not everyone may be adventurous enough to transgress that forbidden ground: IF YOU CAN TAKE IT, SEE GRAVES RAIDED! COFFINS ROBBED! CORPSES CARVED! MIDNIGHT MURDER! BODY BLACKMAIL! STALKING GHOULS! MAD REVENGE! MACABRE MYSTERY! AND DON'T SAY WE DIDN'T WARN YOU!

15 All of it has sort of a pleasant, alliterative ring, doesn't it?

These areas of unease—the political-social-cultural and those of the more mythic, fairy-tale variety—have a tendency to overlap, of course; a good horror picture will put the pressure on at as many points as it can. *They Came from Within*, for instance, is about sexual promiscuity on one level; on another level, it's asking you how you'd like to have a leech jump out of a letter slot and fasten itself onto your face. These are not the same areas of unease at all.

But since we're on the subject of death and decay (a very grave matter, heh-heh-heh), we might look at a couple of films in which this particular area of unease has been used well. The prime example, of course, is *Night of the Living Dead*, in which our horror of these final states is exploited to a point where many audiences found the film well-nigh unbearable. Other taboos are also broken by the film: at one point, a little girl kills her mother with a garden trowel . . . and then begins to eat her. How's that for taboo breaking? Yet the film circles around to its starting point again and again, and the key word in the film's title is not living but dead.

At an early point, the film's female lead, who has barely escaped being killed by a zombie in a graveyard where she and her brother have come to put flowers on their dead father's grave (the brother is not so lucky), stumbles into a lonely farmhouse. As she explores, she hears something dripping . . . dripping . . . dripping. She goes upstairs, sees something, screams . . . and the camera zooms in on the rotting, weeks-old head of a corpse. It is a shocking, memorable moment. Later, a government official tells the watching, beleaguered populace that, although they may not like it (i.e., they will have to cross that taboo line to do it), they must burn their dead; simply soak them with gasoline and light them up. Later still, a local sheriff expresses our own uneasy shock at having come so far over the taboo line. He answers a reporter's question by saying, "Ah, they're dead . . . they're all messed up."

The good horror director must have a clear sense of where the taboo line lies if he is not to lapse into unconscious absurdity, and a gut understanding of what the countryside is like on the far side of it. In *Night of the Living Dead*, George Romero plays a number of instruments, and he plays them like a virtuoso. A lot has been made of this film's graphic violence, but one of the film's most frightening moments comes near the climax, when the heroine's brother makes his reappearance—still wearing his driving gloves and clutching for his sister with the idiotic, implacable single-mindedness of the hungry dead. The film is violent—as is its sequel, *Dawn of the Dead*—but the violence has its own logic, and in the horror genre, logic goes a long way toward proving morality.

20 The crowning horror in Alfred Hitchcock's *Psycho* comes when Vera Miles touches that chair in the cellar and it spins lazily around to reveal Norman's mother at last—a wizened, shriveled corpse from which hollow eye sockets stare up blankly. She is not only dead; she has been stuffed like one of the birds that decorate Norman's office. Norman's subsequent entrance in dress and make-up is almost an anticlimax.

In A.I.P.'s *The Pit and the Pendulum*, we see another facet of the bad death—perhaps the absolute worst. Vincent Price and his cohorts break into a tomb through its brickwork, using pick and shovel. They discover that the lady, his wife, has indeed, been entombed alive; for just a moment, the camera shows us her tortured face, frozen in a rictus of terror, her bulging eyes, her clawlike fingers, the skin stretched tight and gray. This is, I think, the most important moment in the post-1960 horror film, signaling a return to an all-out effort to terrify the audience . . . and a willingness to use any means at hand to do it.

• ○ •

Fiction is full of *economic* horror stories, although very few of them are supernatural; *The Crash of '79* comes to mind, as well as *The Money*

Wolves, The Big Company Look and the wonderful Frank Norris novel *McTeague.*[6] I want to discuss only one movie in this context, *The Amityville Horror*. There may be others, but this one example will serve, I think, to illustrate another idea: that the horror genre is extremely limber, extremely adaptable, extremely useful; the author or filmmaker can use it as a crowbar to lever open locked doors . . . or as a small, slim pick to tease the tumblers into giving. The genre can thus be used to open almost any lock on the fears that lie behind the door, and *The Amityville Horror* is a dollars-and-cents case in point.

It is simple and straightforward, as most horror tales are. The Lutzes, a young married couple with two or three kids (Kathleen Lutz's by a previous marriage), buy a house in Amityville. Previous to their tenancy, a young man has murdered his whole family at the direction of "voices." For this reason, the Lutzes get the house cheaply.

But they soon discover that it wouldn't have been cheap at half the price, because it's haunted. Manifestations include black goop that comes bubbling out of the toilets (and before the festivities are over, it comes oozing out of the walls and the stairs as well), a roomful of flies, a rocking chair that rocks by itself and something in the cellar that causes the dog to dig everlastingly at the wall. A window crashes down on the little boy's fingers. The little girl develops an "invisible friend" who is apparently really there. Eyes glow outside the window at three in the morning. And so on.

25 Worst of all, from the audience's standpoint, Lutz himself (James Brolin) apparently falls out of love with his wife (Margot Kidder) and begins to develop a meaningful relationship with his ax. Before things are done, we are drawn to the inescapable conclusion that he is tuning up for something more than splitting wood.

Stripped of its distracting elements (a puking nun, Rod Steiger shamelessly overacting as a priest who is just discovering the devil after 40 years or so as a man of the cloth, and Margot Kidder doing calisthenics in a pair of bikini panties and one white stocking), *The Amityville Horror* is a perfect example of the tale to be told around the

[6]Financial thriller novels by, respectively, Paul Erdman, Paul Erikson, J. Harvey Howells, and Frank Norris, the last of these being the best known.

campfire. All the teller really has to do is to keep the catalog of inexplicable events in the correct order, so that unease escalates into outright fear.

All of which brings us around to the real watchspring of *Amityville* and the reason it works as well as it does: The picture's subtext is one of economic unease, and that is a theme that director Stuart Rosenberg plays on constantly. In terms of the times—18 percent inflation, mortgage rates out of sight, gasoline selling at a cool $1.40 a gallon—*The Amityville Horror*, like *The Exorcist*, could not have come along at a more opportune moment.

This breaks through most clearly in a scene that is the film's only moment of true and honest drama, a brief vignette that parts the clouds of hokum like a sunray on a drizzly afternoon. The Lutz family is preparing to go to the wedding of Kathleen Lutz's younger brother (who looks as if he might be all of 17). They are, of course, in the Bad House when the scene takes place. The younger brother has lost the $1500 that is due the caterer and is in an understandable agony of panic and embarrassment.

Brolin says he'll write the caterer a check, which he does, and later he stands off the angry caterer, who has specified cash only in a half-whispered washroom argument while the wedding party whoops it up outside. After the wedding, Lutz turns the living room of the Bad House upside down looking for the lost money, which has now become *his* money, and the only way of backing up the bank paper he has issued the caterer. Brolin's check may not have been 100 percent Goodyear rubber, but in his sunken, purple-pouched eyes, we see a man who doesn't really have the money any more than his hapless brother-in-law does. Here is a man tottering on the brink of his own financial crash.

He finds the only trace under the couch: a bank money band with the numerals $500 stamped on it. The band lies there on the rug, tauntingly empty. *"Where is it?"* Brolin screams, his voice vibrating with anger, frustration and fear. At that one moment, we hear the ring of Waterford, clear and true—or if you like, we hear that one quiet phrase of pure music in a film that is otherwise all crash and bash. 30

Everything that *The Amityville Horror* does well is summed up in that scene. Its implications touch on everything about the house's most obvious and insidious effect—and also the only one that seems empirically undeniable: Little by little, it is ruining the Lutz family financially. The movie might as well have been subtitled "The Horror of the Shrinking Bank Account." It's the more prosaic fallout of the place where so many haunted-house stories start. "It's on the market for a song," the realtor says with a big egg-sucking grin. "It's supposed to be haunted."

Well, the house that the Lutzes buy is, indeed, on the market for a song (and there's another good moment—all too short—when Kathleen tells her husband that she will be the first person in her large Catholic family to actually own her own home; "We've always been renters," she says), but it ends up costing them dearly. At the conclusion, the house seems to literally tear itself apart. Windows crash in, black goop comes dribbling out of the walls, the cellar stairs cave in . . . and I found myself wondering not if the Lutz clan would get out alive but if they had adequate homeowner's insurance.

This is a movie for every woman who ever wept over a plugged-up toilet or a spreading water stain on the ceiling from the upstairs shower; for every man who ever did a slow burn when the weight of the snow caused his gutters to give way; for every child who ever jammed his fingers and felt that the door or window that did the jamming was out to get him. As horror goes, *Amityville* is pretty pedestrian. So's beer, but you can get drunk on it.

"Think of the bills," a woman sitting behind me in the theater moaned at one point. I suspect it was her own bills she was thinking about. It was impossible to make a silk purse out of this particular sow's ear, but Rosenberg at least manages to give us Qiana,[7] and the main reason that people went to see it, I think, is that *The Amityville Horror*, beneath its ghost-story exterior, is really a financial demolition derby.

Think of the bills, indeed. 35

• ○ •

If movies are the dreams of the mass culture—one film critic, in fact, has called watching a movie "dreaming with one's eyes open"—and if

[7]A synthetic fabric with a silky texture.

horror movies are the nightmares of the mass culture, then many horror movies of recent times express America's coming to terms with the possibility of nuclear annihilation over political differences.

The contemporary political horror films begin, I think, with *The Thing* (1951), directed by Christian Nyby and produced by Howard Hawks (who also had a hand in the direction, one suspects). It stars Margaret Sheridan, Kenneth Tobey and James Arness as the blood-drinking human carrot from Planet X.

A polar encampment of soldiers and scientists discovers a strong magnetic field emanating from an area where there has been a recent meteor fall; the field is strong enough to throw all the electronic gadgets and gizmos off whack. Further, a camera designed to start shooting pictures when and if the normal background-radiation count suddenly goes up has taken photos of an object that dips, swoops and turns at high speeds—strange behavior for a meteor.

An expedition is dispatched to the spot, and it discovers a flying saucer buried in the ice. The saucer, superhot on touchdown, melted its way into the ice, which then refroze, leaving only the tail fin sticking out (thus relieving the special-effects corps of a potentially big-budget item). The army guys, who demonstrate frostbite of the brain throughout most of the film, promptly destroy the extraterrestrial ship while trying to burn it out of the ice with thermite.

The occupant (Arness) is saved, however, and carted back to the experimental station in a block of ice. He/it is placed in a storage shed, under guard. One of the guards is so freaked out by the thing that he throws a blanket over it. Unlucky man! Quite obviously, all his good stars are in retrograde, his biorhythms low and his mental magnetic poles temporarily reversed. The blanket he's used is of the electric variety, and it miraculously melts the ice without shorting out. The Thing escapes and the fun begins. 40

The fun ends about 60 minutes later with the creature being roasted medium rare on an electric-sidewalk sort of thing that the scientists have set up. A reporter on the scene sends back the news of humankind's first victory over invaders from space, and the film fades out, not with a THE END title card but with a question mark.

The Thing is a small movie done on a low budget. Like *Alien*, which would come more than a quarter century later, it achieves its best effects from feelings of claustrophobia and xenophobia. But, as I said before, the best horror movies will try to get at you on many different levels, and *The Thing* is also operating on a political level. It has grim things to say about eggheads (and knee-jerk liberals—in the early Fifties, you could have put an equal-sign between the two) who would indulge in the crime of appeasement.

The Thing is the first movie of the Fifties to offer us the scientist in the role of The Appeaser, that creature who for reasons either craven or misguided would open the gates to the Garden of Eden and let all the evils fly in (as opposed, say, to those mad labs proprietors of the Thirties, who were more than willing to open Pandora's box[8] and let all the evils fly out—a major distinction, though the results are the same). That scientists should be so constantly vilified in the technohorror films of the Fifties—a decade that was apparently dedicated to the idea of turning out a whole marching corps of men and women in white lab coats—is perhaps not so surprising when we remember that it was science that opened those same gates so that the atomic bomb could be brought into Eden: first by itself and then trundled on missiles.[9]

The average Jane or Joe during those spooky eight or nine years that followed the surrender of Japan had extremely schizoid feelings about science and scientists—recognizing the need for them and, at the same time, loathing the things they had let in forever. On the one hand, the average Jane or Joe had found a new pal, that neat little all-round guy, Reddy Kilowatt;[1] on the other hand, before getting into the first reel of *The Thing*, they had to watch newsreel footage as an army mock-up of a town *just like theirs* was vaporized in a nuclear furnace.

Robert Cornthwaite plays the appeasing scientist in *The Thing*, and 45 we hear from his lips the first verse of a psalm that any filmgoer who

[8]In Greek mythology, the container holding the evils of the world. Pandora opened it out of curiosity.

[9]Twentieth-century science made possible the development of atomic bombs, dropped by the United States on Japan in 1945, precipitating the surrender of Japan in World War II.

[1]Cartoon character used to promote electricity in the first half of the twentieth century.

grew up in the Fifties and Sixties became familiar with very quickly: "We must preserve this creature for science." The second verse goes: "If it comes from a society more advanced than ours, it must come in peace. If we can only establish communications with it, and find out what it wants—"

Twice, near the film's conclusion, Cornthwaite is hauled away by soldiers; at the climax, he breaks free of his guards and faces the creature with his hands open and empty. He begs it to communicate with him and to see that he means it no harm. The creature stares at him for a long, pregnant moment . . . and then bats him casually aside, as you or I might swat a mosquito. The medium-rare roasting on the electric sidewalk follows.

Now, I'm only a journeyman writer and I will not presume to teach history here. I will point out that the Americans of that time were perhaps more paranoid about the idea of appeasement than at any other time before or since. The dreadful humiliation of Neville Chamberlain[2] and England's resulting close squeak at the beginning of Hitler's war was still very much with those Americans, and why not? It had all happened only 12 years prior to *The Thing*'s release, and even Americans who were just turning 21 in 1951 could remember it all very clearly. The moral was simple—such appeasement doesn't work: you gotta cut 'em if they stand and shoot 'em if they run. Otherwise, they'll take you over a bite at a time (and in the case of the Thing, you could take that literally).

If all this seems much too heavy a cargo for a modest little fright flick like *The Thing* to bear, remember that a man's point of view is shaped by the events he experiences and that his politics is shaped by his point of view. I am only suggesting that, given the political temper of the times and the cataclysmic world events that had occurred only a few years before, the viewpoint of this movie is almost preordained. What do you do with a blood-drinking carrot from outer space? Simple. Cut him if he stands and shoot him if he runs. And if you're an appeasing scientist like

[2]British prime minister (1869–1940) known for his policies of appeasement—the attempt to solve international issues with peaceful negotiations.

Cornthwaite (with a yellow streak up your back as wide as the no-passing line on a highway), you simply get bulldozed under.

By contrast, consider the other end of this telescope. The children of World War II produced *The Thing*; 26 years later, a child of Vietnam and the self-proclaimed Love Generation, Steven Spielberg, gives us a fitting balance weight to *The Thing* in *Close Encounters of the Third Kind*. In 1951, the soldier standing sentry duty (the one who has foolishly covered the block of ice with an electric blanket) empties his automatic into the alien when he hears it coming; in 1977, a young guy with a happy, spaced-out smile holds up a sign reading STOP AND BE FRIENDLY. Somewhere between the two, John Foster Dulles evolved into Henry Kissinger and the pugnacious politics of confrontation became *détente*.[3]

In *The Thing*, Tobey occupies himself with building an electric boardwalk to kill the creature; in *Close Encounters*, Richard Dreyfuss occupies himself with building a mock-up of Devil's Butte, the creatures' landing place, in his living room. The Thing is a big, hulking brute who grunts; the creatures from the stars in Spielberg's film are small, delicate, childlike. They do not speak, but their mother ship plays lovely harmonic tones—the music of the spheres, we assume. And Dreyfuss, far from wanting to murder these emissaries from space, goes with them. 50

I'm not saying that Spielberg is or would think of himself as a member of the Love Generation simply because he came to his majority while students were putting daisies in the muzzles of M-1's and Jimi Hendrix and Janis Joplin were playing at Fillmore West. Neither am I saying that Hawks, Nyby, Charles Lederer (who wrote the screenplay for *The Thing*) and John W. Campbell (whose novella *Who Goes There?* formed the basis for the film) fought their way up the beaches of Anzio or helped raise the Stars and Stripes on Iwo Jima. But events determine point of view and point of view determines politics, and *CE3K* seems to me every

[3]Dulles (1888–1959) was Secretary of State Under Dwight D. Eisenhower; Kissinger (b. 1923) served in the same role under Richard Nixon. Dulles favored aggressive promotion of capitalism and action against communism, while Kissinger favored *détente*, or an easing of relations among governments.

bit as preordained as *The Thing*. We can understand that the latter's "Let the military handle this" thesis was a perfectly acceptable one in 1951, because the military had handled the Japs and the Nazis perfectly well in Duke Wayne's Big One,[4] and we can also understand that the former's attitude of "Don't let the military handle this" was a perfectly acceptable one in 1977, following the military's less-than-startling record in Vietnam, or even in 1980 (when *CE3K* was released with additional footage), the year American military personnel lost the chance to free our hostages in Iran following three hours of mechanical fuck-ups.

• ◦ •

It may be that nothing in the world is so hard to comprehend as a terror whose time has come and gone—which may be why parents can scold their children for their fear of the bogeyman, when as children themselves, they had to cope with exactly the same fears (and the same sympathetic but uncomprehending parents). That may be why one generation's nightmare becomes the next generation's sociology, and even those who have walked through the fire have trouble remembering exactly what those burning coals felt like.

In the Fifties, the terror of the bomb and of fallout was real, and it left a scar on those children who wanted to be good, just as the Depression of the Thirties had left a scar on their elders. A newer generation—now teenagers, with no memory of either the Cuban Missile Crisis or of the Kennedy assassination in Dallas, raised on the milk of *détente*—may find it hard to comprehend the terror of these things, but they will undoubtedly have a chance to discover it in the years of tightening belts and heightening tensions that lie ahead . . . and the movies will be there to give their vague fears concrete focusing points in the horror movies yet to come.

I can remember, for instance, that in 1968, when I was 21, the issue of long hair was an extremely nasty, extremely explosive one. That seems as hard to believe now as the idea of people killing each other

[4]American actor John Wayne (1907–79), born Marion Robert Morrison appeared in several movies about World War II.

over whether the sun went around the earth or the earth went around the sun, but that happened, too.

55 I was thrown out of a bar in Brewer, Maine, by a construction worker back in that happy year of 1968. The guy had muscles on his muscles and told me I could come back and finish my beer "after you get a haircut, you faggot fairy." There were the standard catcalls thrown from passing cars (usually old cars with fins and cancer of the rocker panels): Are you a boy or are you a girl? Do you give head, honey? When was the last time you had a bath?

I can remember such things in an intellectual, even analytical way, as I can remember having a dressing that had actually grown into the tissue yanked from the site of a cyst-removal operation that occurred when I was 12. I screamed from the pain and then fainted dead away. I can remember the pulling sensation as the gauze tore free of the new, healthy tissue (the dressing removal was performed by a nurse's aide who apparently had no idea what she was doing), I can remember the scream and I can remember the faint. What I can't remember is the pain itself. It's the same with the hair thing and, in a larger sense, all the other pains associated with coming of age in the decade of napalm and the Nehru jacket.[5]

I've purposely avoided writing a novel with a Sixties time setting because all of that seems, like the pulling of that surgical dressing, very distant to me now—almost as if it had happened to another person. But those things did happen: the hate, paranoia and fear on both sides were all too real. If we doubt it, we need only review that quintessential Sixties counterculture horror film, *Easy Rider*, in which Peter Fonda and Dennis Hopper end up being blown away by a couple of rednecks in a pickup truck as Roger McGuinn sings Bob Dylan's *It's Alright, Ma (I'm Only Bleeding)* on the sound track.

Similarly, it is difficult to remember in any gut way the fears that came with those boom years of atomic technology 25 years ago. The technology itself was strictly Apollonian; as Apollonian as nice guy Larry Talbot, who "said his prayers at night." The atom was not split

[5]Jacket with a standup collar, made famous by Indian Prime Minister Jawaharlal Nehru (1889–1964).

by a gibbering Colin Clive or Boris Karloff in some Eastern European mad lab; it was not done by alchemy and moonlight in the center of a rune-struck circle; it was done by a lot of little guys at Oak Ridge and White Sands who wore tweed jackets and smoked Luckies, guys who worried about dandruff and psoriasis and whether or not they could afford a new car and how to get rid of the goddamn crab grass. Splitting the atom, producing fission, opening that door on a new world that the old scientist speaks of at the end of *Them!*—these things were accomplished on a business-as-usual basis.

People understood this and could live with it (Fifties science books extolled the wonderful world the friendly atom would produce, a world fueled by nice safe nuclear reactors, and grammar school kids got free comic books produced by the power companies), but they suspected and feared the hairy, simian face on the other side of the coin as well: They feared that the atom might be, for a number of reasons both technological and political, essentially uncontrollable. Those feelings of deep unease came out in movies such as *The Beginning of the End, Them!, Tarantula, The Incredible Shrinking Man* (in which radiation combined with a pesticide causes a very personal horror for one man, Scott Carey), *The H-Men* and *The Four-D Man.* The entire cycle reaches its supreme pinnacle of absurdity with *The Night of the Lepus*, in which the world is menaced by giant bunnies.

All of the foregoing are examples of the horror film with a technological subtext . . . sometimes referred to as the "nature run amok" sort of horror picture. In all of them, it is mankind and mankind's technology that must bear the blame. "You brought it on yourselves," they all say; a fitting epitaph for the mass grave of mankind, I think, when the big balloon finally goes up and the ICBMs start to fly. It is here, in the technohorror film, that we really strike the mother lode. No more panning for the occasional nugget, as in the case of the economic horror film or the political horror film; pard, we could dig the gold right out of the ground with our bare hands here, if we wanted to. Here is a corner of the old horror-film corral where even such an abysmal little wet fart of a picture as *The Horror of Party Beach* will yield a technological aspect upon analysis—you see, all those beach-blanket boppers in their bikinis and ball huggers are being menaced by monsters that were cre- 60 ated when drums of radioactive waste leaked. But not to worry; although a few girls get carved up, all comes right in the end in time for one last wiener roast before school starts again.

The concerns of the technohorror films of the Sixties and Seventies change with the concerns of the people who lived through those times; the Big Bug movies give way to pictures such as *The Forbin Project* ("The Software That Conquered the World") and *2001*, which offer us the possibility of the computer as God, or the even nastier idea (ludicrously executed, I'll readily admit) of the computer as satyr that is laboriously produced in *Demon Seed* and *Saturn 3*. In the Sixties, horror proceeds from a vision of technology as an octopus—perhaps sentient—burying us alive in red tape and information retrieval systems that are terrible when they work (*The Forbin Project*) and even more terrible when they don't: In *The Andromeda Strain*, for instance, a small scrap of paper gets caught in the striker of a teletype machine, keeps the bell from ringing and thereby (in a fashion Rube Goldberg[6] certainly would have approved of) nearly causes the end of the world.

Finally, there are the Seventies, culminating in John Frankenheimer's not-very-good but certainly well-meant film *Prophecy*, which is so strikingly similar to those Fifties Big Bug movies (only the first cause has changed), and *The China Syndrome*, a horror movie that synthesizes all three of these major technological fears: fear of radiation, fear for the ecology, fear of the machinery gone out of control.

Even such a much-loved American institution as the motor vehicle has not entirely escaped the troubled dreams of Hollywood: before being run out of his mortgaged house in Amityville, James Brolin had to face the terrors of *The Car* (1977), a customized something or other that looked like a squatty airport limo from one of hell's used-car lots. The movie degenerates into a ho-hum piece of hackwork before the end of the second reel (the sort of movie in which you can safely go out for a popcorn refill at certain intervals because you know the car isn't going to strike again for ten minutes or so), but there is a marvelous opening sequence in which the car chases two bicyclists through Utah's Zion

[6]American cartoonist (1883–1970) known for drawing outrageously complex machines designed to perform simple tasks.

National Park, its horn blatting arrhythmically as it gains on them and finally runs them down. There's something working in that opening that calls up a deep, almost primitive unease about the cars we zip ourselves into, thereby becoming anonymous . . . and perhaps homicidal.

• ◦ •

There have been a few films that have tried to walk the border line between horror and social satire; one of those that seems to me to tread this border line most successfully is *The Stepford Wives*. The film is based on the novel by Ira Levin, and Levin has actually been able to pull this difficult trick off twice, the other case being that of *Rosemary's Baby*. *The Stepford Wives* has some witty things to say about women's liberation and some disquieting things to say about the American male's response to it.

65 It is as satiric as the best of Stanley Kubrick's work (though a good deal less elegant), and I defy an audience not to laugh when Katharine Ross and Paula Prentiss step into the home of a neighbor (he's the local druggist, and a Walter Mitty type if ever there were one) and hear his wife moaning upstairs. "Oh, Frank, you're the greatest . . . Frank, you're the best . . . you're the champ. . . ."

The original Levin story avoided the label "horror novel" (something like the label "pariah dog" in the more exalted circles of literary criticism) because most critics saw it as Levin's sly poke at the women's movement. But the scarier implications of Levin's jape are not directed at women at all; they are aimed unerringly at those men who consider it only their due to leave for the golf course on Saturday morning after breakfast has been served to them and to reappear (loaded, more likely than not) in time for their dinner to be served to them. After some uneasy backing and filling—during which it seems unsure of just what it does want to be—the film does, indeed, become a social horror story.

Katharine Ross and her husband (played by Peter Masterson) move from New York City to Stepford, a Connecticut suburb, because they feel it will be better for the children, and themselves as well. Stepford is a perfect little village where children wait good-humoredly for the school bus, where you can see two or three fellows washing their cars on any given day, where (you feel) the yearly United Fund quota is not only met but exceeded.

Yet there's a strangeness in Stepford. A lot of the wives seem a little, well, spacy. Pretty, always attired in flowing dresses that are almost gowns (a place where the movie slips, I think: as a labeling device, it's pretty crude. These women might as well be wearing stickers pasted to their foreheads that read I AM ONE OF THE WEIRD STEPFORD WIVES), they all drive station wagons, discuss housework with an inordinate degree of enthusiasm and seem to spend any spare time at the supermarket.

One of the Stepford wives (one of the *weird* ones) cracks her head in a minor parking-lot fender bender; later, we see her at a lawn party, repeating over and over again, "I simply *must* get that recipe . . . I simply *must* get that recipe . . . I simply *must*. . . ." The secret of Stepford becomes clear immediately. These women are *robots*. Freud, in a tone that sounded suspiciously like despair, asked, "Woman . . . what does she want?" Bryan Forbes and company ask the opposite question and come up with a stinging answer. Men, the film says, do not want women; they want robots with sex organs.

There are several funny scenes in the movie; my own favorite comes when, at a women's bitch session that Ross and Prentiss have arranged, the Stepford wives begin discussing cleaning products and laundry soaps with a slow and yet earnest intensity; everyone seems to have walked right into one of those commercials Madison Avenue male execs sometimes refer to as "two Cs in a K"—meaning two cunts in a kitchen. 70

But the movie waltzes slowly out of this brightly lit room of social satire and into a darker chamber by far. We feel the ring closing, first around Prentiss, then around Ross.

Stepford, a bedroom community serving a number of high-technology software companies, is exactly the wrong place for New Women such as Prentiss and Ross to have landed, we find. Instead of playing poker and drinking beer at the local Men's Association, the Stepford Husbands are creating counterfeit women: the final sellout in which the real women are replaced with their Malibu Barbie counterparts is left for the viewer to grapple with. The fact that we don't actually know the answers to how some of these things are done, or where the bodies are being buried—if there are, indeed, bodies once the change-over is complete—gives the film a grim, surrealist feel that is almost unique in the annals of modern horror films.

The movie reserves its ultimate horror and its most telling social shot for its closing moments when the "new" Ross walks in on the old one . . . perhaps, we think, to murder her. Under her flowing negligee, which might have come from Frederick's of Hollywood, we see Ross's rather small breasts built up to the size of what men discussing women over beers sometimes refer to as "knockers." And, of course, they are no longer the woman's breasts at all; they now belong solely to her husband. The dummy is not quite complete, however; there are two horrible black pools where the eyes should be. The best social horror movies achieve their effect by implication, and *The Stepford Wives*, by showing us only the surface of things and never troubling to explain exactly how these things are done, implies plenty.

Another film that relies on the unease generated by changing mores is William Friedkin's *The Exorcist*, and I'll not bore you by rehashing the plot: I'll simply assume that if your interest in the genre has been sufficient to sustain you this far, you've probably seen it.

75 If the late Fifties and early Sixties were the curtain raiser on the generation gap, the seven years from 1966 to 1972 were the play itself. Little Richard,[7] who had horrified parents in the Fifties when he leaped atop his piano and began boogieing on it in his lizardskin loafers, looked tame next to John Lennon, who proclaimed that the Beatles were more popular than Jesus—a statement that set off a rash of fundamentalist record burnings.

It was more than a generation gap. The two generations seemed, like the San Andreas Fault, to be moving along opposing plates of social and cultural conscience, commitment and definitions of civilized behavior itself. And with all of this young-vs.-old nuttiness as a backdrop, Friedkin's film appeared and became a social phenomenon in itself. Lines

[7]Richard Wayne Penniman (b. 1932), American rock and roll pioneer. *John Lennon:* Singer and guitarist (1940–80) for the Beatles.

stretched around the block in every major city where it played, and even in towns that normally rolled up their sidewalks promptly at 7:30 P.M., midnight shows were scheduled. Church groups picketed; sociologists pontificated; newscasters did back-of-the-book segments for their programs on slow nights. The country, in fact, went on a two-month possession jag.

The movie (and the novel) is nominally about the attempts of two priests to cast a demon out of young Regan MacNeil, of course, a pretty little subteen played by Linda Blair (who later went on to a *High Noon* showdown with a bathroom plunger in the infamous NBC movie *Born Innocent*). Substantively, however, it is a film about explosive social change, a finely honed focusing point for that entire youth explosion that occurred in the late Sixties and early Seventies. It was a movie for all those parents who felt, in a kind of agony and terror, that they were losing their children and could not understand why or how it was happening. It's the face of the Werewolf, a Jekyll-and-Hyde tale in which sweet, lovely and loving Regan turns into a foul-talking monster strapped into her bed and croaking (in the voice of Mercedes McCambridge) such charming homilies as "You're going to let Jesus fuck you, fuck you, fuck you." Religious trappings aside, every adult in America understood what the film's powerful subtext was saying; they understood that the demon in Regan would have responded enthusiastically to the Fish Cheer at Woodstock.[8]

• ◦ •

A Warner Bros. executive told me recently that movie surveys show the average filmgoer to be 15 years of age, which may be the biggest reason the movies so often seem afflicted with a terminal case of arrested development. For every film like *Julia* or *The Turning Point*, there are a dozen like *Roller Boogie* and *If You Don't Stop It, You'll Go Blind*. But it is worth noting that when the infrequent blockbusters that every film

[8]Acid rock band Country Joe & the Fish engaged its audience with a cheer spelling F-I-S-H ("Gimme an F"); as popular opinion on the Vietnam War began to change, drummer Gary Hirsch suggested changing the cheer to spell a different four-letter word beginning with F. This is the version of the cheer the band performed at the Woodstock concert in 1969.

producer hopes for finally come along—pictures like *Star Wars*, *Jaws*, *American Graffiti*, *The Godfather*, *Gone with the Wind* and, of course, *The Exorcist*—they always break the demographic hammer lock that is the enemy of intelligent film making. It is comparatively rare for horror movies to do this, but *The Exorcist* is a case in point (and we have already spoken of *The Amityville Horror*, another film that has enjoyed a surprisingly old audience).

A film that appealed directly to the 15-year-olds who provide the spike point for moviegoing audiences—and one with a subtext tailored to match—was the Brian De Palma adaptation of my novel *Carrie*. While I believe that both the book and the film depend on largely the same social situations to provide a text and a subtext of horror, there's enough difference to make interesting observations on De Palma's film version.

Both novel and movie have a pleasant *High School Confidential* feel, and while there are some superficial changes from the book in the film (Carrie's mother, for instance, seems to be presented in the film as a kind of weird renegade Roman Catholic), the basic story skeleton is pretty much the same. The story deals with a girl named Carrie White, the browbeaten daughter of a religious fanatic. Because of her strange clothes and shy mannerisms, Carrie is the butt of every class joke, the social outsider in every situation. She also has a mild telekinetic ability that intensifies after her first menstrual period, and she finally uses that power to "bring down the house" following a terrible social disaster at her high school prom. 80

De Palma's approach to the material is lighter and more deft than my own—and a good deal more artistic; the book tries to deal with the loneliness of one girl, her desperate effort to become a part of the peer society in which she must exist, and the failure of that effort. If this deliberate updating of *High School Confidential* has any thesis to offer, it is that high school is a place of almost bottomless conservatism and bigotry, a place where adolescents are no more allowed to rise above their station than a Hindu would be allowed to rise above his caste.

But there's a little more subtext to the book than that—at least, I hope so. If *The Stepford Wives* concerns itself with what men want from women, then *Carrie* is largely about how women find their own channels of power and what men fear about women and women's sexuality—which is only to say that, writing the book in 1973 and out of college only three years, I was fully aware of what women's liberation implied for me and others of my sex. The book is, in its more adult implications, an uneasy masculine shrinking from a future of female equality. For me, Carrie is a sadly misused teenager, an example of the sort of person whose spirit is so often broken for good in that pit of man- and woman-eaters that is your normal suburban high school. But she's also Woman, feeling her powers for the first time, and, like Samson, pulling down the temple[9] on everyone in sight at the end of the book.

Heavy, turgid stuff—but in the novel, it's there only if you want to take it. If you don't, that's OK with me. A subtext works well only if it's unobtrusive (in that, I perhaps succeeded too well: in her review of De Palma's film, Pauline Kael dismissed my novel as "an unassuming potboiler"—as depressing a description as one could imagine but not completely inaccurate).

De Palma's film is up to more ambitious things. As in *The Stepford Wives*, humor and horror exist side by side in *Carrie*, playing off each other, and it is only as the film nears its conclusion that horror takes over completely. We see Billy Nolan (well played by John Travolta) giving the cops a big aw-shucks grin as he hides a beer against his crotch early on; it is a moment reminiscent of *American Graffiti*. Not long after, however, we see him swinging a sledge hammer at the head of a pig in a stockyard—the aw-shucks grin has crossed the line into madness, somehow, and that line crossing is what the film as a whole is about.

85 We see three boys (one of them the film's nominal hero, played by William Katt) trying on tuxedos for the prom in a kind of Gas House Kids routine that includes Donald Duck talk and speeded-up action. We see the girls who have humiliated Carrie in the shower room by throwing tampons and sanitary napkins at her doing penance on the exercise field to tootling, lumbering music that is reminiscent of *Baby*

[9]See Judges 16:29–30.

Elephant Walk. And yet beyond all these sophomoric and mildly amusing high school cut-ups, we sense a vacuous, almost unfocused hate, the almost unplanned revenge upon a girl who is trying to rise above her station. Much of De Palma's film is surprisingly jolly, but we sense that his jocoseness is dangerous: Behind it lurks the aw-shucks grin becoming a frozen rictus, and the girls laboring over their calisthenics are the same girls who shouted "Plug it up, plug it up, plug it up!" at Carrie not long before. Most of all, there is that bucket of pig's blood poised on the beam above the place where Carrie and Tommy will eventually be crowned . . . only waiting its time.

The film came along at a time when movie critics were bewailing the fact that there were no movies being made with good, meaty roles for women in them . . . but none of those critics seems to have noticed that in its film incarnation, *Carrie* belongs almost entirely to the ladies. Billy Nolan, a major—and frightening—character in the book, has been reduced to a semisupporting role in the movie. Tommy, the boy who takes Carrie to the prom, is presented in the novel as a boy who is honestly trying to do something manly—in his own way, he is trying to opt out of the caste system. In the film, however, he becomes little more than his girlfriend's cat's-paw, her tool of atonement for her part in the shower room scene.

"I don't go around with anyone I don't want to," Tommy says patiently. "I'm asking because I want to ask you." Ultimately, he knew this to be the truth.

In the film, however, when Carrie asks Tommy why he is favoring her with an invitation to the prom, he offers her a dizzy sun-'n'-surf grin and says, "Because you liked my poem." Which, by the way, his girlfriend had written.

The novel views high school in a fairly common way: as that pit of man- and woman-eaters already mentioned. De Palma's social stance is more original: he sees this suburban white kids' high school as a kind of matriarchy. No matter where you look, there are girls behind the scenes, pulling invisible wires, rigging elections, using their boyfriends as stalking horses. Against such a backdrop, Carrie becomes doubly pitiful, because she is unable to do any of those things—she can only wait to be saved or damned by the actions of others. Her only power is her telekinetic ability, and both book and movie eventually arrive at the same point: Carrie uses her "wild talent" to pull down the whole rotten society. And one reason for the success of the story in both print and film, I think, lies in this: Carrie's revenge is something that any student who ever had his gym shorts pulled down in phys ed or his glasses thumb-rubbed in study hall could approve of. In Carrie's destruction of the gym (and her destructive walk back home in the book, a sequence left out of the movie because of tight budgeting), we see a dream revolution of the socially downtrodden.

• ○ •

The movies I have been discussing are those that try to link real (if sometimes free-floating) anxieties to the nightmare fears of the horror film. But now, let me put out even this dim light of rationality and discuss a few of those, films whose effects go considerably deeper, past the rational and into those fears that seem universal. 90

Here is where we cross into the taboo lands for sure, and it's best to be frank up front. I think that we're all mentally ill; those of us outside the asylums only hide it a little better—and maybe not all that much better, after all. We've all known people who talk to themselves, people who sometimes squinch their faces into horrible grimaces when they believe no one is watching, people who have some hysterical fear—of snakes, the dark, the tight place, the long drop . . . and, of course, those final worms and grubs that are waiting so patiently underground.

When we pay our four or five bucks and seat ourselves at tenth-row center in a theater showing a horror movie, we are daring the nightmare.

Why? Some of the reasons are simple and obvious. To show that we can, that we are not afraid, that we can ride this roller coaster. Which is not to say that a really good horror movie may not surprise a scream out of us at some point, the way we may scream when the roller coaster twists through a complete 360 or plows through a lake at the bottom of the drop. And horror movies, like roller coasters, have always been the special province of the young; by the time one turns 40 or 50, one's appetite for double twists or 360-degree loops may be considerably depleted.

We also go to re-establish our feeling of essential normality; the horror movie is innately conservative, even reactionary. Freda Jackson as the horrible melting woman in *Die, Monster, Die!* confirms for us that no matter how far we may be removed from the beauty of a Robert Redford or a Diana Ross, we are still light-years from true ugliness.

And we go to have fun. 95

Ah, but this is where the ground starts to slope away, isn't it? Because this is a very peculiar sort of fun, indeed. The fun comes from seeing others menaced—sometimes killed. One critic has suggested that if pro football has become the voyeur's version of combat, then the horror film has become the modern version of the public lynching.

It is true that the mythic, "fairy-tale" horror film intends to take away the shades of gray (which is one reason *When a Stranger Calls* doesn't work; the psycho, well and honestly played by Tony Beckley, is a poor schmuck beset by the miseries of his own psychosis; our unwilling sympathy for him dilutes the film's success as surely as water dilutes Scotch); it urges us to put away our more civilized and adult penchant for analysis and to become children again, seeing things in pure blacks and whites. It may be that horror movies provide psychic relief on this level because this invitation to lapse into simplicity, irrationality and even outright madness is extended so rarely. We are told we may allow our emotions a free rein . . . or no rein at all.

If we are all insane, then sanity becomes a matter of degree. If your insanity leads you to carve up women like Jack the Ripper or the Cleveland Torso Murderer,[1] we clap you away in the funny farm (but neither of those two amateur-night surgeons was ever caught, heh-heh-heh); if, on the other hand, your insanity leads you only to talk to yourself when you're under stress or to pick your nose on your morning bus, then you are left alone to go about your business . . . though it is doubtful that you will ever be invited to the best parties.

The potential lyncher is in almost all of us (excluding saints, past and present; but then most saints have been crazy in their own ways), and every now and then, he has to be let loose to scream and roll around in

[1]Serial killers of London's 1880s and Cleveland, Ohio's 1930s, respectively.

the grass. Our emotions and our fears form their own body, and we recognize that it demands its own exercise to maintain proper muscle tone. Certain of these emotional muscles are accepted—even exalted—in civilized society; they are, of course, the emotions that tend to maintain the status quo of civilization itself. Love, friendship, loyalty, kindness—these are all the emotions that we applaud, emotions that have been immortalized in the couplets of Hallmark cards and in the verses (I don't dare call it poetry) of Leonard Nimoy.[2]

When we exhibit these emotions, society showers us with positive reinforcement; we learn this even before we get out of diapers. When as children, we hug our rotten little puke of a sister and give her a kiss, all the aunts and uncles smile and twit and cry, "Isn't he the sweetest little thing?" Such coveted treats as chocolate-covered graham crackers often follow. But if we deliberately slam the rotten little puke of a sister's fingers in the door, sanctions follow—angry remonstrance from parents, aunts and uncles; instead of a chocolate-covered graham cracker, a spanking. 100

But anticivilization emotions don't go away, and they demand periodic exercise. We have such "sick" jokes as, "What's the difference between a truckload of bowling balls and a truckload of dead babies?" (You can't unload a truckload of bowling balls with a pitchfork . . . a joke, by the way, that I heard originally from a ten-year-old.) Such a joke may surprise a laugh or a grin out of us even as we recoil, a possibility that confirms the thesis: If we share a brotherhood of man, then we also share an insanity of man. None of which is intended as a defense of either the sick joke or insanity but merely as an explanation of why the best horror films, like the best fairy tales, manage to be reactionary, anarchistic and revolutionary all at the same time.

The mythic horror movie, like the sick joke, has a dirty job to do. It deliberately appeals to all that is worst in us. It is morbidity unchained, our most base instincts let free, our nastiest fantasies realized . . . and it all happens, fittingly enough, in the dark. For those reasons, good lib-

[2]American actor (b. 1931) who also wrote poetry; King is probably referring to Nimoy's collection *We Are All Children Searching for Love* (1977).

erals often shy away from horror films. For myself, I like to see the most aggressive of them—*Dawn of the Dead*, for instance—as lifting a trap door in the civilized forebrain and throwing a basket of raw meat to the hungry alligators swimming around in that subterranean river beneath.

Why bother? Because it keeps them from getting out, man. It keeps them down there and me up here. It was Lennon and McCartney who said that all you need is love, and I would agree with that.

As long as you keep the gators fed.

JESSICA MITFORD

Behind the Formaldehyde Curtain

Jessica Mitford (1917–1996) was born into an aristocratic English family and moved in 1939 to the United States, where she became a naturalized American citizen and pursued a career as an investigative reporter. A lifelong activist, Mitford worked on behalf of pacifism and civil rights; when she and her husband, Robert Treuhaft, a lawyer, became aware of funeral costs for working-class families in the San Francisco Bay Area, she published *The American Way of Death* (1963), which sold out on the day of publication. While the work provoked queasiness in some readers and outrage in others (mainly funeral directors), it has become a classic piece of expository prose, anthologized in more than fifty textbooks. Mitford is the author of several books, including *The American Way of Death Revisited* (1998).

This chapter from *The American Way of Death* presents a critical look at the process of embalming bodies and preparing them for burial. Mitford uses an ironically breezy tone to convey her attitude toward the way funerals are conducted in the United States as she describes the procedures used to embalm the fictitious "Mr. Jones." Despite her gruesome subject matter (or perhaps, for some readers, because of it), Mitford's understated sense of humor has made "Behind the Formaldehyde Curtain" enduringly popular.

The drama begins to unfold with the arrival of the corpse at the mortuary.

Alas, poor Yorick![1] How surprised he would be to see how his counterpart of today is whisked off to a funeral parlor and is in short

[1]*Hamlet*, 5.1.171. Hamlet discovers the skull of an old friend in a graveyard.

order sprayed, sliced, pierced, pickled, trussed, trimmed, creamed, waxed, painted, rouged and neatly dressed—transformed from a common corpse into a Beautiful Memory Picture. This process is known in the trade as embalming and restorative art, and is so universally employed in the United States and Canada that the funeral director does it routinely, without consulting corpse or kin. He regards as eccentric those few who are hardy enough to suggest that it might be dispensed with. Yet no law requires embalming, no religious doctrine commends it, nor is it dictated by considerations of health, sanitation, or even of personal daintiness. In no part of the world but in Northern America is it widely used. The purpose of embalming is to make the corpse presentable for viewing in a suitably costly container; and here too the funeral director routinely, without first consulting the family, prepares the body for public display.

Is all this legal? The processes to which a dead body may be subjected are after all to some extent circumscribed by law. In most states, for instance, the signature of next of kin must be obtained before an autopsy may be performed, before the deceased may be cremated, before the body may be turned over to a medical school for research purposes; or such provision must be made in the decedent's will. In the case of embalming, no such permission is required nor is it ever sought. A textbook, *The Principles and Practices of Embalming*, comments on this: "There is some question regarding the legality of much that is done within the preparation room." The author points out that it would be most unusual for a responsible member of a bereaved family to instruct the mortician, in so many words, to *"embalm"* the body of a deceased relative. The very term "embalming" is so seldom used that the mortician must rely upon custom in the matter. The author concludes that unless the family specifies otherwise, the act of entrusting the body to the care of a funeral establishment carries with it an implied permission to go ahead and embalm.

Embalming is indeed a most extraordinary procedure, and one must wonder at the docility of Americans who each year pay hundreds of millions of dollars for its perpetuation, blissfully ignorant of what it is all about, what is done, how it is done. Not one in ten thousand has any idea of what actually takes place. Books on the subject are extremely hard to come by. They are not to be found in most libraries or bookshops.

5 In an era when huge television audiences watch surgical operations in the comfort of their living rooms, when, thanks to the animated cartoon, the geography of the digestive system has become familiar territory even to the nursery school set, in a land where the satisfaction of curiosity about almost all matters is a national pastime, the secrecy surrounding embalming can, surely, hardly be attributed to the inherent gruesomeness of the subject. Custom in this regard has within this century suffered a complete reversal. In the early days of American embalming, when it was performed in the home of the deceased, it was almost mandatory for some relative to stay by the embalmer's side and witness the procedure. Today, family members who might wish to be in attendance would certainly be dissuaded by the funeral director. All others, except apprentices, are excluded by law from the preparation room.

A close look at what does actually take place may explain in large measure the undertaker's intractable reticence concerning a procedure that has become his major *raison d'être.* Is it possible he fears that public information about embalming might lead patrons to wonder if they really want this service? If the funeral men are loath to discuss the subject outside the trade, the reader may, understandably, be equally loath to go on reading at this point. For those who have the stomach for it, let us part the formaldehyde curtain. Others should skip to paragraph 20.

The body is first laid out in the undertaker's morgue—or rather, Mr. Jones is reposing in the preparation room—to be readied to bid the world farewell.

The preparation room in any of the better funeral establishments has the tiled and sterile look of a surgery, and indeed the embalmer-restorative artist who does his chores there is beginning to adopt the term "dermasurgeon" (appropriately corrupted by some mortician-writers as "demisurgeon") to describe his calling. His equipment, consisting of scalpels, scissors, augers, forceps, clamps, needles, pumps, tubes, bowls and basins, is crudely imitative of the surgeon's, as is his technique, acquired in a nine- or twelve-month post-high-school course in an embalming school. He is supplied by an advanced chemical industry with a bewildering array of fluids, sprays, pastes, oils, powders, creams, to fix or soften tissue, shrink or distend it as needed, dry it here, restore the moisture there. There are cosmetics, waxes and paints to fill and cover features, even plaster of Paris to replace entire limbs. There are ingenious aids to prop and stabilize the cadaver: a Vari-Pose Head Rest, the Edwards Arm and Hand Positioner, the Repose Block (to support the shoulders, during the embalming), and the Throop Foot Positioner, which resembles an old-fashioned stocks.

Mr. John H. Eckels, president of the Eckels College of Mortuary Science, thus describes the first part of the embalming procedure: "In the hands of a skilled practitioner, this work may be done in a comparatively short time and without mutilating the body other than by slight incision—so slight that it scarcely would cause serious inconvenience if made upon a living person. It is necessary to remove the blood, and doing this not only helps in the disinfecting, but removes the principal cause of disfigurements due to discoloration."

Another textbook discusses the all-important time element: "The earlier this is done, the better, for every hour that elapses between death and embalming will add to the problems and complications encountered. . . ." Just how soon should one get going on the embalming? The author tells us, "On the basis of such scanty information made available to this profession through its rudimentary and haphazard system of technical research, we must conclude that the best results are to be obtained if the subject is embalmed before life is completely extinct—that is, before cellular death has occurred. In the average case, this would mean within an hour after somatic death." For those who feel that there is something a little rudimentary, not to say haphazard, about this advice, a comforting thought is offered by another writer. Speaking of fears entertained in early days of premature burial, he points out, "One of the effects of embalming by chemical injection, however, has been to dispel fears of live burial." How true; once the blood is removed, chances of live burial are indeed remote. 10

To return to Mr. Jones, the blood is drained out through the veins and replaced by embalming fluid pumped in through the arteries. As noted in *The Principles and Practices of Embalming,* "every operator has a favorite injection and drainage point—a fact which becomes a handicap only if he fails or refuses to forsake his favorites when conditions demand it." Typical favorites are the carotid artery, femoral artery, jugular vein, subclavian vein. There are various choices of embalming fluid. If Flextone is used, it will produce a "mild, flexible rigidity. The skin retains a velvety softness, the tissues are rubbery and pliable. Ideal for women and children." It may be blended with B. and G. Products Company's Lyf-Lyk tint, which is guaranteed to reproduce "nature's own skin texture . . . the velvety appearance of living tissue." Suntone comes in three separate tints: Suntan; Special Cosmetic Tint, a pink shade "especially indicated for young female subjects"; and Regular Cosmetic Tint, moderately pink.

About three to six gallons of a dyed and perfumed solution of formaldehyde, glycerin, borax, phenol, alcohol and water is soon circulating through Mr. Jones, whose mouth has been sewn together with a "needle directed upward between the upper lip and gum and brought out through the left nostril," with the corners raised slightly "for a more pleasant expression." If he should be bucktoothed, his teeth are cleaned with Bon Ami and coated with colorless nail polish. His eyes, meanwhile, are closed with flesh-tinted eye caps and eye cement.

The next step is to have at Mr. Jones with a thing called a trocar. This is a long, hollow needle attached to a tube. It is jabbed into the abdomen, poked around the entrails and chest cavity, the contents of which are pumped out and replaced with "cavity fluid." This done, and the hole in the abdomen sewn up, Mr. Jones's face is heavily creamed (to protect the skin from burns which may be caused by leakage of the chemicals), and he is covered with a sheet and left unmolested for a while. But not for long—there is more, much more, in store for him. He has been embalmed, but not yet restored, and the best time to start the restorative work is eight to ten hours after embalming, when the tissues have become firm and dry.

The object of all this attention to the corpse, it must be remembered, is to make it presentable for viewing in an attitude of healthy repose. "Our customs require the presentation of our dead in the semblance of normality . . . unmarred by the ravages of illness, disease, or mutilation," says Mr. J. Sheridan Mayer in his *Restorative Art.* This is rather a large order since few people die in the full bloom of health, unravaged by illness and unmarked by some disfigurement. The funeral industry is equal to the challenge: "In some cases the gruesome appearance of a mutilated or disease-ridden subject may be quite discouraging. The task of restoration may seem impossible and shake the confidence of the embalmer. This is the time for intestinal fortitude and determination. Once the formative work is begun and affected tissues are cleaned or removed, all doubts of success vanish. It is surprising and gratifying to discover the results which may be obtained."

The embalmer, having allowed an appropriate interval to elapse, returns to the attack, but now he brings into play the skill and equipment of sculptor and cosmetician. Is a hand missing? Casting one in plaster of Paris is a simple matter. "For replacement purposes, only a cast of the back of the hand is necessary; this is within the ability of the average operator and is quite adequate." If a lip or two, a nose or an ear should be missing, the embalmer has at hand a variety of restorative waxes with which to model replacements. Pores and skin texture are simulated by stippling with a little brush, and over this cosmetics are laid on. Head off? Decapitation cases are rather routinely handled. Ragged edges are trimmed, and head joined to torso with a series of splints, wires and sutures. It is a good idea to have a little something at the neck—a scarf or high collar—when time for viewing comes. Swollen mouth? Cut out tissue as needed from inside the lips. If too much is removed, the surface contour can easily be restored by padding with cotton. Swollen necks and cheeks are reduced by removing tissue through vertical incisions made down each side of the neck. "When the deceased is casketed, the pillow will hide the suture incisions . . . as an extra precaution against leakage, the suture may be painted with liquid sealer." 15

The opposite condition is more likely to present itself—that of emaciation. His hypodermic syringe now loaded with massage cream, the embalmer seeks out and fills the hollowed and sunken areas by injection. In this procedure the backs of the hands and fingers and the under-chin area should not be neglected.

Positioning the lips is a problem that recurrently challenges the ingenuity of the embalmer. Closed too tightly, they tend to give a stern, even disapproving expression. Ideally, embalmers feel, the lips should give the impression of being ever so slightly parted, the upper lip protruding slightly for a more youthful appearance. This takes some engineering, however, as the lips tend to drift apart. Lip drift can sometimes be remedied by pushing one or two straight pins through the inner margin of the lower lip and then inserting them between the two front upper teeth. If Mr. Jones happens to have no teeth, the pins can just as easily be anchored in his Armstrong Face Former and Denture Replacer. Another method to maintain lip closure is to dislocate the lower jaw, which is then held in its new position by a wire run through holes which have been drilled through the upper and lower jaws at the midline. As the French are fond of saying, *il faut souffrir pour être belle.*[2]

If Mr. Jones has died of jaundice, the embalming fluid will very likely turn him green. Does this deter the embalmer? Not if he has intestinal fortitude. Masking pastes and cosmetics are heavily laid on, burial garments and casket interiors are color-correlated with particular care, and Jones is displayed beneath rose-colored lights. Friends will say, "How *well* he looks." Death by carbon monoxide, on the other hand, can be rather a good thing from the embalmer's viewpoint: "One advantage is the fact that this type of discoloration is an exaggerated form of a natural pink coloration." This is nice because the healthy glow is already present and needs but little attention.

The patching and filling completed, Mr. Jones is now shaved, washed and dressed. Cream-based cosmetic, available in pink, flesh, suntan, brunette and blond, is applied to his hands and face, his hair is shampooed and combed (and, in the case of Mrs. Jones, set), his hands manicured. For the horny-handed son of toil special care must be taken; cream should be applied to remove ingrained grime, and the nails cleaned. "If he were not in the habit of having them manicured in

[2]In 1963 *Mortuary Management* reports a new development: "Natural Expression Formers," an invention of Funeral Directors Research Company. "They may be used to replace one or both artificial dentures, or over natural teeth; have 'bite-indicator' lines as a closure guide . . . Natural Expression Formers also offer more control of facial expression" [Author's note]. *Il faut souffrir pour être belle:* One must suffer to be beautiful (French).

life, trimming and shaping is advised for better appearance—never questioned by kin."

20 Jones is now ready for casketing (this is the present participle of the verb "to casket"). In this operation his right shoulder should be depressed slightly "to turn the body a bit to the right and soften the appearance of lying flat on the back." Positioning the hands is a matter of importance, and special rubber positioning blocks may be used. The hands should be cupped slightly for a more lifelike, relaxed appearance. Proper placement of the body requires a delicate sense of balance. It should lie as high as possible in the casket, yet not so high that the lid, when lowered, will hit the nose. On the other hand, we are cautioned, placing the body too low "creates the impression that the body is in a box."

Jones is next wheeled into the appointed slumber room where a few last touches may be added—his favorite pipe placed in his hand or, if he was a great reader, a book propped into position. (In the case of little Master Jones a Teddy bear may be clutched.) Here he will hold open house for a few days, visiting hours 10 A.M. to 9 P.M.

All now being in readiness, the funeral director calls a staff conference to make sure that each assistant knows his precise duties. Mr. Wilber Krieger writes: "This makes your staff feel that they are a part of the team, with a definite assignment that must be properly carried out if the whole plan is to succeed. You never heard of a football coach who failed to talk to his entire team before they go on the field. They have drilled on the plays they are to execute for hours and days, and yet the successful coach knows the importance of making even the bench-warming third-string substitute feel that he is important if the game is to be won." The winning of *this* game is predicated upon glass-smooth handling of the logistics. The funeral director has notified the pallbearers whose names were furnished by the family, has arranged for the presence of clergyman, organist, and soloist, has provided transportation for everybody, has organized and listed the flowers sent by friends. In *Psychology of Funeral Service* Mr. Edward A. Martin points out: "He may not always do as much as the family thinks he is doing, but it is his helpful guidance that they appreciate in knowing they are proceeding as they should. . . . The important thing is how well his services can be used to make the family believe they are giving unlimited expression to their own sentiment."

The religious service may be held in a church or in the chapel of the funeral home; the funeral director vastly prefers the latter arrangement, for not only is it more convenient for him but it affords him the opportunity to show off his beautiful facilities to the gathered mourners. After the clergyman has had his say, the mourners queue up to file past the casket for a last look at the deceased. The family is *never* asked whether they want an open-casket ceremony; in the absence of their instruction to the contrary, this is taken for granted. Consequently well over 90 percent of all American funerals feature the open casket—a custom unknown in other parts of the world. Foreigners are astonished by it. An English woman living in San Francisco described her reaction in a letter to the writer:

> I myself have attended only one funeral here—that of an elderly fellow worker of mine. After the service I could not understand why everyone was walking towards the coffin (sorry, I mean casket), but thought I had better follow the crowd. It shook me rigid to get there and find the casket open and poor old Oscar lying there in his brown tweed suit, wearing a suntan makeup and just the wrong shade of lipstick. If I had not been extremely fond of the old boy, I have a horrible feeling that I might have giggled. Then and there I decided that I could never face another American funeral—even dead.

The casket (which has been resting throughout the service on a Classic Beauty Ultra Metal Casket Bier) is now transferred by a hydraulically operated device called Porto-Lift to a balloon-tired, Glide Easy casket carriage which will wheel it to yet another conveyance, the Cadillac Funeral Coach. This may be lavender, cream, light green—anything but black. Interiors, of course, are color-correlated, "for the man who cannot stop short of perfection."

25 At graveside, the casket is lowered into the earth. This office, once the prerogative of friends of the deceased, is now performed by a patented mechanical lowering device. A "Lifetime Green" artificial grass mat is at the ready to conceal the sere earth, and overhead, to con-

ceal the sky, is a portable Steril Chapel Tent ("resists the intense heat and humidity of summer and the terrific storms of winter . . . available in Silver Grey, Rose or Evergreen"). Now is the time for the ritual scattering of earth over the coffin, as the solemn words "earth to earth, ashes to ashes, dust to dust" are pronounced by the officiating cleric. This can today be accomplished "with a mere flick of the wrist with the Gordon Leak-Proof Earth Dispenser. No grasping of a handful of dirt, no soiled fingers. Simple, dignified, beautiful, reverent! The modern way!" The Gordon Earth Dispenser (at $5) is of nickel-plated brass construction. It is not only "attractive to the eye and long wearing"; it is also "one of the 'tools' for building better public relations" if presented as "an appropriate non-commercial gift" to the clergyman. It is shaped something like a saltshaker.

Untouched by human hand, the coffin and the earth are now united.

It is in the function of directing the participants through this maze of gadgetry that the funeral director has assigned to himself his relatively new role of "grief therapist." He has relieved the family of every detail, he has revamped the corpse to look like a living doll, he has arranged for it to nap for a few days in a slumber room, he has put on a well-oiled performance in which the concept of *death* has played no part whatsoever—unless it was inconsiderately mentioned by the clergyman who conducted the religious service. He has done everything in his power to make the funeral a real pleasure for everybody concerned. He and his team have given their all to score an upset victory over death.

PLATO { *Allegory of the Cave*

PLATO (428/427–348/347 BCE), a devoted student of Socrates, became one of ancient Greece's most important philosophers and teachers. Plato's written dialogues explore philosophical questions related to justice, virtue, law, reason, and the soul. The central figure in his writings is Socrates, who taught by posing questions and exploring their implications instead of by lecturing. When Plato was about forty years old he founded the Academy, a school designed to provide rigorous philosophical training to prospective politicians, as Plato believed that public servants must first be seekers of wisdom and truth. His most famous pupil at the Academy was Aristotle.

In the Allegory of the Cave, a section from his best-known work, the *Republic*, Plato presents his belief that while change occurs in the physical realm, all things have their essence in a higher realm. For example, in the physical realm all trees change (they grow and die), but the essence of "tree" exists in the higher realm, the perfect world of permanent and unchanging ideas. The goal of philosophy, according to Plato, is to help the student more clearly see this higher realm. In this dialogue, Socrates asks his student Glaucon to imagine humans chained in a cave so that all they can see are shadows on the back wall. This chained existence of darkness and shadows is all they have ever known. What would happen, Socrates asks, if one were suddenly free of the chains and were able to see that what they had once considered reality was only a shadowy representation of truth?

AND NOW, I SAID, LET me show in a figure how far our nature is enlightened or unenlightened: Behold! human beings living in an underground den, which has a mouth open toward the light and reaching all along the den; here they have been from their childhood, and have their legs and necks chained so that they cannot move, and can see only before them, being prevented by the chains from turning round their heads. Above and behind them a fire is blazing at a distance, and between the fire and the prisoners there is a raised way; and you will see, if you look, a low wall built along the way, like the screen which marionette players have in front of them, over which they show the puppets.

I see.

And do you see, I said, men passing along the wall carrying all sorts of vessels, and statues and figures of animals made of wood and stone and various materials, which appear over the wall? Some of them are talking, others silent.

You have shown me a strange image, and they are strange prisoners.

Like ourselves, I replied; and they see only their own shadows, or the shadows of one another, which the fire throws on the opposite wall of the cave?

True, he said; how could they see anything but the shadows if they were never allowed to move their heads?

And of the objects which are being carried in like manner they would only see the shadows?

Yes, he said.

And if they were able to converse with one another, would they not suppose that they were naming what was actually before them?

Very true.

And suppose further that the prison had an echo which came from the other side, would they not be sure to fancy when one of the passers-by spoke that the voice which they heard came from the passing shadow?

No question, he replied.

To them, I said, the truth would be literally nothing but the shadows of the images.

That is certain.

And now look again, and see what will naturally follow if the prisoners are released and disabused of their error. At first, when any of them is liberated and compelled suddenly to stand up and turn his neck round and walk and look toward the light, he will suffer sharp pains; the glare will distress him and he will be unable to see the realities of which in his former state he had seen the shadows; and then conceive someone saying to him, that what he saw before was an illusion, but that now, when he is approaching nearer to being and his eye is turned toward more real existence, he has a clearer vision—what will be his reply? And you may further imagine that his instructor is pointing to the objects as they pass and requiring him to name them—will he not be perplexed? Will he not fancy that the shadows which he formerly saw are truer than the objects which are now shown to him?

Far truer.

And if he is compelled to look straight at the light, will he not have a pain in his eyes which will make him turn away to take refuge in the objects of vision which he can see, and which he will conceive to be in reality clearer than the things which are now being shown to him?

True, he said.

And suppose once more, that he is reluctantly dragged up a steep and rugged ascent, and held fast until he is forced into the presence of the sun himself, is he not likely to be pained and irritated? When he approaches the light his eyes will be dazzled and he will not be able to see anything at all of what are now called realities.

Not all in a moment, he said. 20

He will require to grow accustomed to the sight of the upper world. And first he will see the shadows best, next the reflections of men and other objects in the water, and then the objects themselves; then he will gaze upon the light of the moon and the stars and the spangled heaven; and he will see the sky and the stars by night better than the sun or the light of the sun by day?

Certainly.

Last of all he will be able to see the sun, and not mere reflections of him in the water, but he will see him in his own proper place, and not in another; and he will contemplate him as he is.

Certainly.

He will then proceed to argue that this is he who gives the season 25 and the years, and is the guardian of all that is in the visible world, and in a certain way the cause of all things which he and his fellows have been accustomed to behold?

Clearly, he said, he would first see the sun and then reason about him.

And when he remembered his old habitation, and the wisdom of the den and his fellow-prisoners, do you not suppose that he would felicitate himself on the change, and pity them?

Certainly, he would.

And if they were in the habit of conferring honors among themselves on those who were quickest to observe the passing shadows and to remark which of them went before, and which followed after, and which were together; and who were therefore best able to draw conclusions as to the future, do you think that he would care for such honors and glories, or envy the possessors of them? Would he not say with Homer, "Better to be the poor servant of a poor master," and to endure anything, rather than think as they do and live after their manner?

Yes, he said, I think that he would rather suffer anything than entertain these false notions and live in this miserable manner. 30

Imagine once more, I said, such a one coming suddenly out of the sun to be replaced in his old situation; would he not be certain to have his eyes full of darkness?

To be sure, he said.

And if there were a contest, and he had to compete in measuring the shadows with the prisoners who had never moved out of the den, while his sight was still weak, and before his eyes had become steady (and the time which would be needed to acquire this new habit of sight might be very considerable) would he not be ridiculous? Men would say of him that up he went and down he came without his eyes; and that it was better not even to think of ascending; and if anyone tried to loose another and lead him up to the light, let them only catch the offender, and they would put him to death.

No question, he said.

This entire allegory, I said, you may now append, dear Glaucon, 35 to the previous argument; the prison-house is the world of sight, the light of the fire is the sun, and you will not misapprehend me if you interpret the journey upwards to be the ascent of the soul into the intellectual world according to my poor belief, which, at your desire, I have expressed—whether rightly or wrongly God knows. But, whether true or false, my opinion is that in the world of knowledge the idea of good appears last of all, and is seen only with an effort; and, when seen, is also inferred to be the universal author of all things beautiful and right, parent of light and of the lord of light in this visible world, and the immediate source of reason and truth in the intellectual; and that this is the power upon which he who would act rationally either in public or private life must have his eye fixed.

I agree, he said, as far as I am able to understand you.

Moreover, I said, you must not wonder that those who attain to this beatific vision are unwilling to descend to human affairs; for their souls are ever hastening into the upper world where they desire to dwell; which desire of theirs is very natural, if our allegory may be trusted.

Yes, very natural.

And is there anything surprising in one who passes from divine contemplations to the evil state of man, misbehaving himself in a ridiculous manner; if, while his eyes are blinking and before he has become accustomed to the surrounding darkness, he is compelled to fight in courts of law, or in other places, about the images or the shadows of images of justice, and is endeavoring to meet the conceptions of those who have never yet seen absolute justice?

Anything but surprising, he replied. 40

Anyone who has common sense will remember that the bewilderments of the eyes are of two kinds, and arise from two causes, either from coming out of the light or from going into the light, which is true of the mind's eye, quite as much as of the bodily eye; and he who remembers this when he sees anyone whose vision is perplexed and weak, will not be too ready to laugh; he will first ask whether that soul of man has come out of the brighter life, and is unable to see because unaccustomed to the dark, or having turned from darkness to the day is dazzled by excess of light. And he will count the one happy in his condition and state of being, and he will pity the other; or, if he have a mind to laugh at the soul which comes from below into the light, there will be more reason in this than in the laugh which greets him who returns from above out of the light into the den.

That, he said, is a very just distinction.

AZAR NAFISI { *Gatsby*

AZAR NAFISI (b. 1947) was born in Iran but educated in England and the United States, where she earned a PhD in American literature from the University of Oklahoma. She returned to Iran in 1979 to teach at the University of Tehran amidst political upheaval that made teaching extremely difficult for a secular woman. In 1981 she was expelled from her position at the university for refusing to wear a traditional veil. She currently works as a visiting professor at Johns Hopkins University in Baltimore and regularly writes for publications such as the *New York Times*, the *Washington Post*, the *Wall Street Journal*, and the *New Republic*.

The following selection comes from Nafisi's book *Reading* Lolita *in Tehran: A Memoir in Books* (2003), which recounts the years Nafisi spent in the Islamic Republic of Iran teaching "forbidden" Western literary texts. The memoir documents her personal history by connecting it to the lives of literary characters from many of her favorite books as well as to the lives of seven female students with whom she meets secretly to discuss these books. Beyond the details of one woman's life, readers will also find her views on teaching, literature, friendship, writing, and politics. The selection you are reading, the "Gatsby" chapter, details Nafisi's first year back in Iran after leaving the United States in 1979.

I

A YOUNG WOMAN STANDS ALONE in the midst of a crowd at the Tehran airport, backpack on her back, a large bag hanging from one shoulder, pushing an oversize carry-on with the tips of her toes. She knows that her husband of two years and her father must be somewhere out there with the suitcases. She stands in the customs area, teary-eyed, desperately looking for a sympathetic face, for someone she can cling to and say, Oh how happy, how glad, how absolutely happy I am to be back home. At long last, here to stay. But no one so much as smiles. The walls of the airport have dissolved into an alien spectacle, with giant posters of an ayatollah staring down reproachfully. Their mood is echoed in the black and bloodred slogans: DEATH TO AMERICA! DOWN WITH IMPERIALISM & ZIONISM! AMERICA IS OUR NUMBER-ONE ENEMY!

Not having registered as yet that the home she had left seventeen years before, at the age of thirteen, was not home anymore, she stands alone, filled with emotions wriggling this way and that, ready to burst at the slightest provocation. I try not to see her, not to bump into her, to pass by unnoticed. Yet there is no way I can avoid her.

This airport, the Tehran airport, has always brought out the worst in me. When I left it the first time, it was a hospitable and magical place, with a fine restaurant that hosted dances on Friday evenings and a coffee shop with big French windows opening onto a balcony. As children my brother and I stood transfixed by those windows, eating ice cream as we counted the planes. Always on arrival there was a particular moment of epiphany, when suddenly a blanket of lights signaled that we had arrived, that Tehran was lying in wait for us below. For seventeen years I dreamed of those lights, so beckoning and seductive. I dreamed of being submerged in them and of never having to leave again.

The dream had finally come true. I was home, but the mood in the airport was not welcoming. It was somber and slightly menacing, like the unsmiling portraits of Ayatollah Khomeini[1] and his anointed successor, Ayatollah Montazeri, that covered the walls. It seemed as if a bad witch with her broomstick had flown over the building and in

[1] Ruhollah Khomeini (1900–89), Iranian cleric and leader of a revolutionary Islamic party that took power in Iran in 1979 and named Khomeini as the Grand Ayatollah—that is, the political and religious authority—of what was now the Islamic Republic of Iran. He is known for framing issues in religious rather than secular terms, and he gained particular notoriety in the United States in 1979 for supporting an Islamist student group that held 52 Americans hostage in the U.S. embassy in Tehran for 444 days.

one sweep had taken away the restaurants, the children and the women in colorful clothes that I remembered. This feeling was confirmed when I noticed the cagey anxiety in the eyes of my mother and friends, who had come to the airport to welcome us home.

As we were leaving the customs area, a morose young man stopped us: he wanted to search me. We've already been searched, I reminded him. Not the carry-on bags, he said curtly. But why? This is my home, I wanted to say, as if this should have offered me protection against suspicion and scrutiny. He needed to search me for alcoholic beverages. I was taken to a corner. Bijan, my husband, observed me anxiously, not knowing whom to fear most, the morose guard or me. His face took on a smile that later became very familiar to me: complicit, reconciling, cynical. Do you argue with a mad dog? someone later asked me. 5

First they emptied my bag: lipstick, pens and pencils, my diary and glasses case. Then they attacked my backpack, from which they extracted my diploma, my marriage license, my books—*Ada, Jews Without Money, The Great Gatsby* . . . [2] The guard picked them up disdainfully, as if handling someone else's dirty laundry. But he did not confiscate them—not then. That came sometime later.

2

During my first years abroad—when I was in school in England and Switzerland, and later, when I lived in America, I attempted to shape other places according to my concept of Iran. I tried to Persianize the landscape and even transferred for a term to a small college in New Mexico, mainly because it reminded me of home. *You see, Frank and Nancy, this little stream surrounded by trees, meandering its way through a parched land, is just like Iran. Just like Iran, just like home.* What impressed me most about Tehran, I told whoever cared to listen, were the mountains and its dry yet generous climate, the trees and flowers that bloomed and thrived on its parched soil and seemed to suck the light out of the sun.

[2] American novels by, respectively, Vladimir Nabokov, Mike Gold, and F. Scott Fitzgerald.

When my father was jailed, I went back home and was allowed to stay for a year. Later, I was insecure enough to marry on the spur of a moment, before my eighteenth birthday. I married a man whose most important credential was that he wasn't like us—he offered a way of life which, in contrast to ours, seemed pragmatic and uncomplicated; and he was so sure of himself. He didn't value books ("the problem with you and your family is that you live more in books than in reality"), he was insanely jealous—jealousy was part of the image he had of himself as a man in command of his destiny and property—he was success-oriented ("When I have my own office, my chair will be higher than those of the visitors, so they'll always feel intimidated by my presence") and he admired Frank Sinatra. The day I said yes, I knew I was going to divorce him. There were no limits to my self-destructive urges and the risks I was prepared to take with my own life.

I moved with him to Norman, Oklahoma, where he was getting his master's in engineering at the University of Oklahoma, and in six months' time I had reached the conclusion that I would divorce him as soon as my father was out of jail. That took another three years. He refused to divorce me ("A woman enters her husband's home in her wedding gown and leaves it in her shroud"). He had underestimated me. He wanted his wife to dress smartly, do her nails, go to the hairdresser every week. I defied him with my long skirts and tattered jeans, wore my hair long and sat on the campus green with my American friends while his friends passing by threw sly glances in our direction.

My father was all in favor of divorce, and threatened to sue for alimony, a woman's only protection under Islamic law. My husband finally consented when I agreed not to sue for alimony and let him have the money in our bank account, the car and the carpets. He returned home while I stayed on in Norman, the only foreign student in the English Department. I shunned the company of the Iranian community, especially the men, who had numerous illusions about a young divorcée's availability. 10

These are my memories of Norman: red earth and fireflies, singing and demonstrating on the Oval, reading Melville, Poe, Lenin and Mao Tse Tung, reading Ovid and Shakespeare on warm spring mornings with a favorite professor, of conservative political leaning, and accompanying another in the afternoons, singing revolutionary songs. At night watching new films by Bergman, Fellini, Godard and Pasolini. As I remember those days, the disparate sights and sounds mix and mingle in my memory: sad stills of Bergman's women merge into the soothing sound of David, my radical professor, singing on his guitar:

> Long-haired preachers come out every night
> And they tell you what's wrong and what's right
> And when you ask them for something to eat
> They tell you in voices so sweet:
> You will eat by and by, in that glorious place in the sky
> Work and pray, live on hay, you will get pie in sky when you die.
> *That's* a lie![3]

We would demonstrate in the mornings, taking over the administration building, singing songs on the green in front of the English Department, called South Oval, watching as the occasional streakers ran across the green towards the redbrick building that was the library. I marched while the suffering ROTC students, in those days of protest against the Vietnam War, tried to ignore our presence on the grass. Later I would go to parties with my true love, who introduced me to Nabokov when he gave me *Ada*, in whose flyleaf he had written: *To Azar, my Ada, Ted.*

My family had always looked down on politics, with a certain rebellious condescension. They prided themselves on the fact that as far back as eight hundred years ago—*fourteen generations*, my mother would proudly emphasize—the Nafisis were known for their contributions to literature and science. The men were called *hakims*, men of knowledge, and later, in this century, the Nafisi women had gone to universities and taught at a time when few women dared leave home. When my father became the mayor of Tehran, instead of celebration there was a sense of unease in the family. My younger uncles, who at the time were university students, refused to acknowledge my father

[3] From "The Preacher and the Slave," a song by American labor activist and songwriter Joe Hill (1879–1915).

as their brother. Later, when my father fell out of favor, my parents managed to make us feel more proud of his term in jail than we had ever been when he was mayor.

I joined the Iranian student movement reluctantly. My father's imprisonment and my family's vague nationalist sympathies had sensitized me towards politics, but I was more of a rebel than a political activist—though in those days there was not much difference between them. One attraction was the fact that the men in the movement didn't try to assault or seduce me. Instead, they held study groups in which we read and discussed Engels's *Origin of the Family, Private Property, and the State* and Marx's *The 18th Brumaire of Louis Bonaparte*.[4] In the seventies, the mood—not just among Iranians, but among American and European students—was revolutionary. There was the Cuban example, and China of course. The revolutionary cant and romantic atmosphere were infectious, and the Iranian students were at the forefront of the struggle. They were active, and even confrontational, going to jail for occupying the Iranian consulate in San Francisco.

The Iranian student group at the University of Oklahoma was a chapter of the World Confederation of Iranian Students, which had members and chapters in most major cities in Europe and the United States. In Oklahoma, it was responsible for the introduction on campus of the RSB, the militant student branch of the Revolutionary Communist Party, and the creation of the Third World Committee Against Imperialism, composed of radical students from different nationalities. The confederation, fashioning itself after Lenin's democratic centralism, exerted a strong hold over its members' lifestyles and social activities. As time went by, the more militant and Marxist elements came to dominate the group, ousting or isolating those with more moderate and nationalist tendencies. Its members usually sported Che Guevara sports jackets and boots; the women usually cropped their hair short, seldom used makeup and wore Mao jackets and khakis.[5]

15

[4] Works written by German political theorists Friedrich Engels (1820–95) and Karl Marx (1818–83), co-authors of *The Communist Manifesto* (1848).

[5] That is, styles inspired by communist icons such as Che Guevara (1928–67), Argentine revolutionary, and Mao Zedong (1893–1976), longtime leader of the People's Republic of China.

I then began a schizophrenic period in my life in which I tried to reconcile my revolutionary aspirations with the lifestyle I most enjoyed. I never fully integrated into the movement. During the long and confrontational meetings between rival factions, I would often leave the room under different pretenses, and sometimes locked myself in the bathroom to escape. I insisted on wearing long dresses outside the meetings and refused to cut my hair. I never gave up the habit of reading and loving "counterrevolutionary" writers—T. S. Eliot, Austen, Plath, Nabokov, Fitzgerald—but I spoke passionately at the rallies; inspired by phrases I had read in novels and poems, I would weave words together into sounds of revolution. My oppressive yearning for home was shaped into excited speeches against the tyrants back home and their American backers, and although I felt alienated from the movement itself, which was never a home to me at any point, I had found an ideological framework within which to justify this unbridled, unreflective passion.

The fall of 1977 was memorable for two events: my marriage in September and the Shah's last official and most dramatic visit to the United States in November. I had met Bijan Naderi two years earlier, at a meeting at Berkeley. He was the leader of the group I most sympathized with. I fell in love with him for all the wrong reasons: not because of his revolutionary rhetoric but because he possessed a sense of confidence in himself and his beliefs that went beyond the hysterics of the movement. He was loyal, passionately committed to whatever he undertook, be it his family, his job or the movement, but his loyalty never made him blind to what the movement would become. I admired him as much for this as for his refusal, later, to follow the revolutionary mandates.

In the many demonstrations in which I participated, shouting slogans against U.S. involvement in Iran, in the protest meetings during which we argued into the night, thinking we were talking about Iran but in reality more concerned with what had happened in China, the picture of home loomed large. It was mine and I could constantly conjure it, and relate to the world through its hazy image.

There were discrepancies, or essential paradoxes, in my idea of "home." There was the familiar Iran I felt nostalgic about, the place of parents and friends and summer nights by the Caspian Sea. Yet just as real was this other, reconstructed, Iran about which we talked in meeting after meeting, quarreling about what the masses in Iran wanted. Apparently, as the movement grew more radical in the seventies, the masses wanted us to serve no alcohol in our celebrations and not to dance or play "decadent" music: only folk and revolutionary music were allowed. They wanted the girls to cut their hair short or wear it in pigtails. They wanted us to avoid the bourgeois habits of studying.

* * *

4

All my memories of those first years[6] revolve around the University of Tehran. It was the navel, the immovable center to which all political and social activities were tied. When in the U.S. we read or heard about the turmoil in Iran, the University of Tehran seemed to be the scene of the most important battles. All groups used the university to make their statements. 20

It was thus not surprising that the new Islamic government took over the university as the site of its weekly Friday prayers. This act gained added significance, because at all times, even after the revolution, the Muslim students, especially the more fanatical ones, were a minority overshadowed by the leftist and secular student groups. It seemed as if with this act, the Islamic faction asserted its victory over other political groups: like a victorious army it positioned itself on the most cherished site of the occupied land, at the heart of the vanquished territory. Every week, one of the most prominent clergymen would stand on the podium to address the thousands who occupied the university grounds, men on one side, women on the other. He would stand with a gun in one hand and offer the sermon of the week, preaching on the most important political issues of the day. Yet it seemed as if the grounds themselves rebelled against this occupation.

[6] That is, the first years after the Islamic Revolution of 1979, when Nafisi was teaching at the University of Tehran.

I felt in those days that there was a turf war going on between different political groups and that this struggle was being fought out mainly at the university. I did not know then that I would also have my own battle to fight. Looking back, I am glad I was unaware of my special vulnerability: with my small collection of books, I was like an emissary from a land that did not exist, with a stock of dreams, coming to reclaim this land as my home. Amid the talk of treason and changes in government, events that now in my mind have become confused and timeless, I sat whenever I had a chance with books and notes scattered around me, trying to shape my classes. I taught a very large seminar in that first semester, called Research, in which we focused on *The Adventures of Huckleberry Finn*, and a survey of twentieth-century fiction.

I tried to be somewhat fair politically. Side by side with *The Great Gatsby* and *A Farewell to Arms*, I would teach works by Maxim Gorky and Mike Gold.[7] I spent most days browsing the bookstores lining the street opposite the university. That street, newly renamed Avenue of the Revolution, was the center for the most important bookstores and publishers in Tehran. It was such a pleasure to go from one store to another and to find an occasional seller or customer who would introduce you to a sudden gem, or startle you by knowing about an obscure English writer by the name of Henry Green.[8]

In the midst of my feverish preparation, I would be summoned to the university for matters that had nothing to do with my classes and books. Almost every week, sometimes every day of the week, there were either demonstrations or meetings, and we were drawn to these like a magnet, independently of our will.

One memory curls itself wantonly and imperceptibly around me, teasing me seductively. With coffee in one hand and a pen and notebook in the other, I was preparing to go to the balcony to work on my 25

[7] Pen name of Itzik Granich (1893–1967), American communist and literary critic best known for the autobiographical novel *Jews Without Money* (1930). *Maxim Gorky*: pen name of Alexey Maximovich Peshkov (1868–1936), Russian/Soviet author and political activist.

[8] Pen name of Henry Vincent Yorke (1905–73), English author best known for the novel *Loving* (1945).

class syllabus. The phone rang. It was the agitated and urgent voice of a friend. She wanted to know if I had heard: Ayatollah Taleghani, a very popular, controversial clergyman, one of the most important figures of the revolution, had died. He was relatively young and radical, and there were already rumors he had been killed. A procession had been scheduled for him beginning at the University of Tehran.

I cannot remember the distance between the phone call and my presence, almost an hour later, at the entrance of the university. There was a traffic jam. Bijan and I got out of the taxi in the vicinity of the university and started to walk. For some reason, after a while, as if pushed by some invisible source of energy, our pace quickened into a run. A huge crowd of mourners had gathered, blocking the streets that led to the university. There were reports of a fight having broken out between members of the Mujahideen, a radical religious organization that claimed to be Taleghani's spiritual and political heir, and those belonging to what was loosely called the Hizbollah, Party of Allah, mainly composed of fanatics and vigilantes determined to implement the laws of God on earth. The fight was over who should have the honor of carrying Taleghani's body. Many were crying, beating their chests and their heads, calling out: "Today is the day of mourning! Taleghani has gone to heaven today."

Over the next two decades, this particular chant would be used for many others, a symptom of the symbiosis between the revolution's founders and death. That was the first time I experienced the desperate, orgiastic pleasure of this form of public mourning: it was the one place where people mingled and touched bodies and shared emotions without restraint or guilt. There was a wild, sexually flavored frenzy in the air. Later, when I saw a slogan by Khomeini saying that the Islamic Republic survives through its mourning ceremonies, I could testify to its truth.

I met many people that day who appeared and disappeared like characters in a cartoon. Was it there that I saw Farideh? She belonged to an extremely radical leftist group—my brother, who knew some of her comrades, had introduced her to me, thinking she could help me settle in. I saw her for a vague second, busy as always, on the verge of attacking someone or something: I saw her and lost her.

I stood in the middle of the whirlpool, struggling to find a familiar face. Always in these demonstrations I would lose sight of those who'd come with me. Now I had lost my husband, and for a while I kept looking for him. The crowd pushed towards me. Voices appeared to be echoing out of different loudspeakers. Posters of Taleghani had mushroomed everywhere: on the walls, on the doors and windows of the bookshops, even on trees. The wide street in front of the university contracted and expanded to accommodate our movements and for a long time I moved senselessly, swaying to the beat of the crowd. Then I found myself beating my fists against a tree and crying, crying, as if the person closest to me had died and I was now all alone in the whole wide world.

5

Before the new term began in September 1979, I spent most of my time hunting for the books on my syllabus. In one bookstore, as I was rummaging through a few copies of *The Great Gatsby* and *A Farewell to Arms*, the owner approached me. "If you're interested in those, you'd better buy them now," he said, shaking his head sadly. I looked at him sympathetically and said smugly, "There's too much demand for them. They can't do anything about that—can they?"

30

He was right. In a few months' time, Fitzgerald and Hemingway were very difficult to find. The government could not remove all of the books from the stores, but gradually it closed down some of the most important foreign-language bookstores and blocked the distribution of foreign books in Iran.

The night before my first class I was very nervous, like a child on her first day of school. I had chosen my clothes with unusual care, and also went over my meager stock of books. I had left most of them in the U.S. with my sister-in-law, along with an antique mirror: my father's present. I thought I would bring them back later, not knowing that I would not return for another eleven years, by which time my sister-in-law had given away most of my books.

That first day, I went to the university armed with my trusty *Gatsby*. It was showing signs of wear: the dearer a book was to my heart, the more battered and bruised it became. *Huckleberry Finn* was still available in bookstores, and I bought a new copy in anticipation. After some hesitation, I also picked up *Ada*, which wasn't on the syllabus, and threw it in as a security blanket.

The university was built during the reign of Reza Shah,[9] in the thirties. The main buildings on campus had very high ceilings, propped up by thick cement columns. They were always a little cold in winter and dank in summer. Memory has given them gargantuan proportions they probably didn't have in reality, but those expansive buildings of the thirties had a strange feel about them. They were made for crowds: you never felt quite at home.

On my way to the English Department, I absentmindedly registered the different stands set out in the big hall at the foot of the overwide staircase. There were long tables—more than ten of them—filled with literature belonging to various revolutionary groups. Students were standing in clusters, talking and sometimes quarreling, ready to defend their territory at a moment's notice. There were no visible enemies, but a sense of menace lingered over the room.

Those were crucial days in Iranian history. A battle was being fought on all levels over the shape of the constitution and the soul of the new regime. The majority of people, among them important clerics, were in favor of a secular constitution. Powerful opposition groups—both secular and religious—were forming to protest the autocratic tendencies within the ruling elite. The strongest of the opposition groups were Ayatollah Shariatmadari's Muslim People's Republican Party and the National Democratic Front, made up of secular progressives who were at the forefront of the struggle to preserve democratic rights, including women's rights and freedom of the press. They were very popular at the time and drew about a million people on the twelfth anniversary of the death of the late nationalist hero Mossadegh[1] to the village of Ahamad Abad, where Mossadegh was buried. They campaigned vigorously for a constituent assembly. The closing down of

[9] Iranian king, or shah (1878–1944), and founder of the Pahlavi dynasty (1925–41).

[1] Mohammad Mossadegh (1882–1967), prime minister of Iran from 1951 until 1953, when he was deposed in a coup backed by the American CIA.

the most popular and progressive paper, *Ayandegan*, had led to a series of large violent demonstrations, in which the demonstrators were attacked by the government-backed vigilantes. In those days it was normal to see these goons on their motorbikes carrying black flags and banners, at times led by a cleric riding in front of them in a bulletproof Mercedes-Benz. Despite these ominous signs, the Communist Tudeh Party and the Marxist Fedayin Organization supported the radical reactionaries against what they called the liberals, and continued to put pressure on Prime Minister Bazargan, whom they suspected of having American sympathies.

The opposition was greeted with brutal violence. "The clog-wearers and the turbaned have given you a chance," Khomeini warned. "After each revolution several thousands of the corrupt elements are executed in public and burned and the story is over. They are not allowed to publish newspapers." Citing the example of the October Revolution[2] and the fact that the state still controlled the press, he went on to say, "We will close all parties except the one, or a few which will act in a proper manner . . . we all made mistakes. We thought we were dealing with human beings. It is evident we are not. We are dealing with wild animals. We will not tolerate them anymore."

It now seems amazing to me, as I relate the events of those years, how focused I was on my work. For I was as anxious about how my class would receive me as I was about the political upheavals.

My first class was in a long room with windows down one side. The room was full when I walked in, but as soon as I took my place behind the desk, my nervousness left me. The students were unusually quiet. My hands were loaded with all the books and Xeroxes I had brought for the class, an eclectic mix of revolutionary writers whose works had been translated into Persian and "elitists" such as Fitzgerald, Faulkner and Woolf.

That class went all right, and the ones after it became easier. I was enthusiastic, naïve and idealistic, and I was in love with my books. The students were curious about me and Dr. K, the curly-haired young 40

[2] Second phase of the Russian Revolution (1917), which brought the Bolsheviks to power and established the Soviet Union under Vladimir Ilyich Lenin.

man I had bumped into at Dr. A's office, strange new recruits at a time when most students were doing their best to expel their professors: they were all "anti-revolutionary," a term that covered a vast range—anything from working with the previous regime to using obscene language in class.

That first day I asked my students what they thought fiction should accomplish, why one should bother to read fiction at all. It was an odd way to start, but I did succeed in getting their attention. I explained that we would in the course of the semester read and discuss many different authors, but that one thing these authors all had in common was their subversiveness. Some, like Gorky or Gold, were overtly subversive in their political aims; others, like Fitzgerald and Mark Twain, were in my opinion more subversive, if less obviously so. I told them we would come back to this term, because my understanding of it was somewhat different from its usual definition. I wrote on the board one of my favorite lines from the German thinker Theodor Adorno:[3] "The highest form of morality is not to feel at home in one's own home." I explained that most great works of the imagination were meant to make you feel like a stranger in your own home. The best fiction always forced us to question what we took for granted. It questioned traditions and expectations when they seemed too immutable. I told my students I wanted them in their readings to consider in what ways these works unsettled them, made them a little uneasy, made them look around and consider the world, like Alice in Wonderland, through different eyes.

At that time, students and faculty were differentiated mainly by their political affiliations. Gradually I matched names to faces, and learned to read them, to know who was with whom against whom and who belonged to what group. It is almost frightening how these images appear out of the void, like the faces of the dead come back to life to execute some unfulfilled task.

I can see Mr. Bahri in the middle row, playing with his pencil, his head down, writing. Is he writing my words, I wonder, or only pre-

[3] German-born sociologist and philosopher (1903–69) associated with the Frankfurt School of social thought.

tending to do so? Every once in a while he lifts his head and gazes at me, as if trying to decipher a puzzle, and then he bends back down and continues with his writing.

In the second row, by the window, is a man whose face I remember well. He sits with both arms folded across his chest, listening defiantly, taking in every word, not so much because he wants or needs to learn but because, for reasons of his own, he has decided not to miss any of this. I will call him Mr. Nyazi.

My most radical students sit in the very back rows, with sardonic 45 smiles. One face I remember well: Mahtab's. She sits self-consciously, looking straight at the blackboard, acutely aware of those sitting to her right and left. She is dark-skinned, with a simple face that seems to have retained its baby fat and resigned, sad eyes. I later discovered that she came from Abadan, an oil city in the south of Iran.

Then of course there is Zarrin, and her friend Vida. They caught my eye on that first day because they looked so different, as if they had no right to be in that class, or on the university grounds for that matter. They didn't fit any of the categories into which students in those days were so clearly divided. Leftists' mustaches covered their upper lips, to distinguish them from the Muslims, who carved out a razor-thin line between upper lip and mustache. Some Muslims also grew beards or what stubble they could muster. The leftist women wore khaki or dull green—large, loose shirts over loose trousers—and the Muslim girls scarves or chadors. In between these two immutable rivers stood the non-political students, who were all mechanically branded as monarchists. But not even the real monarchists stood out like Zarrin and Vida.

Zarrin had fair, fragile skin, eyes the color of melting honey and light brown hair, which she had gathered behind her ears. She and Vida were sitting in the first row, at the far right, near the door. Both were smiling. It seemed slightly rude of them to be there, looking like that, so pastel and serene. Even I, who had abdicated by now all revolutionary claims, was surprised by their appearance.

Vida was more sober, more conventionally academic, but with Zarrin there was always a danger of swerving, of losing control. Unlike many others, they were not defensive about their non-revolutionary attitude, nor did they seem to feel a need for justification. In those days the students canceled classes at the slightest provocation. Almost every day there were new debates, new events, and in the midst of all this Zarrin and her friend—more deliberately than dutifully—attended all classes, looking fresh and neat and immaculate.

I remember one day when my leftist students had canceled classes, protesting the fresh murder of three revolutionaries, I was walking downstairs when they caught up with me. In the previous session I had mentioned that they might have trouble finding copies of some of the books I had assigned. They wanted to tell me about a bookstore with the largest stock of English books in Tehran and eagerly volunteered that it still carried copies of *The Great Gatsby* and *Herzog.*[4]

They had already read *Gatsby.* Were Fitzgerald's other books similar to this? We went on talking Fitzgerald as we walked down the wide staircase, past the various tables with their political goods for sale and the rather large crowd assembled in front of a wall plastered with newspapers. We walked onto the hot asphalt and sat on one of the benches by the stream running through the campus, and talked like children sharing coveted stolen cherries. I felt very young, and we laughed as we talked. Then we went our separate ways. We never became more intimate than that. 50

6

"Criminals should not be tried. The trial of a criminal is against human rights. Human rights demand that we should have killed them in the first place when it became known that they were criminals," proclaimed Ayatollah Khomeini, responding to protests by international human rights organizations of the wave of executions that followed the revolution. "They criticize us because we are executing the brutes." The jubilant mood of celebration and freedom that had followed the Shah's overthrow soon gave way to apprehension and fear as the regime continued to execute and murder "anti-revolutionaries"

[4] Novel by American writer Saul Bellow (1915–2005), winner of the 1965 National Book Award for fiction.

and a new vigilante justice emerged as bands of self-organized militants terrorized the streets.

NAME: Omid Gharib
SEX: male
DATE OF ARREST: 9 June 1980
PLACE OF ARREST: Tehran
PLACE OF DETENTION: Tehran, Qasr Prison
CHARGES: Being Westernized, brought up in a Westernized family; staying too long in Europe for his studies; smoking Winston cigarettes; displaying leftist tendencies.
SENTENCE: three years' imprisonment; death
TRIAL INFORMATION: The accused was tried behind closed doors. He was arrested after the authorities intercepted a letter he had sent to his friend in France. He was sentenced to three years' imprisonment in 1980. On 2 February 1982, while Omid Gharib was serving his prison term, his parents learned that he was executed. The circumstances surrounding his execution are not known.
ADDITIONAL INFORMATION:
DATE OF EXECUTION: 31 January 1982
PLACE OF EXECUTION: Tehran
SOURCE: Amnesty International Newsletter, July 1982, volume XII, number 7.

In those days we were all passersby in the crowded streets of a metropolitan city, faces buried deep in our collars, preoccupied with our own problems. I felt a certain distance from most of my students. When in the States we had shouted Death to this or that, those deaths seemed to be more symbolic, more abstract, as if we were encouraged by the impossibility of our slogans to insist upon them even more. But in Tehran in 1979, these slogans were turning into reality with macabre precision. I felt helpless: all the dreams and slogans were coming true, and there was no escaping them.

By mid-October, we were almost three weeks into classes and I was getting used to the irregular beat of my days at the university. There was seldom a day when our routine was not interrupted by a death or assassination. Meetings and demonstrations were constantly staged at the university for various reasons; almost every week classes were either boycotted or canceled on the smallest pretext. The only way I could give rhyme or rhythm to my life was to read my books and work up my confused classes, which, surprisingly amid all the turmoil, formed fairly regularly and were attended by the majority of the students.

On a mild day in October, I tried to make my way through a crowd that had gathered in front of our building around a well-known leftist professor from the History Department. I stopped impulsively to listen to her. I do not remember much of what she said, but part of my mind picked up some of her words and hid them in a safe corner. She was telling the crowd that for the sake of independence, she was willing to wear the veil. She would wear the veil to fight U.S. imperialists, to show them . . . To show them what?

I hastily made my way up the stairs to the conference room of the English Department, where I had an appointment with a student, Mr. Bahri. Ours was a formal relationship—I was so used to calling and thinking of him by his last name that I have completely forgotten his first name. At any rate, it is irrelevant. What is relevant perhaps, in a roundabout way, are his light complexion and dark hair, the stubborn silence that remained even when he spoke and his seemingly permanent lopsided grin. This grin colored everything he said, giving the impression that what he did not say, what he so blatantly hid and denied his listeners, put him in a superior position.

Mr. Bahri wrote one of the best student papers I had ever read on *The Adventures of Huckleberry Finn*, and ever since that day, for as long as I stayed at the University of Tehran, he somehow appeared beside or behind me all through the agitated meetings. He literally became my shadow, casting the weight of his lopsided silence upon me.

He wanted to inform me that he liked my classes and that "they" approved of my teaching methods. When I had assigned too much reading, the students at first reacted by considering a boycott of the class, but on later consideration they voted against it. He had come to ask or instruct me to add more revolutionary material, to teach more revolutionary writers. A stimulating discussion on the implications of the words *literature*, *radical*, *bourgeois* and *revolutionary* ensued, which proceeded, as I recall, with great emotion and intensity, though little substantial progress was made on the simple matter of definitions. All through this rather heated conversation, we were both standing at the end of a long table surrounded by empty chairs.

At the end of our talk, I was so excited I reached out to him in a gesture of goodwill and friendship. He silently, deliberately, withdrew both his hands behind his back, as if to remove them from even the possibility of a handshake. I was too bewildered, too much of a stranger to the newness of revolutionary ways, to take this gesture in stride. I recounted it later to a colleague, who, with a mocking smile, reminded me that no Muslim man would or should touch a *namahram* woman—a woman other than his wife, mother or sister. He turned to me in disbelief and said, "You really did not know that?"

My experiences, especially my teaching experiences, in Iran have been framed by the feel and touch of that aborted handshake, as much as by that first approach and the glow of our naïve, excited conversation. The image of my student's oblique smile has remained, brilliant yet opaque, while the room, the walls, the chairs and the long conference table have been covered over by layers and layers of what usually in works of fiction is called dust.

7

The first few weeks of classes were spent in a frenzy of meetings. We had department meetings and faculty meetings and meetings with students; we went to meetings in support of women, of workers, of militant Kurdish or Turkmen minorities. In those days I formed alliances and friendships with the head of the department, my brilliant and radical colleague Farideh and others from the departments of psychology, German and linguistics. We would all go to our favorite restaurant near the university for lunch and exchange the latest news and jokes. Already our carefree mood seemed a little out of place, but we had not yet given up hope.

60

During these luncheons we spent a great deal of time joking with or about one of our colleagues, who was worried he'd lose his job: the Muslim students had threatened to expel him for his use of "obscenities" in the classroom. The truth was that this man loved to worry about himself. He had just divorced his wife and had to maintain her, plus his home and swimming pool. We heard endlessly about this swimming pool. Somehow, inappropriately, he kept comparing himself to Gatsby, calling himself Little Great Gatsby. The only similarity, so far as I could see, was the swimming pool. This vanity colored his grasp of all great works of imagination. As it turned out, he was not expelled. He outstayed us all, gradually becoming intolerant of his brightest students, as I discovered years later when two of them, Nima and Manna, paid a high price for disagreeing with his viewpoints. As far as I know, he still teaches and repeats the same material to new students year after year. Little has changed, only he did marry a new and much younger wife.

In between these lunches we went to the Film Club, which had not yet been closed down, and watched Mel Brooks and Antonioni[5] movies, marched off to exhibitions and still believed that the Khomeini crowd could not succeed, that the war was not yet over. Dr. A took us to a photo exhibition of protests and demonstrations during the Shah's time.[6] He walked ahead of us, pointing to various pictures from the first year, saying, "Show me how many mullahs you see demonstrating, show me how many of these sons of . . . were out in the streets shouting for the Islamic Republic." Meanwhile, plots were being hatched, assassinations carried out, some through the novel approach of suicide bombings. The secularists and liberals were being ousted, and Ayatollah Khomeini's rhetoric against the Great Satan[7] and its domestic agents was growing more virulent every day.

It is amazing how everything can fall into a routine. I seemed not to notice the unexpected and breathless quality of everyday life that belied every form of stability. After a while even the revolution found its rhythm: the violence, the executions, public confessions to crimes that had never been committed, judges who coolly talked about ampu-

[5] Michelangelo Antonioni (1912–2007), Italian filmmaker.

[6] That is, the reign of Shah Mohammad Reza Pahlavi, who ruled Iran from the death of his father, Reza Shah Pahlavi, in 1941 until he was overthrown in the Islamic Revolution of 1979.

[7] Epithet for the United States, first used by Khomeini.

tating a thief's hand or legs and killing political prisoners because there was not enough room for them now in jail. One day I sat watching the television, mesmerized by the image of a mother and son. The son belonged to one of the Marxist organizations. His mother was telling him that he deserved to die because he had betrayed the revolution and his faith, and he agreed with her. They both sat there on what seemed to be an empty stage except for their two chairs. They sat opposite each other, talking as they might have of arrangements for his forthcoming marriage. Only they were casually agreeing that his crimes were so heinous that the only way he could atone for them and save his family's honor was to embrace death.

In the mornings, with *The Adventures of Huckleberry Finn* under my arm, I would make my way through the wide, leafy streets leading to the university. As I approached the campus, the number of slogans on the walls and the violence of their demands increased. Never once was there a protest against the killings: the demands were almost always punctually for more blood. I, like others, went about my business. It was only at night and in my diary that my growing desperation, my nightmares, poured out uninhibited.

As I look over the pages of my diary, written in different colored inks in a notebook with a black plastic cover, I find the despair that never impinged upon the surface of my life. In that diary I have registered the deaths, which we seldom talked about, though they dominated the newspapers and the television. 65

One night at home I went to the kitchen for a glass of water and saw on television the battered and bruised face of the former head of the dreaded Ministry of National Security and Information, a general known for his cruelty. He had been one of the officials involved in framing and imprisoning my father. It must have been a rerun of his confession scene, for he had been killed a few months before. I can still remember, when my father was in jail, the number of times my mother would curse this general and his fellow conspirators. And now here he was, in civilian clothes, pleading for forgiveness from judges whose stern brutality even he could not fathom. There was not a shred of humanity in his expression. It was as if he had been forced to negate his former self and in the process he had abdicated his place alongside other men.

I felt strangely connected to him, as if the complete surrender of his dignity had also diminished me. How many times had I dreamt of revenge on this particular man? Was this how one's dreams were to be fulfilled?

The government dailies published his and several other pictures after the next round of executions. These photographs were also published in a cheap pamphlet with yellowing pages sold by street vendors, alongside others on the secrets of health and beauty. I bought one of these poison pamphlets: I wanted to remember everything. Their faces, despite their terrible last moments, were forced to assume the peaceful indifference of death. But what amount of helplessness and desperation did those awful calm faces inspire in us, the survivors?

In the later months and years, every once in a while Bijan and I would be shocked to see the show trials of our old comrades in the U.S. on television. They eagerly denounced their past actions, their old comrades, their old selves, and confessed that they were indeed the enemies of Islam. We would watch these scenes in silence. Bijan was calmer than me, and would rarely show any emotion. He'd sit on the couch, his eyes glued to the television screen, seldom moving a muscle, while I fidgeted and got up to fetch a glass of water or change places. I felt I needed something to hold on to, and would dig harder into the armchair. When I turned to look at Bijan, I would encounter his placid expression; sometimes a whirling of resentment would well up inside of me. How could he be so composed? Once I moved and sat on the floor by his couch. I don't think I have ever felt such utter loneliness. After a few minutes, he rested a hand on my shoulder.

I turned around and asked Bijan, Did you ever dream that this could happen to us? He said, No I didn't, but I should have. After we all helped create this mess, we were not doomed to have the Islamic Republic. And in a sense, he was right. There was a very brief period, between the time the Shah left on January 16, 1979, and Khomeini's return to Iran on February 1, when one of the nationalist leaders, Dr. Shahpour Bakhtiar, had become the prime minister. Bakhtiar was perhaps the most democratic-minded and farsighted of the opposition leaders of that time, who, rather than rallying to his side, had fought against him and joined up with Khomeini. He had immediately disbanded Iran's secret police and set the political prisoners free. In rejecting Bakhtiar and helping to replace the Pahlavi dynasty with a far more reactionary and despotic regime, both the Iranian people and the intellectual elites had shown at best a serious error in judgment. I remember at the time that Bijan's was one lone voice in support of Bakhtiar, while all others, including mine, were only demanding destruction of the old, without much thought to the consequences.

One day, opening the morning paper, I saw pictures of Ali and Faramarz and other friends from the student movement. I knew instantly they had been killed. Unlike the generals, these were not photographs taken after the executions. They were old pictures, passport photos and student I.D.'s. In these insidiously innocent photos they smiled, with a conscious pose for the camera. I tore out the pages and for months hid them in my closet, using them as shoe trees, taking them out almost daily to look again at those faces I had last seen in another country that appeared to me now only in my dreams. 70

HENRY L. ROEDIGER, III

Why Are Textbooks So Expensive?

NEWSLETTERS AND OTHER MISSIVES THAT I receive seem filled with stories about textbooks and textbook prices, with many wringing their hands over why textbooks are so expensive now relative to the more distant past (usually when the author of the article was in college). I suspect some articles arise from middle-aged parents who suddenly must pay for their own children's college textbooks and they recoil when they see a bill of $500 a semester or thereabouts.

What reasons are given for the high price of textbooks? Of course, there's general inflation, but evidence points to textbook prices outpacing inflation. Others point their fingers at the bright colors in many books (relative to older black and white models) and argue that production costs are needlessly pushed up by color. (A quick check of my own bookstore shows that many books without color are more expensive than those with color, probably due to the number of books in the print run.) Another suggested hypothesis is textbook publishers simply seek greater profit margins now than they did in the past. After all, the market used to be dominated by rather genteel textbook companies that really cared about scholarly texts and not so much about being wildly profitable. A comfortable, modest profit line was fine in the old days. Those days are now gone, because traditional textbook companies have been bought up by gigantic conglomerates that look only to the bottom line and seek huge profits. For these companies, so the theory goes, textbooks are just one more product line, no different from detergent or tires or toilet paper, on which to make a profit. The fact that many formerly independent textbook companies are being bought up and merged under the same corporate umbrella could also be partly responsible, if this process reduces competition through having fewer companies. Another facet of the debate is the frequent revision schedule of basic textbooks. Most introductory psychology textbooks are revised every three years, some every two years. Doesn't this constant revision drive up the prices?

Although the reasons listed above may have some merit, I don't think any of them is fundamental to why textbook prices are so high. In fact, I suspect that most of the properties described above are effects and not causes. What is the cause? If I had to bet, the root cause is a feature of the marketplace that has changed greatly over the years and fundamentally reshaped the textbook market: sale of used books.

Let us go back in time to what educational historians refer to as the later Paleolithic era in higher education, that is, the late 1960s, when I was in college. Here was how the used book market worked then. I was a psychology major and was about to take a course in history of psychology. A psychology major in my fraternity, Dave Redmond (now a big-time lawyer in Richmond, Virginia) was going on to law school and wanted to sell some of his psychology textbooks. He asked if I wanted to buy Edna Heidbreder's *Seven Psychologies*, for a dollar. I said OK. The book had cost him $2.95, which is still listed in my copy. (It's a great book, by the way, published in the wonderful Century Psychology Series that was published by Appleton-Century-Crofts, before that company got gobbled up by some other company. It's out of print, but you can still get it on Amazon.com for as low as 55 cents a copy—or as high as $39.)

5 But back to my story. The point is that this was how the used book market worked in my day. One student sold books to another student on a hit or miss basis. Books didn't cost much. Oh, also, most students kept their books and started building a personal library. (This is another idea that seems to have faded with time. Personal library? Today's students assume everything they need to know is on the internet.)

Let's fast forward to 1981. I was teaching at Purdue University and was considering (with Betty Capaldi and several others) writing an introductory psychology textbook, since textbook companies were wooing us to do so. However, neither Betty nor I had ever even taught introductory psychology, so we decided to teach independent sections one semester. We examined a lot of books and decided to use Phil Zimbardo's textbook, *Psychology and Life.* (Some background: The book was originally published by Floyd Ruch, and after many editions became Ruch and Zimbardo, then became Zimbardo and Ruch, then Zimbardo, then Zimbardo and Richard Gerrig, and now it's Gerrig and Zimbardo and in its 17th edition, currently published by Allyn & Bacon). Betty and I were each to teach a section of 475 students, so we ordered 950 books. Nine hundred fifty books was, and is, a big textbook order. Think of the profits to the company and the author!

A few days before classes were to begin, I happened by one of the three Purdue bookstores to buy something. I decided to go see the hundreds of copies of the book I had ordered, gleaming at me on the shelves. I found them, all right, but I was shocked at my discovery. Every single book on the shelf was a used copy! I went through many of them, disbelieving, and saw that quite a few were in poor condition (marked up, spines damaged, etc.), yet the prices were still substantial. How could this be? Zimbardo's book had never been used at Purdue before recent times. Where did all these used copies come from? I decided to walk to the other two bookstores and discovered exactly the same situation; every book for sale was a used book in the other two stores. There wasn't a new book to be found.

The organized used book market represents the great change in the landscape of higher education publishing, but one that has gone relatively unnoticed by most academics (unless they are textbook authors). The implications are huge. Consider the situation in today's dollars (although I am estimating). A single author of a textbook might make a 15 percent royalty on the net price of the book (sometimes a bit more); the net price is the price the bookstore pays the textbook company for the book and the list price is the price set by the bookstore to sell to the student. The net price of an introductory psychology textbook today might be $65 (before the bookstore marks it up), so the author would make $9.75 per book. However, that is only if the book is bought from the company; if the student buys used books, the author makes nothing and neither does the company. If 950 used books are sold, the author would lose (be cheated out of?) $9,262, and the textbook company would perhaps lose a similar or larger amount. (Profit margins probably differ from company to company and book to book. They are a closely guarded secret.) Of course, at Purdue in 1981 the figures would have been smaller, but the principle the same. The fact of modern campus life is that used book companies buy up textbooks on one campus, warehouse them, and ship them to wherever the book is being adopted, and therefore prevent sales of new books.

Consider what this means. The textbook company that invested hundreds of thousands of dollars—maybe millions for introductory textbooks—to sign, develop, review, produce, market, and distribute a book over several years is denied its just profits. The author or authors who wrote the book over many years are denied their royalties. Meanwhile, huge profits are made by the used book companies who did nothing whatsoever to create the product. They are true parasites, deriving profits with no investment (and no value added to the product) while damaging their hosts. The issue here is similar to that in the movie and recording industries for pirated products that are sold very cheaply, denying the companies and the artists their profits. One major dissimilarity in these cases is that pirated movies and music are illegal whereas the used textbook market is legal. (There have been proposals to change this state of affairs. For example, one idea is that when used book companies resell texts they would pay the original textbook company and author a royalty.)

10 The high price of textbooks is the direct result of the used book market. A textbook is customarily used for one semester and (unlike the old days) students rarely keep their books now but sell them back to the bookstore (more on that anon). Therefore, the same text might be used by three to four students, but the textbook company and author profit the first time a book is sold and not thereafter. It stands to reason that textbooks must be priced aggressively, because the profits from the repeated sales will not go to the authors and companies that actually wrote and produced the books, but rather to the companies that specialize in buying and selling used books. Further, the reason textbooks are revised so frequently is to combat the used book market, which further drives up the company's costs. Frequent revisions also add wear and tear on the authors who must perpetually

revise their books. (I've sometimes wanted to have two somewhat different versions of my textbooks and then alternate them.) Most fields of psychology hardly move at such a swift pace as to justify two- to three-year revision cycles of introductory textbooks. The famous textbooks of the 1950s and 1960s were revised every eight to 10 years or so, but after the used textbook market gained steam, revisions became frequent. Moreover, because of the used book market, profitability of many companies was hurt and they became ripe for takeovers, which further consolidated the market. That is why I said in the third paragraph that many factors used to "explain" the high prices of books are probably effects, with the cause being the organized used book companies that prey parasitically on the host publishing companies and threaten to destroy them.

Other changes have also affected the market. College and university bookstores used to be owned by the school and operated as a service to the students and the faculty, but those days are past on most campuses. Now the bookstores are operated by large companies (Follett's, Barnes and Noble, and others), often the same ones who operate used book operations. Most "bookstores" have turned into carnivals where emphasis is placed on selling sweatshirts, trinkets, souvenirs and snacks and, oh, incidentally (used) books.

Another pernicious trend: After universities relinquished their hold on bookstores, the bookstores aggressively raised that the percentage markup on the net price paid to the publisher on new books. Thirty years ago a standard rate of markup was 20 percent and publishers provided list prices on their books (because markups were standard). I can recall the great hue and cry that arose when textbook stores started marking up books by 25 percent. However, a 25 pecent markup for today's bookstores would look like chump change. Publishing companies now sell the bookstore the books based on a net price and the bookstore decides on the list price, often marking up the books 30 to 40 percent in the process. The profits go to the company owning the store and the company pays the college or university for the right to have a monopoly business on campus. However, many students have now learned that it is cheaper and (given the huge lines) sometimes easier to buy textbooks from other sources like Amazon.com.

Let me give you a concrete example. Last summer the eighth edition of my textbook (with Barry Kantowitz and David Elmes), *Experimental Psychology: Understanding Psychological Research*, was published by Wadsworth Publishing Company. The net price (the price the bookstore pays the company for a new book) the first time the book is sold is $73.50. The authors receive 15 percent royalties on the book, so we would split the $11 royalty three ways. However, at the Washington University bookstore, the list price of the book is $99.75, a markup of $26.25 (or 35.7 percent)! Yes, that's right, the authors who wrote the book get $11.02 for their years of hard work whereas the bookstore that ordered the books, let them sit on their shelves for a couple of weeks, and sold them, gets $26.25 per book. (If books are not sold, they are returned to the company for a full price refund. It's a no-risk business.)

Yet the story gets even worse because of the used book problem. After the student uses the book (and if it is in pretty good condition), the bookstore will buy it back from the student at a greatly marked down price, somewhere between 25 and 50 percent. Let's assume that *Experimental Psychology* is bought back for 40 percent of the list price (which is probably a generous assumption at most bookstores). That would be $39.90. After buying it, the bookstore will mark it back up dramatically and resell the book. Suppose the used book is sold for $75, which sounds like a bargain relative to the new book price of $99.75, and it is. However, notice that the profit markup for the bookstore on this used book would then be $35.10, which is higher than the (still very large) profit made on the new book ($26.25). In fact, the primary reason bookstores prefer selling used books to new books is the much higher profit margins on used books. So, on the second (and third and fourth, etc.) sales of the same book, the bookstore and used book company make huge cumulative profits. The textbook company that invested large sums into developing the book (and the authors who invested time and energy and research into writing it) receive exactly zero on these resold books.

15 If this sounds bad, it actually gets worse. Another insidious influence in the textbook industry is the problem of sales of complimentary copies. In order to market their wares to professors, it is customary for textbook companies to give out free copies of their books. All of you

who teach basic courses in the psychology curriculum receive such books. This is just another price of doing business for the book companies. However, many of these books find their way into the used book market because some professors sell books to scavengers from the used book companies who search through university campuses seeking to buy complimentary copies. Now these companies are soliciting professors to sell their complimentary copies by e-mail. I never sell my complimentary books, of course, because I believe it unethical to sell for profit something I was given by a company in good faith. However, apparently many professors do sell their books. Now the textbook company gets hit by a double whammy: The book they produced to give to a professor for possible adoption enters the market and takes away a new book sale in the marketplace!

Is it any wonder that textbook prices are so high? The wonder is that they aren't higher.

What can you as an individual do about the used book problem and the rising cost of textbooks? Unfortunately, the answer is probably "not much" beyond not selling your complimentary copies. (If you have too many books, give them to prisons, or libraries, or deserving students.)

The textbook companies themselves have few alternatives in dealing with this problem. They can and do raise the price of the books so that they try to recoup their investment on the first sale (hence the high price of textbooks). They can revise the book frequently, which renders the previous edition obsolete. They can try to bundle in or shrinkwrap some additional item (a workbook, a CD) with the new text, so that students will need to buy new books to get the free item. This strategy can work, but some bookstores will just unbundle the book from the study guide and sell both! (So, a study guide the bookstore received free can be sold for, say, $15.) Unless and until laws are changed to prevent the organized sale of used books, you can expect textbook prices to keep increasing. Oh, and if an editor comes by to ask you to write a textbook "just by writing up your lecture notes," tell him or her that if you want to make real money, you'll open a university bookstore. That's where the money is.

KATE CHOPIN { *The Story of an Hour*

KATE CHOPIN (1850–1904), popular fiction writer of the late nineteenth century, was born in St. Louis, Missouri. After she and Oscar Chopin married, they moved to his native Louisiana, and their family quickly grew to include six children in nine years. After Oscar's death in 1882, Chopin and her children returned to St. Louis, where she began writing to support her family, but it was Louisiana that provided the setting for much of Chopin's fiction, including her best-known work and first novel, *The Awakening* (1899). Besides two novels, Chopin wrote many short stories. Her work was not well-respected during her lifetime and into the early twentieth century but later twentieth-century readers and critics came to appreciate Chopin's perspectives, particularly on women's issues, and her work is now widely anthologized and read.

Unfolding in real time, "The Story of an Hour," first published in *Vogue* magazine in 1894, narrates a woman's reaction to the news of her husband's death in a railroad accident. As you read, notice how Chopin's physical descriptions of Mrs. Mallard and her environment reflect and shape her emotional responses. Think, too, about the roles that the secondary characters—Richards and Josephine—play as the events unfold.

KNOWING THAT MRS. MALLARD WAS afflicted with a heart trouble, great care was taken to break to her as gently as possible the news of her husband's death.

It was her sister Josephine who told her, in broken sentences; veiled hints that revealed in half concealing. Her husband's friend Richards was there, too, near her. It was he who had been in the newspaper office when intelligence of the railroad disaster was received, with Brently Mallard's name leading the list of "killed." He had only taken the time to assure himself of its truth by a second telegram, and had hastened to forestall any less careful, less tender friend in bearing the sad message.

She did not hear the story as many women have heard the same, with a paralyzed inability to accept its significance. She wept at once, with sudden, wild abandonment, in her sister's arms. When the storm of grief had spent itself she went away to her room alone. She would have no one follow her.

There stood, facing the open window, a comfortable, roomy armchair. Into this she sank, pressed down by a physical exhaustion that haunted her body and seemed to reach into her soul.

She could see in the open square before her house the tops of trees that were all aquiver with the new spring life. The delicious breath of rain was in the air. In the street below a peddler was crying his wares. The notes of a distant song which some one was singing reached her faintly, and countless sparrows were twittering in the eaves. 5

There were patches of blue sky showing here and there through the clouds that had met and piled one above the other in the west facing her window.

She sat with her head thrown back upon the cushion of the chair, quite motionless, except when a sob came up into her throat and shook her, as a child who has cried itself to sleep continues to sob in its dreams.

She was young, with a fair, calm face, whose lines bespoke repression and even a certain strength. But now there was a dull stare in her eyes, whose gaze was fixed away off yonder on one of those patches of blue sky. It was not a glance of reflection, but rather indicated a suspension of intelligent thought.

There was something coming to her and she was waiting for it, fearfully. What was it? She did not know; it was too subtle and elusive to name. But she felt it, creeping out of the sky, reaching toward her through the sounds, the scents, the color that filled the air.

Now her bosom rose and fell tumultuously. She was beginning to recognize this thing that was approaching to possess her, and she was striving to beat it back with her will—as powerless as her two white slender hands would have been. 10

When she abandoned herself a little whispered word escaped

her slightly parted lips. She said it over and over under her breath: "free, free, free!" The vacant stare and the look of terror that had followed it went from her eyes. They stayed keen and bright. Her pulses beat fast, and the coursing blood warmed and relaxed every inch of her body.

She did not stop to ask if it were or were not a monstrous joy that held her. A clear and exalted perception enabled her to dismiss the suggestion as trivial.

She knew that she would weep again when she saw the kind, tender hands folded in death; the face that had never looked save with love upon her, fixed and gray and dead. But she saw beyond that bitter moment a long procession of years to come that would belong to her absolutely. And she opened and spread her arms out to them in welcome.

There would be no one to live for her during those coming years; she would live for herself. There would be no powerful will bending hers in that blind persistence with which men and women believe they have a right to impose a private will upon a fellow-creature. A kind intention or a cruel intention made the act seem no less a crime as she looked upon it in that brief moment of illumination.

And yet she had loved him—sometimes. Often she had not. What did it matter! What could love, the unsolved mystery, count for in face of this possession of self-assertion which she suddenly recognized as the strongest impulse of her being! 15

"Free! Body and soul free!" she kept whispering.

Josephine was kneeling before the closed door with her lips to the keyhold, imploring for admission. "Louise, open the door! I beg; open the door—you will make yourself ill. What are you doing, Louise? For heaven's sake open the door."

"Go away. I am not making myself ill." No; she was drinking in a very elixir of life through that open window.

Her fancy was running riot along those days ahead of her. Spring days, and summer days, and all sorts of days that would be her own. She breathed a quick prayer that life might be long. It was only yesterday she had thought with a shudder that life might be long.

She arose at length and opened the door to her sister's importuni- 20 ties. There was a feverish triumph in her eyes, and she carried herself unwittingly like a goddess of Victory. She clasped her sister's waist, and together they descended the stairs. Richards stood waiting for them at the bottom.

Some one was opening the front door with a latchkey. It was Brently Mallard who entered, a little travel-stained, composedly carrying his grip-sack and umbrella. He had been far from the scene of the accident, and did not even know there had been one. He stood amazed at Josephine's piercing cry; at Richards' quick motion to screen him from the view of his wife.

But Richards was too late.

When the doctors came they said she had died of heart disease—of joy that kills.

F. SCOTT FITZGERALD { *The Ice Palace*

F. Scott Fitzgerald (1896–1940) is the American writer most associated with the 1920s, a decade he described as the "Jazz Age." Most famous for his novel *The Great Gatsby* (1925), Fitzgerald authored four other novels as well as many short stories, poems, plays, and essays. His literary aspirations began at a young age with contributions to school newspapers in his native Minnesota; much of his time as a student at Princeton University was spent writing musical comedies and his first novel. In 1920 that book, *This Side of Paradise*, became a phenomenal best seller; Fitzgerald married an Alabama beauty named Zelda Sayre; and he was launched on a meteoric career that eventually crashed in what Fitzgerald himself called the "crack-up" of Zelda's mental illness and his own heavy drinking, as well as shifting literary tastes and the 1929 collapse of the stock market. He died in obscurity at an early age; later generations of readers and critics have placed Fitgerald among the great American writers of the twentieth century.

"The Ice Palace," like nearly all of Fitzgerald's fiction, features his trademark preoccupation with wealth and social status, but notice too how much the characters' actions, motivations, and identities are shaped and influenced by their understanding of places—specifically a cemetery and a palace built of ice, and more generally the deep South and the Northern plains. As you read, pay particular attention to how the two main characters—Sally Carrol Happer and Harry Bellamy—each identify with monuments that signify their respective homes.

THE SUNLIGHT DRIPPED OVER THE house like golden paint over an art jar, and the freckling shadows here and there only intensified the rigor of the bath of light. The Butterworth and Larkin houses flanking were intrenched behind great stodgy trees; only the Happer house took the full sun, and all day long faced the dusty road-street with a tolerant kindly patience. This was the city of Tarleton in southernmost Georgia, September afternoon.

Up in her bedroom window Sally Carrol Happer rested her nineteen-year-old chin on a fifty-two-year-old sill and watched Clark Darrow's ancient Ford turn the corner. The car was hot—being partly metallic it retained all the heat it absorbed or evolved—and Clark Darrow sitting bolt upright at the wheel wore a pained, strained expression as though he considered himself a spare part, and rather likely to break. He laboriously crossed two dust ruts, the wheels squeaking indignantly at the encounter, and then with a terrifying expression he gave the steering-gear a final wrench and deposited self and car approximately in front of the Happer steps. There was a plaintive heaving sound, a death-rattle, followed by a short silence; and then the air was rent by a startling whistle.

Sally Carrol gazed down sleepily. She started to yawn, but finding this quite impossible unless she raised her chin from the windowsill, changed her mind and continued silently to regard the car, whose owner sat brilliantly if perfunctorily at attention as he waited for an answer to his signal. After a moment the whistle once more split the dusty air.

"Good mawnin'."

With difficulty Clark twisted his tall body round and bent a distorted glance on the window. 5

" 'Tain't mawnin', Sally Carrol."

"Isn't it, sure enough?"

"What you doin'?"

"Eatin' 'n apple."

"Come on go swimmin'—want to?" 10

"Reckon so."

"How 'bout hurrin' up?"

"Sure enough."

Sally Carrol sighed voluminously and raised herself with profound inertia from the floor, where she had been occupied in alternately destroying parts of a green apple and painting paper dolls for her younger sister. She approached a mirror, regarded her expression with a pleased and pleasant languor, dabbed two spots of rouge on her lips and a grain of powder on her nose, and covered her bobbed corn-colored hair with a rose-littered sunbonnet. Then she kicked over the painting water, said, "Oh, damn!"—but let it lay—and left the room.

"How you, Clark?" she inquired a minute later as she slipped nimbly over the side of the car. 15

"Mighty fine, Sally Carrol."

"Where we go swimmin'?"

"Out to Walley's Pool. Told Marylyn we'd call by an' get her an' Joe Ewing."

Clark was dark and lean, and when on foot was rather inclined to stoop. His eyes were ominous and his expression somewhat petulant except when startlingly illuminated by one of his frequent smiles. Clark had "a income"—just enough to keep himself in ease and his car in gasoline—and he had spent the two years since he graduated from Georgia Tech in dozing round the lazy streets of his hometown, discussing how he could best invest his capital for an immediate fortune.

Hanging round he found not at all difficult; a crowd of little girls had grown up beautifully, the amazing Sally Carrol foremost among them; and they enjoyed being swum with and danced with and made love to in the flower-filled summery evenings—and they all liked Clark immensely. When feminine company palled there were half a dozen other youths who were always just about to do something, and meanwhile were quite willing to join him in a few holes of golf, or a game of billiards, or the consumption of a quart of "hard yella licker." Every once in a while one of these contemporaries made a farewell round of calls before going up to New York or Philadelphia or Pittsburgh to go into business, but mostly they just stayed round in this languid paradise of dreamy skies and firefly evenings and noisy niggery street fairs—and especially of gracious, soft-voiced girls, who were brought up on memories instead of money. 20

The Ford having been excited into a sort of restless, resentful life, Clark and Sally Carrol rolled and rattled down Valley Avenue into

Jefferson Street, where the dust road became a pavement; along opiate Millicent Place, where there were half a dozen prosperous, substantial mansions; and on into the downtown section. Driving was perilous here, for it was shopping time; the population idled casually across the streets and a drove of low-moaning oxen were being urged along in front of a placid streetcar; even the shops seemed only yawning their doors and blinking their windows in the sunshine before retiring into a state of utter and finite coma.

"Sally Carrol," said Clark suddenly, "it a fact that you're engaged?"

She looked at him quickly.

"Where'd you hear that?"

"Sure enough, you engaged?" 25

" 'At's a nice question!"

"Girl told me you were engaged to a Yankee you met up in Asheville last summer."

Sally Carrol sighed.

"Never saw such an old town for rumors."

"Don't marry a Yankee, Sally Carrol. We need you round here." 30

Sally Carrol was silent a moment.

"Clark," she demanded suddenly, "who on earth shall I marry?"

"I offer my services."

"Honey, you couldn't support a wife," she answered cheerfully. "Anyway, I know you too well to fall in love with you."

" 'At doesn't mean you ought to marry a Yankee," he persisted. 35

"S'pose I love him?"

He shook his head.

"You couldn't. He'd be a lot different from us, every way."

He broke off as he halted the car in front of a rambling, dilapidated house. Marylyn Wade and Joe Ewing appeared in the doorway.

" 'Lo, Sally Carrol." 40

"Hi!"

"How you-all?"

"Sally Carrol," demanded Marylyn as they started off again, "you engaged?"

"Lawdy, where'd all this start? Can't I look at a man 'thout everybody in town engagin' me to him?"

Clark stared straight in front of him at a bolt on the clattering windshield. 45

"Sally Carrol," he said with a curious intensity, "don't you like us?"

"What?"

"Us down here?"

"Why, Clark, you know I do. I adore all you boys."

"Then why you gettin' engaged to a Yankee?" 50

"Clark, I don't know. I'm not sure what I'll do, but—well, I want to go places and see people. I want my mind to grow. I want to live where things happen on a big scale."

"What you mean?"

"Oh, Clark, I love you, and I love Joe here, and Ben Arrot, and you-all, but you'll—you'll——"

"We'll all be failures?"

"Yes. I don't mean only money failures, but just sort of—of ineffectual and sad, and—oh, how can I tell you?" 55

"You mean because we stay here in Tarleton?"

"Yes, Clark; and because you like it and never want to change things or think or go ahead."

He nodded and she reached over and pressed his hand.

"Clark," she said softly, "I wouldn't change you for the world. You're sweet the way you are. The things that'll make you fail I'll love always—the living in the past, the lazy days and nights you have, and all your carelessness and generosity."

"But you're goin' away?" 60

"Yes—because I couldn't ever marry you. You've a place in my heart no one else ever could have, but tied down here I'd get restless. I'd feel I was—wastin' myself. There's two sides to me, you see. There's the sleepy old side you love; an' there's a sort of energy—the feelin' that makes me do wild things. That's the part of me that may be useful somewhere, that'll last when I'm not beautiful anymore."

She broke off with characteristic suddenness and sighed, "Oh, sweet cooky!" as her mood changed.

Half closing her eyes and tipping back her head till it rested on the seat-back she let the savory breeze fan her eyes and ripple the fluffy curls of her bobbed hair. They were in the country now, hurrying between tangled growths of bright-green coppice and grass and tall trees that sent sprays of foliage to hang a cool welcome over the road. Here and there they passed a battered Negro cabin, its oldest white-haired inhabitant smoking a corncob pipe beside the door, and half a dozen scantily clothed pickaninnies parading tattered dolls on the wild-grown grass in front. Farther out were lazy cotton-fields, where even the workers seemed intangible shadows lent by the sun to the earth, not for toil, but to while away some age-old tradition in the golden September fields. And round the drowsy picturesqueness, over the trees and shacks and muddy rivers, flowed the heat, never hostile, only comforting, like a great warm nourishing bosom for the infant earth.

"Sally Carrol, we're here!"

"Poor chile's soun' asleep."

"Honey, you dead at last outa sheer laziness?"

"Water, Sally Carrol! Cool water waitin' for you!"

Her eyes opened sleepily.

"Hi!" she murmured, smiling.

II

In November Harry Bellamy, tall, broad, and brisk, came down from his Northern city to spend four days. His intention was to settle a matter that had been hanging fire since he and Sally Carrol had met in Asheville, North Carolina, in midsummer. The settlement took only a quiet afternoon and an evening in front of a glowing open fire, for Harry Bellamy had everything she wanted; and, besides, she loved him—loved him with that side of her she kept especially for loving. Sally Carrol had several rather clearly defined sides.

On his last afternoon they walked, and she found their steps tending half-unconsciously toward one of her favorite haunts, the cemetery. When it came in sight, gray-white and golden-green under the cheerful late sun, she paused, irresolute, by the iron gate.

"Are you mournful by nature, Harry?" she asked with a faint smile.

"Mournful? Not I."

"Then let's go in here. It depresses some folks, but I like it."

They passed through the gateway and followed a path that led through a wavy valley of graves—dusty-gray and mouldy for the fifties;[1] quaintly carved with flowers and jars for the seventies; ornate and hideous for the nineties, with fat marble cherubs lying in sodden sleep on stone pillows, and great impossible growths of nameless granite flowers. Occasionally they saw a kneeling figure with tributary flowers, but over most of the graves lay silence and withered leaves with only the fragrance that their own shadowy memories could waken in living minds. 75

They reached the top of a hill where they were fronted by a tall, round headstone, freckled with dark spots of damp and half grown over with vines.

"Margery Lee," she read, "1844–1873. Wasn't she nice? She died when she was twenty-nine. Dear Margery Lee," she added softly. "Can't you see her, Harry?"

"Yes, Sally Carrol."

He felt a little hand insert itself into his.

"She was dark, I think; and she always wore her hair with a ribbon in it, and gorgeous hoopskirts of Alice blue and old rose." 80

"Yes."

"Oh, she was sweet, Harry! And she was the sort of girl born to stand on a wide, pillared porch and welcome folks in. I think perhaps a lot of men went away to war meanin' to come back to her; but maybe none of 'em ever did."

He stooped down close to the stone, hunting for any record of marriage.

"There's nothing here to show."

"Of course not. How could there be anything there better than just 'Margery Lee,' and that eloquent date?" 85

She drew close to him and an unexpected hump came into his throat as her yellow hair brushed his cheek.

"You see how she was, don't you, Harry?"

[1] That is, the 1850s.

"I see," he agreed gently. "I see through your precious eyes. You're beautiful now, so I know she must have been."

Silent and close they stood, and he could feel her shoulders trembling a little. An ambling breeze swept up the hill and stirred the brim of her floppidy hat.

"Let's go down there!" 90

She was pointing to a flat stretch on the other side of the hill where along the green turf were a thousand grayish-white crosses stretching in endless, ordered rows like the stacked arms of a battalion.

"Those are the Confederate dead," said Sally Carrol simply.

They walked along and read the inscriptions, always only a name and a date, sometimes quite indecipherable.

"The last row is the saddest—see, 'way over there. Every cross has just a date on it, and the word 'Unknown.'"

She looked at him and her eyes brimmed with tears. 95

"I can't tell you how real it is to me, darling—if you don't know."

"How you feel about it is beautiful to me."

"No, no, it's not me, it's them—that old time that I've tried to have live in me. These were just men, unimportant evidently or they wouldn't have been 'unknown'; but they died for the most beautiful thing in the world—the dead South. You see," she continued, her voice still husky, her eyes glistening with tears, "people have these dreams they fasten onto things, and I've always grown up with that dream. It was so easy because it was all dead and there weren't any disillusions comin' to me. I've tried in a way to live up to those past standards of noblesse oblige[2]—there's just the last remnants of it, you know, like the roses of an old garden dying all round us—streaks of strange courtliness and chivalry in some of these boys an' stories I used to hear from a Confederate soldier who lived next door, and a few old darkies. Oh, Harry, there was something, there was something! I couldn't ever make you understand, but it was there."

"I understand," he assured her again quietly.

[2] Literally, "nobility obligates" (French); the responsibility to behave honorably and generously toward those of lower social standing.

Sally Carrol smiled and dried her eyes on the tip of a handkerchief protruding from his breast pocket. 100

"You don't feel depressed, do you, lover? Even when I cry I'm happy here, and I get a sort of strength from it."

Hand in hand they turned and walked slowly away. Finding soft grass she drew him down to a seat beside her with their backs against the remnants of a low broken wall.

"Wish those three old women would clear out," he complained. "I want to kiss you, Sally Carrol."

"Me, too."

They waited impatiently for the three bent figures to move off, and then she kissed him until the sky seemed to fade out and all her smiles and tears to vanish in an ecstasy of eternal seconds. 105

Afterward they walked slowly back together, while on the corners twilight played at somnolent black-and-white checkers with the end of day.

"You'll be up about mid-January," he said, "and you've got to stay a month at least. It'll be slick. There's a winter carnival on, and if you've never really seen snow it'll be like fairy-land to you. There'll be skating and skiing and tobagganing and sleigh-riding, and all sorts of torchlight parades on snowshoes. They haven't had one for years, so they're going to make it a knockout."

"Will I be cold, Harry?" she asked suddenly.

"You certainly won't. You may freeze your nose, but you won't be shivery cold. It's hard and dry, you know."

"I guess I'm a summer child. I don't like any cold I've ever seen." 110

She broke off, and they were both silent for a minute.

"Sally Carrol," he said very slowly, "what do you say to—March?"

"I say I love you."

"March?"

"March, Harry." 115

III

All night in the Pullman[3] it was very cold. She rang for the porter to ask for another blanket, and when he couldn't give her one she tried vainly, by squeezing down into the bottom of her berth and doubling back the bedclothes, to snatch a few hours' sleep. She wanted to look her best in the morning.

She rose at six and sliding uncomfortably into her clothes stumbled up to the diner[4] for a cup of coffee. The snow had filtered into the vestibules and covered the floor with a slippery coating. It was intriguing, this cold, it crept in everywhere. Her breath was quite visible and she blew into the air with a naïve enjoyment. Seated in the diner she stared out the window at white hills and valleys and scattered pines whose every branch was a green platter for a cold feast of snow. Sometimes a solitary farmhouse would fly by, ugly and bleak and lone on the white waste; and with each one she had an instant of chill compassion for the souls shut in there waiting for spring.

As she left the diner and swayed back into the Pullman she experienced a surging rush of energy and wondered if she was feeling the bracing air of which Harry had spoken. This was the North, the North—her land now!

"Then blow, ye winds, heigho!
A-roving I will go,"

she chanted exultantly to herself.

"What's 'at?" inquired the porter politely.

"I said: 'Brush me off.' " 120

The long wires of the telegraph poles doubled; two tracks ran up beside the train—three—four; came a succession of white-roofed houses, a glimpse of a trolley-car with frosted windows, streets—more streets—the city.

[3] A railroad car, designed in the late nineteenth century, that provided passengers with amenities such as stewards, comfortable seats, and private sleeping berths. Pullman cars were used mainly by wealthy passengers traveling long distances.

[4] That is, the dining car of a passenger train.

She stood for a dazed moment in the frosty station before she saw three fur-bundled figures descending upon her.

"There she is!"

"Oh, Sally Carrol!"

Sally Carrol dropped her bag. 125

"Hi!"

A faintly familiar icy-cold face kissed her, and then she was in a group of faces all apparently emitting great clouds of heavy smoke; she was shaking hands. There were Gordon, a short, eager man of thirty who looked like an amateur knocked-about model for Harry, and his wife, Myra, a listless lady with flaxen hair under a fur automobile cap. Almost immediately Sally Carrol thought of her as vaguely Scandinavian. A cheerful chauffeur adopted her bag, and amid ricochets of half-phrases, exclamations, and perfunctory listless "my dears" from Myra, they swept each other from the station.

Then they were in a sedan bound through a crooked succession of snowy streets where dozens of little boys were hitching sleds behind grocery wagons and automobiles.

"Oh," cried Sally Carrol, "I want to do that! Can we, Harry?"

"That's for kids. But we might——" 130

"It looks like such a circus!" she said regretfully.

Home was a rambling frame house set on a white lap of snow, and there she met a big, gray-haired man of whom she approved, and a lady who was like an egg, and who kissed her—these were Harry's parents. There was a breathless, indescribable hour crammed full of half-sentences, hot water, bacon and eggs and confusion; and after that she was alone with Harry in the library, asking him if she dared smoke.

It was a large room with a Madonna over the fireplace and rows upon rows of books in covers of light gold and dark gold and shiny red. All the chairs had little lace squares where one's head should rest, the couch was just comfortable, the books looked as if they had been read—some—and Sally Carrol had an instantaneous vision of the battered old library at home, with her father's huge medical books, and the oil paintings of her three great-uncles, and the old couch that had been mended up for forty-five years and was still luxurious to dream in. This room struck her as being neither attractive nor particularly otherwise. It was simply a room with a lot of fairly expensive things in it that all looked about fifteen years old.

"What do you think of it up here?" demanded Harry eagerly. "Does it surprise you? Is it what you expected, I mean?"

"You are, Harry," she said quietly, and reached out her arms to him. 135

But after a brief kiss he seemed anxious to extort enthusiasm from her.

"The town, I mean. Do you like it? Can you feel the pep in the air?"

"Oh, Harry," she laughed, "you'll have to give me time. You can't just fling questions at me."

She puffed at her cigarette with a sigh of contentment.

"One thing I want to ask you," he began rather apologetically. "You Southerners put quite an emphasis on family, and all that—not that it isn't quite all right, but you'll find it a little different here. I mean—you'll notice a lot of things that'll seem to you sort of vulgar display at first, Sally Carrol; but just remember that this is a three-generation town. Everybody has a father, and about half of us have grandfathers. Back of that we don't go." 140

"Of course," she murmured.

"Our grandfathers, you see, founded the place, and a lot of them had to take some pretty queer jobs while they were doing the founding. For instance, there's one woman who at present is about the social model for the town; well, her father was the first public ash man[5]—things like that."

"Why," said Sally Carrol, puzzled, "did you s'pose I was goin' to make remarks about people?"

"Not at all," interrupted Harry, "and I'm not apologizing for anyone either. It's just that—well, a Southern girl came up here last summer and said some unfortunate things, and—oh, I just thought I'd tell you."

Sally Carrol felt suddenly indignant—as though she had been unjustly spanked—but Harry evidently considered the subject closed, for he went on with a great surge of enthusiasm. 145

[5] Municipal garbage collector.

"It's carnival time, you know. First in ten years. And there's an ice palace they're building now that's the first they've had since eighty-five. Built out of blocks of the clearest ice they could find—on a tremendous scale."

She rose and walking to the window pushed aside the heavy Turkish portières and looked out.

"Oh!" she cried suddenly. "There's two little boys makin' a snow man! Harry, do you reckon I can go out an' help 'em?"

"You dream! Come here and kiss me."

She left the window rather reluctantly. 150

"I don't guess this is a very kissable climate, is it? I mean, it makes you so you don't want to sit round, doesn't it?"

"We're not going to. I've got a vacation for the first week you're here, and there's a dinner-dance tonight."

"Oh, Harry," she confessed, subsiding in a heap, half in his lap, half in the pillows, "I sure do feel confused. I haven't got an idea whether I'll like it or not, an' I don't know what people expect, or anythin'. You'll have to tell me, honey."

"I'll tell you," he said softly, "if you'll just tell me you're glad to be here."

"Glad—just awful glad!" she whispered, insinuating herself into 155 his arms in her own peculiar way. "Where you are is home for me, Harry."

And as she said this she had the feeling for almost the first time in her life that she was acting a part.

That night, amid the gleaming candles of a dinner party, where the men seemed to do most of the talking while the girls sat in a haughty and expensive aloofness, even Harry's presence on her left failed to make her feel at home.

"They're a good-looking crowd, don't you think?" he demanded. "Just look round. There's Spud Hubbard, tackle at Princeton last year, and Junie Morton—he and the red-haired fellow next to him were both Yale hockey captains; Junie was in my class. Why, the best athletes in the world come from these states round here. This is a man's country, I tell you. Look at John J. Fishburn!"

"Who's he?" asked Sally Carrol innocently.

"Don't you know?" 160

"I've heard the name."

"Greatest wheat man in the Northwest, and one of the greatest financiers in the country."

She turned suddenly to a voice on her right.

"I guess they forgot to introduce us. My name's Roger Patton."

"My name is Sally Carrol Happer," she said graciously. 165

"Yes, I know. Harry told me you were coming."

"You a relative?"

"No, I'm a professor."

"Oh," she laughed.

"At the university. You're from the South, aren't you?" 170

"Yes; Tarleton, Georgia."

She liked him immediately—a reddish-brown mustache under watery blue eyes that had something in them that these other eyes lacked, some quality of appreciation. They exchanged stray sentences through dinner, and she made up her mind to see him again.

After coffee she was introduced to numerous good-looking young men who danced with conscious precision and seemed to take it for granted that she wanted to talk about nothing except Harry.

'Heavens,' she thought, 'they talk as if my being engaged made me older than they, are—as if I'd tell their mothers on them!'

In the South an engaged girl, even a young married woman, 175 expected the same amount of half-affectionate badinage and flattery that would be accorded a débutante, but here all that seemed banned. One young man, after getting well started on the subject of Sally Carrol's eyes, and how they had allured him ever since she entered the room, went into a violent confusion when he found she was visiting the Bellamys—was Harry's fiancée. He seemed to feel as though he had made some risqué and inexcusable blunder, became immediately formal, and left her at the first opportunity.

She was rather glad when Roger Patton cut in on her and suggested that they sit out a while.

"Well," he inquired, blinking cheerily, "how's Carmen from the South?"

"Mighty fine. How's—how's Dangerous Dan McGrew?[6] Sorry, but he's the only Northerner I know much about."

He seemed to enjoy that.

"Of course," he confessed, "as a professor of literature I'm not supposed to have read Dangerous Dan McGrew." 180

"Are you a native?"

"No, I'm a Philadelphian. Imported from Harvard to teach French. But I've been here ten years."

"Nine years, three hundred an' sixty-four days longer than me."

"Like it here?"

"Uh-huh. Sure do!" 185

"Really?"

"Well, why not? Don't I look as if I were havin' a good time?"

"I saw you look out the window a minute ago—and shiver."

"Just my imagination," laughed Sally Carrol. "I'm used to havin' everythin' quiet outside, an' sometimes I look out an' see a flurry of snow, an' it's just as if somethin' dead was movin'."

He nodded appreciatively. 190

"Ever been North before?"

"Spent two Julys in Asheville, North Carolina."

"Nice-looking crowd, aren't they?" suggested Patton, indicating the swirling floor.

Sally Carrol started. This had been Harry's remark.

"Sure are! They're—canine." 195

"What?"

She flushed.

"I'm sorry; that sounded worse than I meant it. You see, I always think of people as feline or canine, irrespective of sex."

"Which are you?"

"I'm feline. So are you. So are most Southern men an' most of these girls here." 200

[6] A reference to "The Shooting of Dan McGrew," a popular poem by Robert Service about the Yukon Gold Rush, first published in 1907. "Carmen" refers to the opera *Carmen* by Georges Bizet (1838–75).

"What's Harry?"

"Harry's canine distinctly. All the men I've met tonight seem to be canine."

"What does 'canine' imply? A certain conscious masculinity as opposed to subtlety?"

"Reckon so. I never analyzed it—only I just look at people an' say 'canine' or 'feline' right off. It's right absurd, I guess."

"Not at all. I'm interested. I used to have a theory about these people. I think they're freezing up." 205

"What?"

"I think they're growing like Swedes—Ibsenesque,[7] you know. Very gradually getting gloomy and melancholy. It's these long winters. Ever read any Ibsen?"

She shook her head.

"Well, you find in his characters a certain brooding rigidity. They're righteous, narrow, and cheerless, without infinite possibilities for great sorrow or joy."

"Without smiles or tears?" 210

"Exactly. That's my theory. You see there are thousands of Swedes up here. They come, I imagine, because the climate is very much like their own, and there's been a gradual mingling. There're probably not half a dozen here tonight, but—we've had four Swedish governors. Am I boring you?

"I'm mighty interested."

"Your future sister-in-law is half Swedish. Personally I like her, but my theory is that Swedes react rather badly on us as a whole. Scandinavians, you know, have the largest suicide rate in the world."

"Why do you live here if it's so depressing?"

"Oh, it doesn't get me. I'm pretty well cloistered, and I suppose books mean more than people to me anyway." 215

"But writers all speak about the South being tragic. You know—Spanish señoritas, black hair and daggers an' haunting music."

He shook his head.

[7] Characteristic of the writing of Norwegian playwright Henrik Ibsen (1828–1906).

"No, the Northern races are the tragic races—they don't indulge in the cheering luxury of tears."

Sally Carrol thought of her graveyard. She supposed that that was vaguely what she had meant when she said it didn't depress her.

"The Italians are about the gayest people in the world—but it's a dull subject," he broke off. "Anyway, I want to tell you you're marrying a pretty fine man." 220

Sally Carrol was moved by an impulse of confidence.

"I know. I'm the sort of person who wants to be taken care of after a certain point, and I feel sure I will be."

"Shall we dance? You know," he continued as they rose, "it's encouraging to find a girl who knows what she's marrying for. Nine-tenths of them think of it as a sort of walking into a moving-picture sunset."

She laughed, and liked him immensely.

Two hours later on the way home she nestled near Harry in the back seat. 225

"Oh, Harry," she whispered, "it's so co-old!"

"But it's warm in here, darling girl."

"But outside it's cold; and oh, that howling wind!"

She buried her face deep in his fur coat and trembled involuntarily as his cold lips kissed the tip of her ear.

IV

The first week of her visit passed in a whirl. She had her promised toboggan ride at the back of an automobile through a chill January twilight. Swathed in furs she put in a morning tobogganing on the country club hill; even tried skiing, to sail through the air for a glorious moment and then land in a tangled laughing bundle on a soft snowdrift. She liked all the winter sports, except an afternoon spent snowshoeing over a glaring plain under pale yellow sunshine, but she soon realized that these things were for children—that she was being humored and that the enjoyment round her was only a reflection of her own. 230

At first the Bellamy family puzzled her. The men were reliable and she liked them; to Mr. Bellamy especially, with his iron-gray hair and energetic dignity, she took an immediate fancy, once she found that he was born in Kentucky; this made of him a link between the old life and the new. But toward the women she felt a definite hostility. Myra, her future sister-in-law, seemed the essence of spiritless conventionality. Her conversation was so utterly devoid of personality that Sally Carrol, who came from a country where a certain amount of charm and assurance could be taken for granted in the women, was inclined to despise her.

"If those women aren't beautiful," she thought, "they're nothing. They just fade out when you look at them. They're glorified domestics. Men are the centre of every mixed group."

Lastly there was Mrs. Bellamy, whom Sally Carrol detested. The first day's impression of an egg had been confirmed—an egg with a cracked, veiny voice and such an ungracious dumpiness of carriage that Sally Carrol felt that if she once fell she would surely scramble. In addition, Mrs. Bellamy seemed to typify the town in being innately hostile to strangers. She called Sally Carrol "Sally," and could not be persuaded that the double name was anything more than a tedious, ridiculous nickname. To Sally Carrol this shortening of her name was like presenting her to the public half clothed. She loved "Sally Carrol"; she loathed "Sally." She knew also that Harry's mother disapproved of her bobbed hair; and she had never dared smoke downstairs after that first day when Mrs. Bellamy had come into the library sniffing violently.

Of all the men she met she preferred Roger Patton, who was a frequent visitor at the house. He never again alluded to the Ibsenesque tendency of the populace, but when he came in one day and found her curled upon the sofa bent over "Peer Gynt,"[8] he laughed and told her to forget what he'd said—that it was all rot.

And then one afternoon in her second week she and Harry hovered 235
on the edge of a dangerously steep quarrel. She considered that he precipitated it entirely, though the Serbia in the case was an unknown man who had not had his trousers pressed.[9]

[8] Ibsen play that satirizes the Norwegian personality (1867).

[9] A Serbian nationalist's 1914 assassination of Archduke Franz Ferdinand of Austria, heir to the Austro-Hungarian empire, is often viewed as the spark that ignited World War I.

They had been walking homeward between mounds of high-piled snow and under a sun which Sally Carrol scarcely recognized. They passed a little girl done up in gray wool until she resembled a small Teddy bear, and Sally Carrol could not resist a gasp of maternal appreciation.

"Look! Harry!"

"What?"

"That little girl—did you see her face?"

"Yes, why?" 240

"It was red as a little strawberry. Oh, she was cute!"

"Why, your own face is almost as red as that already! Everybody's healthy here. We're out in the cold as soon as we're old enough to walk. Wonderful climate!"

She looked at him and had to agree. He was mighty healthy-looking; so was his brother. And she had noticed the new red in her own cheeks that very morning.

Suddenly their glances were caught and held, and they stared for a moment at the street corner ahead of them. A man was standing there, his knees bent, his eyes gazing upward with a tense expression as though he were about to make a leap toward the chilly sky. And then they both exploded into a shout of laughter, for coming closer they discovered it had been a ludicrous momentary illusion produced by the extreme bagginess of the man's trousers.

"Reckon that's one on us," she laughed. 245

"He must be a Southerner, judging by those trousers," suggested Harry mischievously.

"Why, Harry!"

Her surprised look must have irritated him.

"Those damn Southerners!"

Sally Carrol's eyes flashed. 250

"Don't call 'em that!"

"I'm sorry, dear," said Harry, malignantly apologetic, "but you know what I think of them. They're sort of—sort of degenerates—not at all like the old Southerners. They've lived so long down there with all the colored people that they've gotten lazy and shiftless."

"Hush your mouth, Harry!" she cried angrily. They're not! They may be lazy—anybody would be in that climate—but they're my best friends, an' I don't want to hear 'em criticised in any such sweepin' way. Some of 'em are the finest men in the world."

"Oh, I know. They're all right when they come North to college, but of all the hangdog, ill-dressed, slovenly lot I ever saw, a bunch of small-town Southerners are the worst!"

Sally Carrol was clenching her gloved hands and biting her lip 255 furiously.

"Why," continued Harry, "there was one in my class at New Haven, and we all thought that at last we'd found the true type of Southern aristocrat, but it turned out that he wasn't an aristocrat at all—just the son of a Northern carpetbagger[1] who owned about all the cotton round Mobile."

"A Southerner wouldn't talk the way you're talking now," she said evenly.

"They haven't the energy!"

"Or the somethin' else."

"I'm sorry, Sally Carrol, but I've heard you say yourself that you'd 260 never marry—"

That's quite different. I told you I wouldn't want to tie my life to any of the boys that are round Tarleton now, but I never made any sweepin' generalities."

They walked along in silence.

"I probably spread it on a bit thick, Sally Carrol. I'm sorry."

She nodded but made no answer. Five minutes later as they stood in the hallway she suddenly threw her arms round him.

"Oh, Harry," she cried, her eyes brimming with tears, "let's get 265 married next week. I'm afraid of having fusses like that. I'm afraid, Harry. It wouldn't be that way if we were married."

But Harry, being in the wrong, was still irritated.

"That'd be idiotic. We decided on March."

The tears in Sally Carrol's eyes faded; her expression hardened slightly.

[1] Derogatory term used by Southerners to describe Northerners who came to the South after the Civil War to exploit economic opportunities amidst the severe problems the region faced. (A typical traveler's suitcase of the period was made of an upholstered material that resembled carpeting.)

"Very well—I suppose I shouldn't have said that."

Harry melted. 270

"Dear little nut!" he cried. "Come and kiss me and let's forget."

That very night at the end of a vaudeville performance the orchestra played "Dixie," and Sally Carrol felt something stronger and more enduring than her tears and smiles of the day brim up inside her. She leaned forward gripping the arms of her chair until her face grew crimson.

"Sort of get you, dear?" whispered Harry.

But she did not hear him. To the spirited throb of the violins and the inspiring beat of the kettledrums her own old ghosts were marching by and on into the darkness, and as fifes whistled and sighed in the low encore they seemed so nearly out of sight that she could have waved good-by.

> "Away, Away,
> Away down South in Dixie!
> Away, away,
> Away down South in Dixie!"

V

It was a particularly cold night. A sudden thaw had nearly cleared the streets the day before, but now they were traversed again with a powdery wraith of loose snow that traveled in wavy lines before the feet of the wind, and filled the lower air with a fine-particled mist. There was no sky—only a dark, ominous tent that draped in the tops of the streets and was in reality a vast approaching army of snowflakes—while over it all, chilling away the comfort from the brown-and-green glow of lighted windows and muffling the steady trot of the horse pulling their sleigh, interminably washed the north wind. It was a dismal town after all, she thought—dismal. 275

Sometimes at night it had seemed to her as though no one lived here—they had all gone long ago—leaving lighted houses to be covered in time by tombing heaps of sleet. Oh, if there should be snow on her grave! To be beneath great piles of it all winter long, where even her headstone would be a light shadow against light shadows. Her grave—a grave that should be flower-strewn and washed with sun and rain.

She thought again of those isolated country houses that her train had passed, and of the life there the long winter through—the ceaseless glare through the windows, the crust forming on the soft drifts of snow, finally the slow, cheerless melting, and the harsh spring of which Roger Patton had told her. Her spring—to lose it forever—with its lilacs and the lazy sweetness it stirred in her heart. She was laying away that spring—afterward she would lay away that sweetness.

With a gradual insistence the storm broke. Sally Carrol felt a film of flakes melt quickly on her eyelashes, and Harry reached over a furry arm and drew down her complicated flannel cap. Then the small flakes came in skirmish line, and the horse bent his neck patiently as a transparency of white appeared momentarily on his coat.

"Oh, he's cold, Harry," she said quickly.

"Who? The horse? Oh, no, he isn't. He likes it!" 280

After another ten minutes they turned a corner and came in sight of their destination. On a tall hill, outlined in vivid glaring green against the wintry sky, stood the ice palace. It was three stories in the air, with battlements and embrasures and narrow icicled windows, and the innumerable electric lights inside made a gorgeous transparency of the great central hall. Sally Carrol clutched Harry's hand under the fur robe.

"It's beautiful!" he cried excitedly. "My golly, it's beautiful, isn't it! They haven't had one here since eighty-five!"

Somehow the notion of there not having been one since eighty-five oppressed her. Ice was a ghost, and this mansion of it was surely peopled by those shades of the eighties, with pale faces and blurred snow-filled hair.

"Come on, dear," said Harry.

She followed him out of the sleigh and waited while he hitched the 285 horse. A party of four—Gordon, Myra, Roger Patton, and another girl—drew up beside them with a mighty jingle of bells. There was quite a crowd already, bundled in fur or sheepskin, shouting and calling to each other as they moved through the snow, which was now so thick that people could scarcely be distinguished a few yards away.

"It's a hundred and seventy feet tall," Harry was saying to a muffled figure beside him as they trudged toward the entrance, "covers six thousand square yards."

She caught snatches of conversation: "One main hall"—"walls twenty to forty inches thick"—"and the ice cave has almost a mile of—"—"this Canuck who built it—"

They found their way inside, and dazed by the magic of the great crystal walls Sally Carrol found herself repeating over and over two lines from "Kubla Khan":[2]

> "It was a miracle of rare device,
> A sunny pleasure-dome with caves of ice!"

In the great glittering cavern with the dark shut out she took a seat on a wooden bench, and the evening's oppression lifted. Harry was right—it was beautiful; and her gaze traveled the smooth surface of the walls, the blocks for which had been selected for their purity and clearness to obtain this opalescent, translucent effect.

"Look! Here we go—oh, boy!" cried Harry. 290

A band in a far corner struck up "Hail, Hail, the Gang's All Here!" which echoed over to them in wild muddled acoustics, and then the lights suddenly went out; silence seemed to flow down the icy sides and sweep over them. Sally Carrol could still see her white breath in the darkness, and a dim row of pale faces over on the other side.

The music eased to a sighing complaint, and from outside drifted in the full-throated resonant chant of the marching clubs. It grew louder like some pæan of a viking tribe traversing an ancient wild; it swelled—they were coming nearer; then a row of torches appeared, and another and another, and keeping time with their moccasined feet a long column of gray-mackinawed figures swept in, snowshoes slung at their shoulders, torches soaring and flickering as their voices rose along the great walls.

[2] Poem written by Samuel Taylor Coleridge, published in 1816. Historically, Kublai Khan was a leader of the Mongol Empire in the thirteenth century; his extravagant palace in the city of Xanadu has frequently been used as a metaphor for luxury and opulence.

The gray column ended and another followed, the light streaming luridly this time over red toboggan caps and flaming crimson mackinaws, and as they entered they took up the refrain; then came a long platoon of blue and white, of green, of white, of brown and yellow.

"Those white ones are the Wacouta Club," whispered Harry eagerly. "Those are the men you've met round at dances."

The volume of the voices grew; the great cavern was a phantasmagoria of torches waving in great banks of fire, of colors and the rhythm of soft-leather steps. The leading column turned and halted, platoon deployed in front of platoon until the whole procession made a solid flag of flame, and then from thousands of voices burst a mighty shout that filled the air like a crash of thunder, and sent the torches wavering. It was magnificent, it was tremendous! To Sally Carrol it was the North offering sacrifice on some mighty altar to the gray pagan God of Snow. As the shout died the band struck up again and there came more singing, and then long reverberating cheers by each club. She sat very quiet, listening while the staccato cries rent the stillness; and then she started, for there was a volley of explosion, and great clouds of smoke went up here and there through the cavern—the flash-light photographers at work—and the council was over. With the band at their head the clubs formed in column once more, took up their chant, and began to march out. 295

"Come on!" shouted Harry. "We want to see the labyrinths downstairs before they turn the lights off!"

They all rose and started toward the chute—Harry and Sally Carrol in the lead, her little mitten buried in his big fur gantlet. At the bottom of the chute was a long empty room of ice, with the ceiling so low that they had to stoop—and their hands were parted. Before she realized what he intended Harry had darted down one of the half-dozen glittering passages that opened into the room and was only a vague receding blot against the green shimmer.

"Harry!" she called.

"Come on!" he cried back.

She looked round the empty chamber; the rest of the party had evidently decided to go home, were already outside somewhere in the blundering snow. She hesitated and then darted in after Harry. 300

"Harry!" she shouted.

She had reached a turning point thirty feet down; she heard a faint muffled answer far to the left, and with a touch of panic fled toward it. She passed another turning, two more yawning alleys.

"Harry!"

No answer. She started to run straight forward, and then turned like lightning and sped back the way she had come, enveloped in a sudden icy terror.

She reached a turn—was it here?—took the left and came to what should have been the outlet into the long, low room, but it was only another glittering passage with darkness at the end. She called again, but the walls gave back a flat, lifeless echo with no reverberations. Retracing her steps she turned another corner, this time following a wide passage. It was like the green lane between the parted waters of the Red Sea, like a damp vault connecting empty tombs. 305

She slipped a little now as she walked, for ice had formed on the bottom of her overshoes; she had to run her gloves along the half-slippery, half-sticky walls to keep her balance.

"Harry!"

Still no answer. The sound she made bounced mockingly down to the end of the passage.

Then on an instant the lights went out, and she was in complete darkness. She gave a small, frightened cry, and sank down into a cold little heap on the ice. She felt her left knee do something as she fell, but she scarcely noticed it as some deep terror far greater than any fear of being lost settled upon her. She was alone with this presence that came out of the North, the dreary loneliness that rose from ice-bound whalers in the Arctic seas, from smokeless, trackless wastes where were strewn the whitened bones of adventure. It was an icy breath of death; it was rolling down low across the land to clutch at her.

With a furious, despairing energy she rose again and started blindly down the darkness. She must get out. She might be lost in here for days, freeze to death and lie embedded in the ice like corpses she had read of, kept perfectly preserved until the melting of a glacier. Harry probably thought she had left with the others—he had gone by now; 310

no one would know until late next day. She reached pitifully for the wall. Forty inches thick, they had said—forty inches thick!

"Oh!"

On both sides of her along the walls she felt things creeping, damp souls that haunted this palace, this town, this North.

"Oh, send somebody—send somebody!" she cried aloud.

Clark Darrow—he would understand; or Joe Ewing; she couldn't be left here to wander forever—to be frozen, heart, body, and soul. This her—this Sally Carrol! Why, she was a happy thing. She was a happy little girl. She liked warmth and summer and Dixie. These things were foreign—foreign.

"You're not crying," something said aloud. "You'll never cry any- 315 more. Your tears would just freeze; all tears freeze up here!"

She sprawled full length on the ice.

"Oh, God!" she faltered.

A long single file of minutes went by, and with a great weariness she felt her eyes closing. Then someone seemed to sit down near her and take her face in warm, soft hands. She looked up gratefully.

"Why, it's Margery Lee," she crooned softly to herself. "I knew you'd come." It really was Margery Lee, and she was just as Sally Carrol had known she would be, with a young, white brow, and wide, welcoming eyes, and a hoop-skirt of some soft material that was quite comforting to rest on.

"Margery Lee." 320

It was getting darker now and darker—all those tombstones ought to be repainted, sure enough, only that would spoil 'em, of course. Still, you ought to be able to see 'em.

Then after a succession of moments that went fast and then slow, but seemed to be ultimately resolving themselves into a multitude of blurred rays converging toward a pale-yellow sun, she heard a great cracking noise break her new-found stillness.

It was the sun, it was a light; a torch, and a torch beyond that, and another one, and voices; a face took flesh below the torch, heavy arms raised her, and she felt something on her cheek—it felt wet. Someone had seized her and was rubbing her face with snow. How ridiculous—with snow!

"Sally Carrol! Sally Carrol!"

It was Dangerous Dan McGrew; and two other faces she didn't know. 325

"Child, child! We've been looking for you two hours! Harry's half crazy!"

Things came rushing back into place—the singing, the torches, the great shout of the marching clubs. She squirmed in Patton's arms and gave a long, low cry.

"Oh, I want to get out of here! I'm going back home. Take me home"—her voice rose to a scream that sent a chill to Harry's heart as he came racing down the next passage—"tomorrow!" she cried with delirious, unrestrained passion—"Tomorrow! Tomorrow! Tomorrow!"

VI

The wealth of golden sunlight poured a quite enervating yet oddly comforting heat over the house where daylong it faced the dusty stretch of road. Two birds were making a great to-do in a cool spot found among the branches of a tree next door, and down the street a colored woman was announcing herself melodiously as a purveyor of strawberries. It was April afternoon.

Sally Carrol Happer, resting her chin on her arm, and her arm on 330 an old window seat, gazed sleepily down over the spangled dust whence the heat waves were rising for the first time this spring. She was watching a very ancient Ford turn a perilous corner and rattle and groan to a jolting stop at the end of the walk. She made no sound, and in a minute a strident familiar whistle rent the air. Sally Carrol smiled and blinked.

"Good mawnin'."

A head appeared tortuously from under the cartop below.

" 'Tain't mawnin', Sally Carrol."

"Sure enough!" she said in affected surprise. "I guess maybe not."

"What you doin?" 335

"Eatin' green peach. 'Spect to die any minute."

Clark twisted himself a last impossible notch to get a view of her face.

"Water's warm as a kettla steam, Sally Carrol. Wanta go swimmin'?"

"Hate to move," sighed Sally Carrol lazily, "but I reckon so."

LANGSTON HUGHES { *Theme for English B*

LANGSTON HUGHES (1902–1967) was born in Joplin, Missouri. He lived with his maternal grandmother in Lawrence, Kansas, after his parents divorced and then with family friends after her death before returning to his mother in Lincoln, Illinois. Hughes was elected class poet, though he suspected it was because of a stereotype in the largely white school that blacks had "rhythm." As a teen he was able to travel to Africa and Europe as a crewman on the *SS Malone*. Returning to the United States, he assisted the historian Carter G. Woodson before entering Lincoln University in Pennsylvania, earning a BA in 1929. He then moved to Harlem, in the midst of the Harlem Renaissance, a period when the African American community's artistic talent flourished. However, Hughes took issue with some of the shepherds of the Renaissance, such as W. E. B. Du Bois and Alain Locke, because he felt that their approach was too assimilationist. Instead, Hughes celebrated blackness unapologetically and focused his work on racial pride, employing rhythms from jazz and folk music. He also wrote fiction, nonfiction, plays, and children's books. His best-known works include *The Weary Blues* (1926), *The Big Sea* (1940), and *Mule Bone* (1931), the last written with Zora Neale Hurston.

"Theme for English B" depicts an African American student's reaction to being assigned an essay by a white instructor. The assignment seems simple enough, but as the speaker talks about himself, he shows how it is loaded with cultural assumptions. Has the speaker written something that's "true"?

The instructor said,

Go home and write
a page tonight.
And let that page come out of you—
Then, it will be true. 5

I wonder if it's that simple?
I am twenty-two, colored, born in Winston-Salem.
I went to school there, then Durham, then here
to this college on the hill above Harlem.
I am the only colored student in my class. 10
The steps from the hill lead down into Harlem,
through a park, then I cross St. Nicholas,
Eighth Avenue, Seventh, and I come to the Y,
the Harlem Branch Y, where I take the elevator
up to my room, sit down, and write this page: 15

It's not easy to know what is true for you or me
at twenty-two, my age. But I guess I'm what
I feel and see and hear, Harlem, I hear you:
hear you, hear me—we two—you, me, talk on this page.
(I hear New York, too.) Me—who? 20
Well, I like to eat, sleep, drink, and be in love.
I like to work, read, learn, and understand life.
I like a pipe for a Christmas present,
or records—Bessie, bop, or Bach.
I guess being colored doesn't make me *not* like 25
the same things other folks like who are other races.
So will my page be colored that I write?
Being me, it will not be white.
But it will be
a part of you, instructor. 30
You are white—
yet a part of me, as I am a part of you.
That's American.

Sometimes perhaps you don't want to be a part of me.
Nor do I often want to be a part of you. 35
But we are, that's true!
As I learn from you,
I guess you learn from me—
although you're older—and white—
and somewhat more free. 40

This is my page for English B.

URSULA K. LEGUIN

The Ones who Walk Away from Omelas

(VARIATIONS ON A THEME BY WILLIAM JAMES)

THE CENTRAL IDEA OF THIS psychomyth, the scapegoat, turns up in Dostoyevsky's Brothers Karamazov, *and several people have asked me, rather suspiciously, why I gave the credit to William James. The fact is, I haven't been able to re-read Dostoyevsky, much as I loved him, since I was twenty-five, and I'd simply forgotten he used the idea. But when I met it in James's "The Moral Philosopher and the Moral Life," it was with a shock of recognition. Here is how James puts it:*

> *Or if the hypothesis were offered us of a world in which Messrs. Fourier's and Bellamy's and Morris's Utopias should all be outdone, and millions kept permanently happy on the one simple condition that a certain lost soul on the far-off edge of things should lead a life of lonely torment, what except a specifical and independent sort of emotion can it be which would make us immediately feel, even though an impulse arose within us to clutch at the happiness so offered, how hideous a thing would be its enjoyment when deliberately accepted as the fruit of such a bargain?*

The dilemma of the American conscience can hardly be better stated. Dostoyevsky was a great artist, and a radical one, but his early social radicalism reversed itself, leaving him a violent reactionary. Whereas the American James, who seems so mild, so naively gentlemanly—look how he says "us," assuming all his readers are as decent as himself!—was, and remained, and remains, a genuinely radical thinker. Directly after the "lost soul" passage he goes on,

All the higher, more penetrating ideals are revolutionary. They present themselves far less in the guise of effects of past experience than in that of probable causes of future experience, factors to which the environment and the lessons it has so far taught us must learn to bend.

5

The application of those two sentences to this story, and to science fiction, and to all thinking about the future, is quite direct. Ideals as "the probable causes of future experience"—that is a subtle and an exhilarating remark!

Of course I didn't read James and sit down and say, Now I'll write a story about that "lost soul." It seldom works that simply. I sat down and started a story, just because I felt like it, with nothing but the word "Omelas" in mind. It came from a road sign: Salem (Oregon) backwards. Don't you read road signs backwards? POTS. WOLS nerdlihc. Ocsicnarf Nas . . . Salem equals schelomo equals salaam equals Peace. Melas. O melas. Omelas. Homme hélas. "Where do *you get your ideas from, Ms Le Guin?" From forgetting Dostoyevsky and reading road signs backwards, naturally. Where else?*

With a clamor of bells that set the swallows soaring, the Festival of Summer came to the city Omelas, bright-towered by the sea. The rigging of the boats in harbor sparkled with flags. In the streets between houses with red roofs and painted walls, between old moss-grown gardens and under avenues of trees, past great parks and public buildings, processions moved. Some were decorous: old people in long stiff robes of mauve and grey, grave master workmen, quiet, merry women carrying their babies and chatting as they walked. In other streets the music beat faster, a shimmering of gong and tambourine, and the people went dancing, the procession was a dance. Children dodged in and out, their high calls rising like the swallows' crossing flights over the music and the singing. All the processions wound towards the north side of the city, where on the great water-meadow called the Green Fields boys and girls, naked in the bright air, with mud-stained feet and ankles and long, lithe arms, exercised their restive horses before the race. The horses wore no gear at all but a halter without bit. Their manes were braided with streamers of silver, gold, and green. They flared their nostrils and pranced and boasted to one another; they were vastly excited, the horse being the only animal who has adopted our ceremonies as his own. Far off to the north and west the mountains stood up half encircling Omelas on her bay. The air of morning was so clear that the snow still crowning the Eighteen Peaks burned with white-gold fire across the miles of sunlit air, under the dark blue of the sky. There was just enough wind to make the banners that marked the racecourse snap and flutter now and then. In the silence of the broad green meadows one could hear the music winding through the city streets, farther and nearer and ever approaching, a cheerful faint sweetness of the air that from time to time trembled and gathered together and broke out into the great joyous clanging of the bells.

Joyous! How is one to tell about joy? How describe the citizens of Omelas?

They were not simple folk, you see, though they were happy. But we do not say the words of cheer much any more. All smiles have become archaic. Given a description such as this one tends to make certain assumptions. Given a description such as this one tends to look next for the King, mounted on a splendid stallion and surrounded by his noble knights, or perhaps in a golden litter borne by great-muscled slaves. But there was no king. They did not use swords, or keep slaves. They were not barbarians. I do not know the rules and laws of their society, but I suspect that they were singularly few. As they did without monarchy and slavery, so they also got on without the stock exchange, the advertisement, the secret police, and the bomb. Yet I repeat that these were not simple folk, not dulcet shepherds, noble savages, bland utopians. They were not less complex than us. The trouble is that we have a bad habit, encouraged by pedants and sophisticates, of considering happiness as something rather stupid. Only pain is intellectual, only evil interesting. This is the treason of the artist: a refusal to admit the banality of evil and the terrible boredom of pain. If you can't lick 'em, join 'em. If it hurts, repeat it. But to praise despair is to condemn delight, to embrace violence is to lose hold of everything else. We have almost lost hold; we can no longer describe a happy man, nor make any celebration of joy. How can I tell you about the people of Omelas? They were not naïve and happy children—though their children were, in fact, happy. They were mature, intelligent, passionate adults whose lives were not wretched. O miracle! but I wish I could describe it better. I wish I could convince you. Omelas sounds in my words like a city in a fairy tale, long ago and far away, once upon a time. Perhaps it would be best if you imagined it as your own fancy bids, assuming it will rise to the occasion, for certainly I cannot suit you all. For instance, how about technology? I think that there would be no cars or helicopters in and above the streets; this follows from the fact that the people of Omelas are happy people. Happiness is based on a just discrimination of what is necessary, what is neither necessary nor destructive, and what is destructive. In the middle category, however—that of the unnecessary but undestructive, that of comfort, luxury, exuberance, etc.—they could perfectly well have central heating, subway trains, washing machines, and all kinds of marvelous devices not yet invented here, floating light-sources, fuelless power, a cure for the common cold. Or they could have none of that: it doesn't matter. As you like it. I incline to think that people from towns up and down the coast have been coming in to Omelas during the last days before the Festival on very fast little trains and double-decked trams, and that the train station of Omelas is actually the handsomest building in town, though plainer than the magnificent Farmers' Market. But even granted trains, I fear that Omelas so far strikes some of you as goody-goody. Smiles, bells, parades, horses, bleh. If so, please add an orgy. If an orgy would help, don't hesitate. Let us not, however, have temples from which issue beautiful nude priests and priestesses already half in ecstasy and ready to copulate with any man or woman, lover or stranger, who desires union with the deep godhead of the blood, although that was my first idea. But really it would be better not to have any temples in Omelas—at least, not manned temples. Religion yes, clergy no. Surely the beautiful nudes can just wander about, offering themselves like divine soufflés to the hunger of the needy and the rapture of the flesh. Let them join the processions. Let tambourines be struck above the copulations, and the glory of desire be proclaimed upon the gongs, and (a not unimportant point) let the offspring of these delightful rituals be beloved and looked after by all. One thing I know there is none of in Omelas is guilt. But what else should there be? I thought at first there were no drugs, but that is puritanical. For those who like it, the faint insistent sweetness of *drooz* may perfume the ways of the city, *drooz* which first brings a great lightness and brilliance to the mind and limbs, and then after some hours a dreamy languor, and wonderful visions at last of the very arcana and inmost secrets of the Universe, as well as exciting the pleasure of sex beyond all belief; and it is not habit-forming. For more modest tastes I think there ought to be beer. What else, what else belongs in the joyous city? The sense of victory, surely, the celebration of courage. But as we did without clergy, let us do without soldiers. The joy built upon successful slaughter is not the right kind of joy; it will not do; it is fearful and it is trivial. A boundless and generous contentment, a magnanimous triumph felt not against some outer enemy but in communion with the finest and fairest in the souls of all men everywhere and the splendor of the world's summer: this is what swells the hearts of the people of Omelas, and the victory they celebrate is that of life. I really don't think many of them need to take *drooz.*

Most of the processions have reached the Green Fields by now. A marvelous smell of cooking goes forth from the red and blue tents of the provisioners. The faces of small children are amiably sticky; in the benign grey beard of a man a couple of crumbs of rich pastry are entangled. The youths and girls have mounted their horses and are beginning to group around the starting line of the course. An old woman, small, fat, and laughing, is passing out flowers from a basket, and tall young men wear her flowers in their shining hair. A child of nine or ten sits at the edge of the crowd, alone, playing on a wooden flute. People pause to listen, and they smile, but they do not speak to him, for he never ceases playing and never sees them, his dark eyes wholly rapt in the sweet, thin magic of the tune.

He finishes, and slowly lowers his hands holding the wooden flute.

As if that little private silence were the signal, all at once a trumpet sounds from the pavilion near the starting line: imperious, melancholy, piercing. The horses rear on their slender legs, and some of them neigh in answer. Sober-faced, the young riders stroke the horses' necks and soothe them, whispering, "Quiet, quiet, there my beauty, my hope. . . ." They begin to form in rank along the starting line. The crowds along the racecourse are like a field of grass and flowers in the wind. The Festival of Summer has begun.

Do you believe? Do you accept the festival, the city, the joy? No? Then let me describe one more thing.

In a basement under one of the beautiful public buildings of Omelas, or perhaps in the cellar of one of its spacious private homes, there is a room. It has one locked door, and no window. A little light seeps in dustily between cracks in the boards, secondhand from a cobwebbed window somewhere across the cellar. In one corner of the little room a couple of mops, with stiff, clotted, foul-smelling heads, stand near a rusty bucket. The floor is dirt, a little damp to the touch, as cellar dirt usually is. The room is about three paces long and two wide: a mere broom closet or disused tool room. In the room a child is sitting. It could be a boy or a girl. It looks about six, but actually is nearly ten. It is feeble-minded. Perhaps it was born defective, or perhaps it has become imbecile through fear, malnutrition, and neglect. It picks its nose and occasionally fumbles vaguely with its toes or genitals, as it sits bunched in the corner farthest from the bucket and the two mops. It is afraid of the mops. It finds them horrible. It shuts its eyes, but it knows the mops are still standing there; and the door is locked; and nobody will come. The door is always locked; and nobody ever comes, except that sometimes—the child has no understanding of time or interval—sometimes the door rattles terribly and opens, and a person, or several people, are there. One of them may come in and kick the child to make it stand up. The others never come close, but peer in at it with frightened, disgusted eyes. The food bowl and the water jug are hastily filled, the door is locked, the eyes disappear. The people at the door never say anything, but the child, who has not always lived in the tool room, and can remember sunlight and its mother's voice, sometimes speaks. "I will be good," it says. "Please let me out. I will be good!" They never answer. The child used to scream for help at night, and cry a good deal, but now it only makes a kind of whining, "eh-haa, eh-haa," and it speaks less and less often. It is so thin there are no calves to its legs; its belly protrudes; it lives on a half-bowl of corn meal and grease a day. It is naked. Its buttocks and thighs are a mass of festered sores, as it sits in its own excrement continually.

They all know it is there, all the people of Omelas. Some of them have come to see it, others are content merely to know it is there. They all know that it has to be there. Some of them understand why, and some do not, but they all understand that their happiness, the beauty of their city, the tenderness of their friendships, the health of their children, the wisdom of their scholars, the skill of their makers, even the abundance of their harvest and the kindly weathers of their skies, depend wholly on this child's abominable misery.

This is usually explained to children when they are between eight and twelve, whenever they seem capable of understanding; and most of those who come to see the child are young people, though often enough an adult comes, or comes back, to see the child. No matter how well the matter has been explained to them, these young spectators are always shocked and sickened at the sight. They feel disgust, which they had thought themselves superior to. They feel anger, outrage, impotence, despite all the explanations. They would like to do something for the child. But there is nothing they can do. If the child were brought up into the sunlight out of that vile place, if it were cleaned and fed and comforted, that would be a good thing, indeed; but if it were done, in that day and hour all the prosperity and beauty and delight of Omelas would wither and be destroyed. Those are the terms. To exchange all the goodness and grace of every life in Omelas for that single, small improvement: to throw away the happiness of thousands for the chance of the happiness of one: that would be to let guilt within the walls indeed.

The terms are strict and absolute; there may not even be a kind word spoken to the child.

Often the young people go home in tears, or in a tearless rage, when they have seen the child and faced this terrible paradox. They may brood over it for weeks or years. But as time goes on they begin to realize that even if the child could be released, it would not get much good of its freedom: a little vague pleasure of warmth and food, no doubt, but little more. It is too degraded and imbecile to know any real joy. It has been afraid too long ever to be free of fear. Its habits are too uncouth for it to respond to humane treatment. Indeed, after so long it would probably be wretched without walls about it to protect it, and darkness for its eyes, and its own excrement to sit in. Their tears at the bitter injustice dry when they begin to perceive the terrible justice of reality, and to accept it. Yet it is their tears and anger, the trying of their generosity and the acceptance of their helplessness, which are perhaps the true source of the splendor of their lives. Theirs is no vapid, irresponsible happiness. They know that they, like the child, are not free. They know compassion. It is the existence of the child, and their knowledge of its existence, that makes possible the nobility of their architecture, the poignancy of their music, the profundity of their science. It is because of the child that they are so gentle with children. They know that if the wretched one were not there snivelling in the dark, the other one, the flute-player, could make no joyful music as the young riders line up in their beauty for the race in the sunlight of the first morning of summer.

Now do you believe in them? Are they not more credible? But there is one more thing to tell, and this is quite incredible. 20

At times one of the adolescent girls or boys who go to see the child does not go home to weep or rage, does not, in fact, go home at all. Sometimes also a man or woman much older falls silent for a day or two, and then leaves home. These people go out into the street, and walk down the street alone. They keep walking, and walk straight out of the city of Omelas, through the beautiful gates. They keep walking across the farmlands of Omelas. Each one goes alone, youth or girl, man or woman. Night falls; the traveler must pass down village streets, between the houses with yellow-lit windows, and on out into the darkness of the fields. Each alone, they go west or north, towards the mountains. They go on. They leave Omelas, they walk ahead into the darkness, and they do not come back. The place they go towards is a place even less imaginable to most of us than the city of happiness. I cannot describe it at all. It is possible that it does not exist. But they seem to know where they are going, the ones who walk away from Omelas.

FLANNERY O'CONNOR { *A Good Man Is Hard to Find*

Flannery O'Connor (1925–1964), novelist, short-story writer, and essayist, was born in Savannah, Georgia. She graduated from Georgia State College for Women in 1945 and earned an MFA from the Iowa Writers' Workshop in 1947. O'Connor, whose Catholicism figures prominently in her work, is considered a "Southern Gothic" writer; the genre is defined by disturbing and often grotesque incidents set in the southern United States. O'Connor wrote two novels—Wise Blood (1952) and The Violent Bear It Away (1960)—and six collections of stories, essays, and letters. Her Complete Short Stories, published posthumously in 1971, won the National Book Award.

The following is the title story from *A Good Man Is Hard to Find and Other Stories* (1955). It depicts a family's ill-fated vacation: a wrong turn, a road accident, a confrontation with three escaped convicts. Both humorous and horrifying, the story explores themes of good and evil, religious hypocrisy, and grace. As you read, notice the foreshadowing, the many instances of irony, and the detached narrative tone. Pay attention to the details that O'Connor uses to craft the personalities of each character.

THE GRANDMOTHER DIDN'T WANT TO go to Florida. She wanted to visit some of her connections in east Tennessee and she was seizing every chance to change Bailey's mind. Bailey was the son she lived with, her only boy. He was sitting on the edge of his chair at the table, bent over the orange sports section of the *Journal.* "Now look here, Bailey," she said, "see here, read this," and she stood with one hand on her thin hip and the other rattling the newspaper at his bald head. "Here this fellow that calls himself The Misfit is aloose from the Federal Pen and headed toward Florida and you read here what it says he did to these people. Just you read it. I wouldn't take my children in any direction with a criminal like that aloose in it. I couldn't answer to my conscience if I did."

Bailey didn't look up from his reading so she wheeled around then and faced the children's mother; a young woman in slacks, whose face was as broad and innocent as a cabbage and was tied around with a green headkerchief that had two points on the top like rabbit's ears. She was sitting on the sofa, feeding the baby his apricots out of a jar. "The children have been to Florida before," the old lady said. "You all ought to take them somewhere else for a change so they would see different parts of the world and be broad. They never have been to east Tennessee."

The children's mother didn't seem to hear her, but the eight-year-old boy, John Wesley, a stocky child with glasses, said, "If you don't want to go to Florida, why dontcha stay at home?" He and the little girl, June Star, were reading the funny papers on the floor.

"She wouldn't stay at home to be queen for a day," June Star said without raising her yellow head.

"Yes, and what would you do if this fellow, The Misfit, caught you?" the grandmother asked. 5

"I'd smack his face," John Wesley said.

"She wouldn't stay at home for a million bucks," June Star said. "Afraid she'd miss something. She has to go everywhere we go."

"All right, Miss," the grandmother said. "Just remember that the next time you want me to curl your hair."

June Star said her hair was naturally curly.

The next morning the grandmother was the first one in the car, ready to go. She had her big black valise that looked like the head of a hippopotamus in one corner, and underneath it she was hiding a basket with Pitty Sing,[1] the cat, in it. She didn't intend for the cat to be left 10

[1]The name of a character in Gilbert and Sullivan's comic opera *The Mikado* (1885).

alone in the house for three days because he would miss her too much and she was afraid he might brush against one of the gas burners and accidentally asphyxiate himself. Her son, Bailey, didn't like to arrive at a motel with a cat.

She sat in the middle of the back seat with John Wesley and June Star on either side of her. Bailey and the children's mother and the baby sat in the front and they left Atlanta at eight forty-five with the mileage on the car at 55890. The grandmother wrote this down because she thought it would be interesting to say how many miles they had been when they got back. It took them twenty minutes to reach the outskirts of the city.

The old lady settled herself comfortably, removing her white cotton gloves and putting them up with her purse on the shelf in front of the back window. The children's mother still had on slacks and still had her head tied up in a green kerchief, but the grandmother had on a navy blue straw sailor hat with a bunch of white violets on the brim and a navy blue dress with a small white dot in the print. Her collar and cuffs were white organdy trimmed with lace and at her neckline she had pinned a purple spray of cloth violets containing a sachet. In case of an accident, anyone seeing her dead on the highway would know at once that she was a lady.

She said she thought it was going to be a good day for driving, neither too hot nor too cold, and she cautioned Bailey that the speed limit was fifty-five miles an hour and that the patrolmen hid themselves behind billboards and small clumps of trees and sped out after you before you had a chance to slow down. She pointed out interesting details of the scenery: Stone Mountain;[2] the blue granite that in some places came up to both sides of the highway; the brilliant red clay banks slightly streaked with purple; and the various crops that made rows of green lace-work on the ground. The trees were full of silver-white sunlights and the meanest of them sparkled. The children were reading comic magazines and their mother had gone back to sleep.

[2]Memorial to the Confederate States of America near Atlanta, Georgia; it consists of large bas-relief images of generals Stonewall Jackson and Robert E. Lee, and Confederate President Jefferson Davis carved into an immense granite outcrop.

"Let's go through Georgia fast so we won't have to look at it much," John Wesley said.

"If I were a little boy," said the grandmother, "I wouldn't talk about my native state that way. Tennessee has the mountains and Georgia has the hills." 15

"Tennessee is just a hillbilly dumping ground," John Wesley said, "and Georgia is a lousy state too."

"You said it," June Star said.

"In my time," said the grandmother, folding her thin veined fingers, "children were more respectful of their native states and their parents and everything else. People did right then. Oh look at the cute little pickaninny!" she said and pointed to a Negro child standing in the door of a shack. "Wouldn't that make a picture, now?" she asked and they all turned and looked at the little Negro out of the back window. He waved.

"He didn't have any britches on," June Star said.

"He probably didn't have any," the grandmother explained. "Little niggers in the country don't have things like we do. If I could paint, I'd paint that picture," she said. 20

The children exchanged comic books.

The grandmother offered to hold the baby and the children's mother passed him over the front seat to her. She set him on her knee and bounced him and told him about the things they were passing. She rolled her eyes and screwed up her mouth and stuck her leathery thin face into his smooth bland one. Occasionally he gave her a faraway smile. They passed a large cotton field with five or six graves fenced in the middle of it, like a small island. "Look at the graveyard!" the grandmother said, pointing it out. "That was the old family burying ground. That belonged to the plantation."

"Where's the plantation?" John Wesley asked.

"Gone With the Wind,"[3] said the grandmother. "Ha. Ha."

When the children finished all the comic books they had brought, they opened the lunch and ate it. The grandmother ate a peanut but- 25

[3]Title of the best-selling 1936 novel by Margaret Mitchell about the Civil War and the passing of the old South, made into one of the most successful films of all time.

ter sandwich and an olive and would not let the children throw the box and the paper napkins out the window. When there was nothing else to do they played a game by choosing a cloud and making the other two guess what shape it suggested. John Wesley took one the shape of a cow and June Star guessed a cow and John Wesley said, no, an automobile, and June Star said he didn't play fair, and they began to slap each other over the grandmother.

The grandmother said she would tell them a story if they would keep quiet. When she told a story, she rolled her eyes and waved her head and was very dramatic. She said once when she was a maiden lady she had been courted by a Mr. Edgar Atkins Teagarden from Jasper, Georgia. She said he was a very good-looking man and a gentleman and that he brought her a watermelon every Saturday afternoon with his initials cut in it, E.A.T. Well, one Saturday, she said, Mr. Teagarden brought the watermelon and there was nobody at home and he left it on the front porch and returned in his buggy to Jasper, but she never got the watermelon, she said, because a nigger boy ate it when he saw the initials, E.A.T.! This story tickled John Wesley's funny bone and he giggled and giggled but June Star didn't think it was any good. She said she wouldn't marry a man that just brought her a watermelon on Saturday. The grandmother said she would have done well to marry Mr. Teagarden because he was a gentleman and had bought Coca-Cola stock when it first came out and that he had died only a few years ago, a very wealthy man.

They stopped at The Tower for barbecued sandwiches. The Tower was a part-stucco and part-wood filling station and dance hall set in a clearing outside of Timothy. A fat man named Red Sammy Butts ran it and there were signs stuck here and there on the building and for miles up and down the highway saying, TRY RED SAMMY'S FAMOUS BARBECUE. NONE LIKE FAMOUS RED SAMMY'S! RED SAM! THE FAT BOY WITH THE HAPPY LAUGH. A VETERAN! RED SAMMY'S YOUR MAN!

Red Sammy was lying on the bare ground outside The Tower with his head under a truck while a gray monkey about a foot high, chained to a small chinaberry tree, chattered nearby. The monkey sprang back into the tree and got on the highest limb as soon as he saw the children jump out of the car and run toward him.

Inside, The Tower was a long dark room with a counter at one end and tables at the other and dancing space in the middle. They all sat down at a broad table next to the nickelodeon[4] and Red Sam's wife, a tall burnt-brown woman with hair and eyes lighter than her skin, came and took their order. The children's mother put a dime in the machine and played "The Tennessee Waltz," and the grandmother said that tune always made her want to dance. She asked Bailey if he would like to dance but he only glared at her. He didn't have a naturally sunny disposition like she did and trips made him nervous. The grandmother's brown eyes were very bright. She swayed her head from side to side and pretended she was dancing in her chair. June Star said play something she could tap to so the children's mother put in another dime and played a fast number and June Star stepped out onto the dance floor and did her tap routine.

"Ain't she cute?" Red Sam's wife said, leaning over the counter. "Would you like to come be my little girl?" 30

"No, I certainly wouldn't," June Star said. "I wouldn't live in a broken-down place like this for a million bucks!" and she ran back to the table.

"Ain't she cute?" the woman repeated, stretching her mouth politely.

"Aren't you ashamed?" hissed the grandmother.

Red Sam came in and told his wife to quit lounging on the counter and hurry up with these people's order. His khaki trousers reached just to his hip bones and his stomach hung over them like a sack of meal swaying under his shirt. He came over and sat down at a table nearby and let out a combination sigh and yodel. "You can't win," he said. "You can't win," and he wiped his sweating red face off with a gray handkerchief. "These days you don't know who to trust," he said. "Ain't that the truth?"

"People are certainly not nice like they used to be," said the grandmother. 35

"Two fellers come in here last week," Red Sammy said, "driving a Chrysler. It was an old beat-up car but it was a good one and these boys looked all right to me. Said they worked at the mill and you know I let them fellers charge the gas they bought? Now why did I do that?"

"Because you're a good man!" the grandmother said at once.

[4]Jukebox.

"Yes'm, I suppose so," Red Sam said as if he were struck with this answer.

His wife brought the orders, carrying the five plates all at once without a tray, two in each hand and one balanced on her arm. "It isn't a soul in this green world of God's that you can trust," she said. "And I don't count nobody out of that, not nobody," she repeated, looking at Red Sammy.

"Did you read about that criminal, The Misfit, that's escaped?" asked the grandmother. 40

"I wouldn't be a bit surprised if he didn't attack this place right here," said the woman. "If he hears about it being here, I wouldn't be none surprised to see him. If he hears it's two cent in the cash register, I wouldn't be a tall surprised if he . . ."

"That'll do," Red Sam said. "Go bring these people their Co'-Colas," and the woman went off to get the rest of the order.

"A good man is hard to find," Red Sammy said. "Everything is getting terrible. I remember the day you could go off and leave your screen door unlatched. Not no more."

He and the grandmother discussed better times. The old lady said that in her opinion Europe was entirely to blame for the way things were now. She said the way Europe acted you would think we were made of money and Red Sam said it was no use talking about it, she was exactly right. The children ran outside into the white sunlight and looked at the monkey in the lacy chinaberry tree. He was busy catching fleas on himself and biting each one carefully between his teeth as if it were a delicacy.

They drove off again into the hot afternoon. The grandmother took cat naps and woke up every few minutes with her own snoring. Outside of Toombsboro she woke up and recalled an old plantation that she had visited in this neighborhood once when she was a young lady. She said the house had six white columns across the front and that there was an avenue of oaks leading up to it and two little wooden trellis arbors on either side in front where you sat down with your suitor after a stroll in the garden. She recalled exactly which road to turn off to get to it. She knew that Bailey would not be willing to lose any time looking at an old house, but the more she talked about it, the 45 more she wanted to see it once again and find out if the little twin arbors were still standing. "There was a secret panel in this house," she said craftily, not telling the truth but wishing that she were, "and the story went that all the family silver was hidden in it when Sherman[5] came through but it was never found . . ."

"Hey!" John Wesley said. "Let's go see it! We'll find it! We'll poke all the woodwork and find it! Who lives there? Where do you turn off at? Hey Pop, can't we turn off there?"

"We never have seen a house with a secret panel!" June Star shrieked. "Let's go to the house with the secret panel! Hey, Pop, can't we go see the house with the secret panel!"

"It's not far from here, I know," the grandmother said. "It wouldn't take over twenty minutes."

Bailey was looking straight ahead. His jaw was as rigid as a horseshoe. "No," he said.

50 The children began to yell and scream that they wanted to see the house with the secret panel. John Wesley kicked the back of the front seat and June Star hung over her mother's shoulder and whined desperately into her ear that they never had any fun even on their vacation, that they could never do what THEY wanted to do. The baby began to scream and John Wesley kicked the back of the seat so hard that his father could feel the blows in his kidney.

"All right!" he shouted and drew the car to a stop at the side of the road. "Will you all shut up? Will you all just shut up for one second? If you don't shut up, we won't go anywhere."

"It would be very educational for them," the grandmother murmured.

"All right," Bailey said, "but get this. This is the only time we're going to stop for anything like this. This is the one and only time."

"The dirt road that you have to turn down is about a mile back," the grandmother directed. "I marked it when we passed."

55 "A dirt road," Bailey groaned.

After they had turned around and were headed toward the dirt road,

[5]In 1864 the Union army led by General William Tecumseh Sherman marched from Atlanta to Savannah, destroying civilian farms and houses along the way.

the grandmother recalled other points about the house, the beautiful glass over the front doorway and the candle lamp in the hall. John Wesley said that the secret panel was probably in the fireplace.

"You can't go inside this house," Bailey said. "You don't know who lives there."

"While you all talk to the people in front, I'll run around behind and get in a window," John Wesley suggested.

"We'll all stay in the car," his mother said.

They turned onto the dirt road and the car raced roughly along in a swirl of pink dust. The grandmother recalled the times when there were no paved roads and thirty miles was a day's journey. The dirt road was hilly and there were sudden washes in it and sharp curves on dangerous embankments. All at once they would be on a hill, looking down over the blue tops of trees for miles around, then the next minute, they would be in a red depression with the dust-coated trees looking down on them. 60

"This place had better turn up in a minute," Bailey said, "or I'm going to turn around."

The road looked as if no one had traveled on it in months.

"It's not much farther," the grandmother said and just as she said it, a horrible thought came to her. The thought was so embarrassing that she turned red in the face and her eyes dilated and her feet jumped up, upsetting her valise in the corner. The instant the valise moved, the newspaper top she had over the basket under it rose with a snarl and Pitty Sing, the cat, sprang onto Bailey's shoulder.

The children were thrown to the floor and their mother, clutching the baby, was thrown out the door onto the ground; the old lady was thrown into the front seat. The car turned over once and landed right-side-up in a gulch on the side of the road. Bailey remained in the driver's seat with the cat—gray-striped with a broad white face and an orange nose—clinging to his neck like a caterpillar.

As soon as the children saw they could move their arms and legs, they scrambled out of the car, shouting, "We've had an ACCIDENT!" The grandmother was curled up under the dashboard, hoping she was injured so that Bailey's wrath would not come down on her all at 65 once. The horrible thought she had had before the accident was that the house she had remembered so vividly was not in Georgia but in Tennessee.

Bailey removed the cat from his neck with both hands and flung it out the window against the side of a pine tree. Then he got out of the car and started looking for the children's mother. She was sitting against the side of the red gutted ditch, holding the screaming baby, but she only had a cut down her face and a broken shoulder. "We've had an ACCIDENT!" the children screamed in a frenzy of delight.

"But nobody's killed," June Star said with disappointment as the grandmother limped out of the car, her hat still pinned to her head but the broken front brim standing up at a jaunty angle and the violet spray hanging off the side. They all sat down in the ditch, except the children, to recover from the shock. They were all shaking.

"Maybe a car will come along," said the children's mother hoarsely.

"I believe I have injured an organ," said the grandmother, pressing her side, but no one answered her. Bailey's teeth were clattering. He had on a yellow sport shirt with bright blue parrots designed in it and his face was as yellow as the shirt. The grandmother decided that she would not mention that the house was in Tennessee.

70 The road was about ten feet above and they could see only the tops of the trees on the other side of it. Behind the ditch they were sitting in there were more woods, tall and dark and deep. In a few minutes they saw a car some distance away on top of a hill, coming slowly as if the occupants were watching them. The grandmother stood up and waved both arms dramatically to attract their attention. The car continued to come on slowly, disappeared around a bend and appeared again, moving even slower, on top of the hill they had gone over. It was a big black battered hearselike automobile. There were three men in it.

It came to a stop over them and for some minutes, the driver looked down with a steady expressionless gaze to where they were sitting, and didn't speak. Then he turned his head and muttered something to the other two and they got out. One was a fat boy in black trousers and a red sweat shirt with a silver stallion embossed on the front of it. He moved around on the right side of them and stood staring, his mouth partly open in a kind of loose grin. The other had on khaki pants and a blue striped coat and a gray hat pulled down very low, hiding most of his face. He came around slowly on the left side. Neither spoke.

The driver got out of the car and stood by the side of it, looking down at them. He was an older man than the other two. His hair was just beginning to gray and he wore silver-rimmed spectacles that gave him a scholarly look. He had a long creased face and didn't have on any shirt or undershirt. He had on blue jeans that were too tight for him and was holding a black hat and a gun. The two boys also had guns.

"We've had an ACCIDENT!" the children screamed.

The grandmother had the peculiar feeling that the bespectacled man was someone she knew. His face was as familiar to her as if she had known him all her life but she could not recall who he was. He moved away from the car and began to come down the embankment, placing his feet carefully so that he wouldn't slip. He had on tan and white shoes and no socks, and his ankles were red and thin. "Good afternoon," he said. "I see you all had you a little spill."

"We turned over twice!" said the grandmother. 75

"Oncet," he corrected. "We seen it happen. Try their car and see will it run, Hiram," he said quietly to the boy with the gray hat.

"What you got that gun for?" John Wesley asked. "Whatcha gonna do with that gun?"

"Lady," the man said to the children's mother, "would you mind calling them children to sit down by you? Children make me nervous. I want all you all to sit down right together there where you're at."

"What are you telling us what to do for?" June Star asked.

Behind them the line of woods gaped like a dark open mouth. 80 "Come here," said their mother.

"Look here now," Bailey began suddenly, "we're in a predicament! We're in . . ."

The grandmother shrieked. She scrambled to her feet and stood staring.

"You're The Misfit!" she said. "I recognized you at once!"

"Yes'm," the man said, smiling slightly as if he were pleased in spite of himself to be known, "but it would have been better for all of you, lady, if you hadn't of reckernized me."

Bailey turned his head sharply and said something to his mother 85 that shocked even the children. The old lady began to cry and The Misfit reddened.

"Lady," he said, "don't you get upset. Sometimes a man says things he don't mean. I don't reckon he meant to talk to you thataway."

"You wouldn't shoot a lady, would you?" the grandmother said and removed a clean handkerchief from her cuff and began to slap at her eyes with it.

The Misfit pointed the toe of his shoe into the ground and made a little hole and then covered it up again. "I would hate to have to," he said.

"Listen," the grandmother almost screamed, "I know you're a good man. You don't look a bit like you have common blood. I know you must come from nice people!"

"Yes mam," he said, "finest people in the world." When he smiled he showed a row of strong white teeth. "God never made a finer woman than my mother and my daddy's heart was pure gold," he said. The boy with the red sweat shirt had come around behind them and was standing with his gun at his hip. The Misfit squatted down on the ground. "Watch them children, Bobby Lee," he said. "You know they make me nervous." He looked at the six of them huddled together in front of him and he seemed to be embarrassed as if he couldn't think of anything to say. "Ain't a cloud in the sky," he remarked, looking up at it. "Don't see no sun but don't see no cloud neither." 90

"Yes, it's a beautiful day," said the grandmother. "Listen," she said, "you shouldn't call yourself The Misfit because I know you're a good man at heart. I can just look at you and tell."

"Hush!" Bailey yelled. "Hush! Everybody shut up and let me handle this!" He was squatting in the position of a runner about to spring forward but he didn't move.

"I pre-chate that, lady," The Misfit said and drew a little circle in the ground with the butt of his gun.

"It'll take a half a hour to fix this here car," Hiram called, looking over the raised hood of it.

"Well, first you and Bobby Lee get him and that little boy to step over yonder with you," The Misfit said, pointing to Bailey and John Wesley. "The boys want to ask you something," he said to Bailey. "Would you mind stepping back in them woods there with them?" 95

"Listen," Bailey began, "we're in a terrible predicament! Nobody realizes what this is," and his voice cracked. His eyes were as blue and intense as the parrots in his shirt and he remained perfectly still.

The grandmother reached up to adjust her hat brim as if she were going to the woods with him but it came off in her hand. She stood staring at it and after a second she let it fall on the ground. Hiram pulled Bailey up by the arm as if he were assisting an old man. John Wesley caught hold of his father's hand and Bobby Lee followed. They went off toward the woods and just as they reached the dark edge, Bailey turned and supporting himself against a gray naked pine trunk, he shouted, "I'll be back in a minute, Mamma, wait on me!"

"Come back this instant!" his mother shrilled but they all disappeared into the woods.

"Bailey Boy!" the grandmother called in a tragic voice but she found she was looking at The Misfit squatting on the ground in front of her. "I just know you're a good man," she said desperately. "You're not a bit common!"

"Nome, I ain't a good man," The Misfit said after a second as if he had considered her statement carefully, "but I ain't the worst in the world neither. My daddy said I was a different breed of dog from my brothers and sisters. 'You know,' Daddy said, 'it's some that can live their whole life out without asking about it and it's others has to know why it is, and this boy is one of the latters. He's going to be into everything!'" He put on his black hat and looked up suddenly and then away deep into the woods as if he were embarrassed again. "I'm sorry I don't have on a shirt before you ladies," he said, hunching his shoulders slightly. "We buried our clothes that we had on when we escaped and we're just making do until we can get better. We borrowed these from some folks we met," he explained. 100

"That's perfectly all right," the grandmother said. "Maybe Bailey has an extra shirt in his suitcase."

"I'll look and see terrectly," The Misfit said.

"Where are they taking him?" the children's mother screamed.

"Daddy was a card himself," The Misfit said. "You couldn't put anything over on him. He never got in trouble with the Authorities though. Just had the knack of handling them."

"You could be honest too if you'd only try," said the grandmother. "Think how wonderful it would be to settle down and live a comfortable life and not have to think about somebody chasing you all the time." 105

The Misfit kept scratching in the ground with the butt of his gun as if he were thinking about it. "Yes'm, somebody is always after you," he murmured.

The grandmother noticed how thin his shoulder blades were just behind his hat because she was standing up looking down on him. "Do you ever pray?" she asked.

He shook his head. All she saw was the black hat wiggle between his shoulder blades. "Nome," he said.

There was a pistol shot from the woods, followed closely by another. Then silence. The old lady's head jerked around. She could hear the wind move through the tree tops like a long satisfied insuck of breath. "Bailey Boy!" she called.

"I was a gospel singer for a while," The Misfit said. "I been most everything. Been in the arm service, both land and sea, at home and abroad, been twict married, been an undertaker, been with the railroads, plowed Mother Earth, been in a tornado, seen a man burnt alive oncet," and he looked up at the children's mother and the little girl who were sitting close together, their faces white and their eyes glassy; "I even seen a woman flogged," he said. 110

"Pray, pray," the grandmother began, "pray, pray . . ."

"I never was a bad boy that I remember of," The Misfit said in an almost dreamy voice, "but somewheres along the line I done something wrong and got sent to the penitentiary. I was buried alive," and he looked up and held her attention to him by a steady stare.

"That's when you should have started to pray," she said. "What did you do to get sent to the penitentiary that first time?"

"Turn to the right, it was a wall," The Misfit said, looking up again at the cloudless sky. "Turn to the left, it was a wall. Look up it was a ceiling, look down it was a floor. I forget what I done, lady. I set there and set there, trying to remember what it was I done and I ain't recalled it to this day. Oncet in a while, I would think it was coming to me, but it never come."

"Maybe they put you in by mistake," the old lady said vaguely. 115

"Nome," he said. "It wasn't no mistake. They had the papers on me."

"You must have stolen something," she said.

The Misfit sneered slightly. "Nobody had nothing I wanted," he said. "It was a head-doctor at the penitentiary said what I had done was kill my daddy but I known that for a lie. My daddy died in nineteen ought nineteen of the epidemic flu[6] and I never had a thing to do with it. He was buried in the Mount Hopewell Baptist churchyard and you can go there and see for yourself."

"If you would pray," the old lady said, "Jesus would help you."

"That's right," The Misfit said. 120

"Well then, why don't you pray?" she asked trembling with delight suddenly.

"I don't want no hep," he said. "I'm doing all right by myself."

Bobby Lee and Hiram came ambling back from the woods. Bobby Lee was dragging a yellow shirt with bright blue parrots in it.

"Throw me that shirt, Bobby Lee," The Misfit said. The shirt came flying at him and landed on his shoulder and he put it on. The grandmother couldn't name what the shirt reminded her of. "No, lady," The Misfit said while he was buttoning up, "I found out the crime don't matter. You can do one thing or you can do another, kill a man or take a tire off his car, because sooner or later you're going to forget what it was you done and just be punished for it."

The children's mother had begun to make heaving noises as if she couldn't get her breath. "Lady," he asked, "would you and that little girl like to step off yonder with Bobby Lee and Hiram and join your husband?" 125

"Yes, thank you," the mother said faintly. Her left arm dangled helplessly and she was holding the baby, who had gone to sleep, in the other. "Hep that lady up, Hiram," The Misfit said as she struggled to climb out of the ditch, "and Bobby Lee, you hold onto that little girl's hand."

[6]The so-called "Spanish flu" spread through much of the world in 1918–19, killing millions.

"I don't want to hold hands with him," June Star said. "He reminds me of a pig."

The fat boy blushed and laughed and caught her by the arm and pulled her off into the woods after Hiram and her mother.

Alone with The Misfit, the grandmother found that she had lost her voice. There was not a cloud in the sky nor any sun. There was nothing around her but woods. She wanted to tell him that he must pray. She opened and closed her mouth several times before anything came out. Finally she found herself saying, "Jesus, Jesus," meaning, Jesus will help you, but the way she was saying it, it sounded as if she might be cursing.

"Yes'm," The Misfit said as if he agreed. "Jesus thrown everything off balance. It was the same case with Him as with me except He hadn't committed any crime and they could prove I had committed one because they had the papers on me. Of course," he said, "they never shown me my papers. That's why I sign myself now. I said long ago, you get you a signature and sign everything you do and keep a copy of it. Then you'll know what you done and you can hold up the crime to the punishment and see do they match and in the end you'll have something to prove you ain't been treated right. I call myself The Misfit," he said, "because I can't make what all I done wrong fit what all I gone through in punishment." 130

There was a piercing scream from the woods, followed closely by a pistol report. "Does it seem right to you, lady, that one is punished a heap and another ain't punished at all?"

"Jesus!" the old lady cried. "You've got good blood! I know you wouldn't shoot a lady! I know you come from nice people! Pray! Jesus, you ought not to shoot a lady. I'll give you all the money I've got!"

"Lady," The Misfit said, looking beyond her far into the woods, "there never was a body that give the undertaker a tip."

There were two more pistol reports and the grandmother raised her head like a parched old turkey hen crying for water and called, "Bailey Boy, Bailey Boy!" as if her heart would break.

"Jesus was the only One that ever raised the dead," The Misfit continued, "and He shouldn't have done it. He thrown everything off balance. If He did what He said, then it's nothing for you to do but throw 135 away everything and follow Him, and if He didn't then it's nothing for you to do but enjoy the few minutes you got left the best way you can—by killing somebody or burning down his house or doing some other meanness to him. No pleasure but meanness," he said and his voice had become almost a snarl.

"Maybe He didn't raise the dead," the old lady mumbled, not knowing what she was saying and feeling so dizzy that she sank down in the ditch with her legs twisted under her.

"I wasn't there so I can't say He didn't," The Misfit said, "I wisht I had of been there," he said, hitting the ground with his fist. "It ain't right I wasn't there because if I had of been there I would of known. Listen lady," he said in a high voice, "if I had of been there I would of known and I wouldn't be like I am now." His voice seemed about to crack and the grandmother's head cleared for an instant. She saw the man's face twisted close to her own as if he were going to cry and she murmured, "Why, you're one of my babies. You're one of my own children!" She reached out and touched him on the shoulder. The Misfit sprang back as if a snake had bitten him and shot her three times through the chest. Then he put his gun down on the ground and took off his glasses and began to clean them.

Hiram and Bobby Lee returned from the woods and stood over the ditch, looking down at the grandmother who half sat and half lay in a puddle of blood with her legs crossed under her like a child's and her face smiling up at the cloudless sky.

Without his glasses, The Misfit's eyes were red-rimmed and pale and defenseless-looking. "Take her off and throw her where you thrown the others," he said, picking up the cat that was rubbing itself against his leg.

"She was a talker, wasn't she?" Bobby Lee said, sliding down the ditch with a yodel. 140

"She would of been a good woman," The Misfit said, "if it had been somebody there to shoot her every minute of her life."

"Some fun!" Bobby Lee said.

"Shut up, Bobby Lee," The Misfit said. "It's no real pleasure in life."

DYLAN THOMAS — *Do Not Go Gentle into That Good Night*

DYLAN THOMAS (1914–1953) was born in Swansea, South Wales. His first collection, *18 Poems,* was published when Thomas was nineteen, and he was immediately heralded as an exciting new voice. In addition to writing poems, screenplays, and short stories, Thomas worked in radio and theater and even served as an anti-aircraft gunner in World War II. Between 1950 and 1953 he made three lecture tours of the United States, where large, appreciative audiences were drawn by his captivating voice, his dramatic persona, and his notoriously bohemian lifestyle. Reckless with money and with his health, Thomas was a profligate spender and heavy drinker; he died in New York City at age thirty-nine when he slipped into a coma after days of drinking. Thomas had just published his *Collected Poems: 1934–1953.*

"Do Not Go Gentle into That Good Night" is from *Poems of Dylan Thomas* (1952). The poem is a villanelle, a form that requires five tercets (three-line stanzas) followed by a quatrain and features an intricate pattern of repeating lines. As you read, follow Thomas's argument. Notice the examples the speaker uses to urge his father to fight rather than yield passively to death.

Do not go gentle into that good night,
Old age should burn and rave at close of day;
Rage, rage against the dying of the light.

Though wise men at their end know dark is right,
Because their words had forked no lightning they   5
Do not go gentle into that good night.

Good men, the last wave by, crying how bright
Their frail deeds might have danced in a green bay,
Rage, rage against the dying of the light.

Wild men who caught and sang the sun in flight, 10
And learn, too late, they grieved it on its way,
Do not go gentle into that good night.

Grave men, near death, who see with blinding sight
Blind eyes could blaze like meteors and be gay,
Rage, rage against the dying of the light. 15

And you, my father, there on the sad height,
Curse, bless, me now with your fierce tears, I pray.
Do not go gentle into that good night.
Rage, rage against the dying of the light.

ALICE WALKER { *Everyday Use*

ALICE WALKER (b. 1944), poet, novelist, and essayist, was born in Eatonton, Georgia, and earned her BA at Sarah Lawrence College in New York. Much of Walker's writing addresses civil rights issues, particularly the racism and sexism leveled at African-American women. She coined the now-common term "womanist" to describe the particular experiences of women of color. Walker's many novels include the Pulitzer Prize–winning *The Color Purple* (1982), *The Temple of My Familiar* (1989), and *Possessing the Secret of Joy* (1992); her books of nonfiction include *Living by the Word* (1988) and *We Are the Ones We Have Been Waiting For* (2006).

"Everyday Use" was first published in Walker's collection of short fiction *In Love and Trouble* (1973). The story explores the relationship between Mama and her two daughters, one educated and self-centered, the other simple and sweet natured, each with a distinct sense of ethnic heritage. Should family artifacts be showcased as works of art or should they be put to the "everyday use" for which they were intended? As you read, notice how physical details can function as symbols for larger, more abstract issues.

---

for your grandmamma

I WILL WAIT FOR HER in the yard that Maggie and I made so clean and wavy yesterday afternoon. A yard like this is more comfortable than most people know. It is not just a yard. It is like an extended living room. When the hard clay is swept clean as a floor and the fine sand around the edges lined with tiny, irregular grooves, anyone can come and sit and look up into the elm tree and wait for the breezes that never come inside the house.

Maggie will be nervous until after her sister goes: she will stand hopelessly in corners, homely and ashamed of the burn scars down her arms and legs, eying her sister with a mixture of envy and awe. She thinks her sister has held life always in the palm of one hand, that "no" is a word the world never learned to say to her.

You've no doubt seen those TV shows where the child who has "made it" is confronted, as a surprise, by her own mother and father, tottering in weakly from backstage. (A pleasant surprise, of course: What would they do if parent and child came on the show only to curse out and insult each other?) On TV mother and child embrace and smile into each other's faces. Sometimes the mother and father weep, the child wraps them in her arms and leans across the table to tell how she would not have made it without their help. I have seen these programs.

Sometimes I dream a dream in which Dee and I are suddenly brought together on a TV program of this sort. Out of a dark and soft-seated limousine I am ushered into a bright room filled with many people. There I meet a smiling, gray, sporty man like Johnny Carson[1] who shakes my hand and tells me what a fine girl I have. Then we are on the stage and Dee is embracing me with tears in her eyes. She pins on my dress a large orchid, even though she has told me once that she thinks orchids are tacky flowers.

5 In real life I am a large, big-boned woman with rough, man-working hands. In the winter I wear flannel nightgowns to bed and overalls during the day. I can kill and clean a hog as mercilessly as a man. My fat keeps me hot in zero weather. I can work outside all day, breaking ice to get water for washing; I can eat pork liver cooked over the open fire minutes after it comes steaming from the hog. One winter I knocked a bull calf straight in the brain between the eyes with a sledge hammer and had the meat hung up to chill before nightfall. But of course all this does not show on television. I am the way my daughter would want me

[1]American comedian (1925–2005), best known as host of *The Tonight Show* on television.

to be: a hundred pounds lighter, my skin like an uncooked barley pancake. My hair glistens in the hot bright lights. Johnny Carson has much to do to keep up with my quick and witty tongue.

But that is a mistake. I know even before I wake up. Who ever knew a Johnson with a quick tongue? Who can even imagine me looking a strange white man in the eye? It seems to me I have talked to them always with one foot raised in flight, with my head turned in whichever way is farthest from them. Dee, though. She would always look anyone in the eye. Hesitation was no part of her nature.

"How do I look, Mama?" Maggie says, showing just enough of her thin body enveloped in pink skirt and red blouse for me to know she's there, almost hidden by the door.

"Come out into the yard," I say.

Have you ever seen a lame animal, perhaps a dog run over by some careless person rich enough to own a car, sidle up to someone who is ignorant enough to be kind to them? That is the way my Maggie walks. She has been like this, chin on chest, eyes on ground, feet in shuffle, ever since the fire that burned the other house to the ground.

Dee is lighter than Maggie, with nicer hair and a fuller figure. She's a woman now, though sometimes I forget. How long ago was it that the other house burned? Ten, twelve years? Sometimes I can still hear the flames and feel Maggie's arms sticking to me, her hair smoking and her dress falling off her in little black papery flakes. Her eyes seemed stretched open, blazed open by the flames reflected in them. And Dee. I see her standing off under the sweet gum tree she used to dig gum out of; a look of concentration on her face as she watched the last dingy gray board of the house fall in toward the red-hot brick chimney. Why don't you do a dance around the ashes? I'd wanted to ask her. She had hated the house that much. 10

I used to think she hated Maggie, too. But that was before we raised the money, the church and me, to send her to Augusta to school. She used to read to us without pity; forcing words, lies, other folks' habits, whole lives upon us two, sitting trapped and ignorant underneath her voice. She washed us in a river of make-believe, burned us with a lot of knowledge we didn't necessarily need to know. Pressed us to her with the serious way she read, to shove us away at just the moment, like dimwits, we seemed about to understand.

Dee wanted nice things. A yellow organdy dress to wear to her graduation from high school; black pumps to match a green suit she'd made from an old suit somebody gave me. She was determined to stare down any disaster in her efforts. Her eyelids would not flicker for minutes at a time. Often I fought off the temptation to shake her. At sixteen she had a style of her own: and knew what style was.

I never had an education myself. After second grade the school was closed down. Don't ask me why: in 1927 colored asked fewer questions than they do now. Sometimes Maggie reads to me. She stumbles along good naturedly but can't see well. She knows she is not bright. Like good looks and money, quickness passed her by. She will marry John Thomas (who has mossy teeth in an earnest face) and then I'll be free to sit here and I guess just sing church songs to myself. Although I never was a good singer. Never could carry a tune. I was always better at a man's job. I used to love to milk till I was hooked[2] in the side in '49. Cows are soothing and slow and don't bother you, unless you try to milk them the wrong way.

I have deliberately turned my back on the house. It is three rooms, just like the one that burned, except the roof is tin; they don't make shingle roofs anymore. There are no real windows, just some holes cut in the sides, like the portholes in a ship, but not round and not square, with rawhide holding the shutters up on the outside. This house is in a pasture, too, like the other one. No doubt when Dee sees it she will want to tear it down. She wrote me once that no matter where we "choose" to live, she will manage to come see us. But she will never bring her friends. Maggie and I thought about this and Maggie asked me, "Mama, when did Dee ever *have* any friends?"

She had a few. Furtive boys in pink shirts hanging about on washday after school. Nervous girls who never laughed. Impressed with her they worshiped the well-turned phrase, the cute shape, the scalding humor that erupted like bubbles in lye. She read to them. 15

[2]That is, gored by the horn of a cow.

When she was courting Jimmy T she didn't have much time to pay to us, but turned all her faultfinding power on him. He *flew* to marry a cheap city girl from a family of ignorant flashy people. She hardly had time to recompose herself.

When she comes I will meet—but there they are!

Maggie attempts to make a dash for the house, in her shuffling way, but I stay her with my hand. "Come back here," I say. And she stops and tries to dig a well in the sand with her toe.

It is hard to see them clearly through the strong sun. But even the first glimpse of leg out of the car tells me it is Dee. Her feet were always neat-looking, as if God himself had shaped them with a certain style. From the other side of the car comes a short, stocky man. Hair is all over his head a foot long and hanging from his chin like a kinky mule tail. I hear Maggie suck in her breath. "Uhnnnh," is what it sounds like. Like when you see the wriggling end of a snake just in front of your foot on the road. "Uhnnnh."

Dee next. A dress down to the ground, in this hot weather. A dress so loud it hurts my eyes. There are yellows and oranges enough to throw back the light of the sun. I feel my whole face warming from the heat waves it throws out. Earrings gold, too, and hanging down to her shoulders. Bracelets dangling and making noises when she moves her arm up to shake the folds of the dress out of her armpits. The dress is loose and flows, and as she walks closer, I like it. I hear Maggie go "Uhnnnh" again. It is her sister's hair. It stands straight up like the wool on a sheep. It is black as night and around the edges are two long pigtails that rope about like small lizards disappearing behind her ears. 20

"Wa-su-zo-Tean-o!" she says, coming on in that gliding way the dress makes her move. The short stocky fellow with the hair to his navel is all grinning and he follows up with "Asalamalakim,[3] my mother and sister!" He moves to hug Maggie but she falls back, right up against the back of my chair. I feel her trembling there and when I look up I see the perspiration falling off her chin.

[3]Transliteration of a Muslim greeting; literally, "Peace be with you." "Wa-su-zo-Tean-o" is a similar rendering of a Ugandan salutation.

"Don't get up," says Dee. Since I am stout it takes something of a push. You can see me trying to move a second or two before I make it. She turns, showing white heels through her sandals, and goes back to the car. Out she peeks next with a Polaroid. She stoops down quickly and lines up picture after picture of me sitting there in front of the house with Maggie cowering behind me. She never takes a shot without making sure the house is included. When a cow comes nibbling around the edge of the yard she snaps it and me and Maggie *and* the house. Then she puts the Polaroid in the back seat of the car, and comes up and kisses me on the forehead.

Meanwhile Asalamalakim is going through motions with Maggie's hand. Maggie's hand is as limp as a fish, and probably as cold, despite the sweat, and she keeps trying to pull it back. It looks like Asalamalakim wants to shake hands but wants to do it fancy. Or maybe he don't know how people shake hands. Anyhow, he soon gives up on Maggie.

"Well," I say. "Dee."

"No, Mama," she says. "Not 'Dee,' Wangero Leewanika Kemanjo!" 25

"What happened to 'Dee'?" I wanted to know.

"She's dead," Wangero said. "I couldn't bear it any longer, being named after the people who oppress me."

"You know as well as me you was named after your aunt Dicie," I said. Dicie is my sister. She named Dee. We called her "Big Dee" after Dee was born.

"But who was *she* named after?" asked Wangero.

"I guess after Grandma Dee," I said. 30

"And who was she named after?" asked Wangero.

"Her mother," I said, and saw Wangero was getting tired. "That's about as far back as I can trace it," I said. Though, in fact, I probably could have carried it back beyond the Civil War through the branches.

"Well," said Asalamalakim, "there you are."

"Uhnnnh," I heard Maggie say.

"There I was not," I said, "before 'Dicie' cropped up in our family, 35 so why should I try to trace it that far back?"

He just stood there grinning, looking down on me like somebody inspecting a Model A car. Every once in a while he and Wangero sent eye signals over my head.

"How do you pronounce this name?" I asked.

"You don't have to call me by it if you don't want to," said Wangero.

"Why shouldn't I?" I asked. "If that's what you want us to call you, we'll call you."

"I know it might sound awkward at first," said Wangero. 40

"I'll get used to it," I said. "Ream it out again."

Well, soon we got the name out of the way. Asalamalakim had a name twice as long and three times as hard. After I tripped over it two or three times he told me to just call him Hakim-a-barber. I wanted to ask him was he a barber, but I didn't really think he was, so I didn't ask.

"You must belong to those beef-cattle peoples down the road," I said. They said "Asalamalakim" when they met you, too, but they didn't shake hands. Always too busy: feeding the cattle, fixing the fences, putting up salt-lick shelters, throwing down hay. When the white folks poisoned some of the herd the men stayed up all night with rifles in their hands. I walked a mile and a half just to see the sight.

Hakim-a-barber said, "I accept some of their doctrines, but farming and raising cattle is not my style." (They didn't tell me, and I didn't ask, whether Wangero (Dee) had really gone and married him.)

We sat down to eat and right away he said he didn't eat collards and pork was unclean. Wangero, though, went on through the chitlins and corn bread, the greens and everything else. She talked a blue streak over the sweet potatoes. Everything delighted her. Even the fact that we still used the benches her daddy made for the table when we couldn't afford to buy chairs. 45

"Oh, Mama!" she cried. Then turned to Hakim-a-barber. "I never knew how lovely these benches are. You can feel the rump prints," she said running her hands underneath her and along the bench. Then she gave a sigh and her hand closed over Grandma Dee's butter dish. "That's it!" she said. "I knew there was something I wanted to ask you if I could have." She jumped up from the table and went over in the corner where the churn stood, the milk in it clabber[4] by now. She looked at the churn and looked at it.

[4]Curdled.

"This churn top is what I need," she said. "Didn't Uncle Buddy whittle it out of a tree you all used to have?"

"Yes," I said.

"Uh huh," she said happily. "And I want the dasher,[5] too."

"Uncle Buddy whittle that, too?" asked the barber. 50

Dee (Wangero) looked up at me.

"Aunt Dee's first husband whittled the dash," said Maggie so low you almost couldn't hear her. "His name was Henry, but they called him Stash."

"Maggie's brain is like an elephant's," Wangero said, laughing. "I can use the churn top as a centerpiece for the alcove table," she said, sliding a plate over the churn, "and I'll think of something artistic to do with the dasher."

When she finished wrapping the dasher the handle stuck out. I took it for a moment in my hands. You didn't even have to look close to see where hands pushing the dasher up and down to make butter had left a kind of sink in the wood. In fact, there were a lot of small sinks; you could see where thumbs and fingers had sunk into the wood. It was beautiful light yellow wood, from a tree that grew in the yard where Big Dee and Stash had lived.

After dinner Dee (Wangero) went to the trunk at the foot of my bed 55 and started rifling through it. Maggie hung back in the kitchen over the dishpan. Out came Wangero with two quilts. They had been pieced by Grandma Dee and then Big Dee and me had hung them on the quilt frames on the front porch and quilted them. One was in the Lone Star pattern. The other was Walk Around the Mountain. In both of them were scraps of dresses Grandma Dee had worn fifty and more years ago. Bits and pieces of Grandpa Jarrell's Paisley shirts. And one teeny faded blue piece, about the size of a penny matchbox, that was from Great Grandpa Ezra's uniform that he wore in the Civil War.

"Mama," Wangero said sweet as a bird. "Can I have these old quilts?"

I heard something fall in the kitchen, and a minute later the kitchen door slammed.

[5]A device for stirring the cream in a churn.

"Why don't you take one or two of the others?" I asked. "These old things was just done by me and Big Dee from some tops your grandma pieced before she died."

"No," said Wangero. "I don't want those. They are stitched around the borders by machine."

"That'll make them last better," I said. 60

"That's not the point," said Wangero. "These are all pieces of dresses Grandma used to wear. She did all this stitching by hand. Imagine!" She held the quilts securely in her arms, stroking them.

"Some of the pieces, like those lavender ones, come from old clothes her mother handed down to her," I said, moving up to touch the quilts. Dee (Wangero) moved back just enough so that I couldn't reach the quilts. They already belonged to her.

"Imagine!" she breathed again, clutching them closely to her bosom.

"The truth is," I said, "I promised to give them quilts to Maggie, for when she marries John Thomas."

She gasped like a bee had stung her. 65

"Maggie can't appreciate these quilts!" she said. "She'd probably be backward enough to put them to everyday use."

"I reckon she would," I said. "God knows I been saving 'em for long enough with nobody using 'em. I hope she will!" I didn't want to bring up how I had offered Dee (Wangero) a quilt when she went away to college. Then she had told me they were old-fashioned, out of style.

"But they're *priceless*!" she was saying now, furiously; for she has a temper. "Maggie would put them on the bed and in five years they'd be in rags. Less than that!"

"She can always make some more," I said. "Maggie knows how to quilt."

Dee (Wangero) looked at me with hatred. "You just will not understand. The point is these quilts, *these* quilts!" 70

"Well," I said, stumped. "What would *you* do with them?"

"Hang them," she said. As if that was the only thing you *could* do with quilts.

Maggie by now was standing in the door. I could almost hear the sound her feet made as they scraped over each other.

"She can have them, Mama," she said, like somebody used to never winning anything, or having anything reserved for her. "I can 'member Grandma Dee without the quilts."

I looked at her hard. She had filled her bottom lip with checkerberry snuff and it gave her a face a kind of dopey, hangdog look. It was Grandma Dee and Big Dee who taught her how to quilt herself. She stood there with her scarred hands hidden in the folds of her skirt. She looked at her sister with something like fear but she wasn't mad at her. This was Maggie's portion. This was the way she knew God to work. 75

When I looked at her like that something hit me in the top of my head and ran down to the soles of my feet. Just like when I'm in church and the spirit of God touches me and I get happy and shout. I did something I never had done before: hugged Maggie to me, then dragged her on into the room, snatched the quilts out of Miss Wangero's hands and dumped them into Maggie's lap. Maggie just sat there on my bed with her mouth open.

"Take one or two of the others," I said to Dee.

But she turned without a word and went out to Hakim-a-barber.

"You just don't understand," she said, as Maggie and I came out to the car.

"What don't I understand?" I wanted to know. 80

"Your heritage," she said. And then she turned to Maggie, kissed her, and said, "You ought to try to make something of yourself, too, Maggie. It's really a new day for us. But from the way you and Mama still live you'd never know it."

She put on some sunglasses that hid everything above the tip of her nose and her chin.

Maggie smiled; maybe at the sunglasses. But a real smile, not scared. After we watched the car dust settle I asked Maggie to bring me a dip of snuff. And then the two of us sat there just enjoying, until it was time to go in the house and go to bed.

VIRGINIA WOOLF { *The Death of the Moth*

VIRGINIA WOOLF (1882–1941), English novelist, feminist essayist, and literary critic, was born into a respected literary family in London. She was educated by her father and private tutors and by reading extensively in her father's large library. As part of the Bloomsbury group—an influential community of experimental artists and writers who lived in and around London in the early twentieth century—Woolf led an intellectually rich, if unconventional, life. She began writing for the *Times Literary Supplement* in 1905 and, with her husband Leonard Woolf, founded the Hogarth Press, which published works by T. S. Eliot and Sigmund Freud. In addition to writing many novels, Woolf authored *A Room of One's Own* (1929), a seminal feminist work in which she argues that if a woman is to write, she must have "money and a room of her own"—in other words, she must be both financially and intellectually independent.

The following essay originally appeared in *The Death of the Moth and Other Essays* (1942). In it, Woolf contemplates the nature of life and death as she watches a moth die on her windowsill. When Woolf first observes the moth flying back and forth on her windowpane, it is merely a curiosity; however, as the moth begins to die, its struggle becomes richly symbolic for her. As you read, pay particular attention to the language Woolf uses to describe life, death, and the moth's final moments. Consider how word choice reveals her purpose.

MOTHS THAT FLY BY DAY are not properly to be called moths; they do not excite that pleasant sense of dark autumn nights and ivy-blossom which the commonest yellow-underwing asleep in the shadow of the curtain never fails to rouse in us. They are hybrid creatures, neither gay like butterflies nor somber like their own species. Nevertheless the present specimen, with his narrow hay-coloured wings, fringed with a tassel of the same colour, seemed to be content with life. It was a pleasant morning, mid-September, mild, benignant, yet with a keener breath than that of the summer months. The plough was already scoring the field opposite the window, and where the share[1] had been, the earth was pressed flat and gleamed with moisture. Such vigour came rolling in from the fields and the down[2] beyond that it was difficult to keep the eyes strictly turned upon the book. The rooks too were keeping one of their annual festivities; soaring round the tree tops until it looked as if a vast net with thousands of black knots in it had been cast up into the air; which, after a few moments sank slowly down upon the trees until every twig seemed to have a knot at the end of it. Then, suddenly, the net would be thrown into the air again in a wider circle this time, with the utmost clamour and vociferation, as though to be thrown into the air and settle slowly down upon the tree tops were a tremendously exciting experience.

The same energy which inspired the rooks, the ploughmen, the horses, and even, it seemed, the lean bare-backed downs, sent the moth fluttering from side to side of his square of the window-pane. One could not help watching him. One was, indeed, conscious of a queer feeling of pity for him. The possibilities of pleasure seemed that morning so enormous and so various that to have only a moth's part in life, and a day moth's at that, appeared a hard fate, and his zest in enjoying his meagre opportunities to the full, pathetic. He flew vigorously to one corner of his compartment, and, after waiting there a second, flew across to the other. What remained for him but to fly to a third corner and then to a fourth? That was all he could do, in spite of the size of the downs, the width of the sky, the far-off smoke of houses, and the romantic voice, now and then, of a steamer out at sea. What he could do he did. Watching him, it seemed as if a fibre, very thin but pure, of the enormous energy of the world had been thrust into his frail and

[1]That is, the blade of the plow ("plough"), which cuts and turns the soil.
[2]Hill.

diminutive body. As often as he crossed the pane, I could fancy that a thread of vital light became visible. He was little or nothing but life.

Yet, because he was so small, and so simple a form of the energy that was rolling in at the open window and driving its way through so many narrow and intricate corridors in my own brain and in those of other human beings, there was something marvellous as well as pathetic about him. It was as if someone had taken a tiny bead of pure life and decking it as lightly as possible with down and feathers, had set it dancing and zigzagging to show us the true nature of life. Thus displayed one could not get over the strangeness of it. One is apt to forget all about life, seeing it humped and bossed and garnished and cumbered so that it has to move with the greatest circumspection and dignity. Again, the thought of all that life might have been had he been born in any other shape caused one to view his simple activities with a kind of pity.

After a time, tired by his dancing apparently, he settled on the window ledge in the sun, and, the queer spectacle being at an end, I forgot about him. Then, looking up, my eye was caught by him. He was trying to resume his dancing, but seemed either so stiff or so awkward that he could only flutter to the bottom of the window-pane; and when he tried to fly across it he failed. Being intent on other matters I watched these futile attempts for a time without thinking, unconsciously waiting for him to resume his flight, as one waits for a machine, that has stopped momentarily, to start again without considering the reason of its failure. After perhaps a seventh attempt he slipped from the wooden ledge and fell, fluttering his wings, on to his back on the window sill. The helplessness of his attitude roused me. It flashed upon me that he was in difficulties; he could no longer raise himself; his legs struggled vainly. But, as I stretched out a pencil, meaning to help him to right himself, it came over me that the failure and awkwardness were the approach of death. I laid the pencil down again.

The legs agitated themselves once more. I looked as if for the enemy against which he struggled. I looked out of doors. What had happened there? Presumably it was midday, and work in the fields had stopped. Stillness and quiet had replaced the previous animation. The birds had taken themselves off to feed in the brooks. The horses stood still. 5

Yet the power was there all the same, massed outside indifferent, impersonal, not attending to anything in particular. Somehow it was opposed to the little hay-coloured moth. It was useless to try to do anything. One could only watch the extraordinary efforts made by those tiny legs against an oncoming doom which could, had it chosen, have submerged an entire city, not merely a city, but masses of human beings; nothing, I knew, had any chance against death. Nevertheless after a pause of exhaustion the legs fluttered again. It was superb this last protest, and so frantic that he succeeded at last in righting himself. One's sympathies, of course, were all on the side of life. Also, when there was nobody to care or to know, this gigantic effort on the part of an insignificant little moth, against a power of such magnitude, to retain what no one else valued or desired to keep, moved one strangely. Again, somehow, one saw life, a pure bead. I lifted the pencil again, useless though I knew it to be. But even as I did so, the unmistakable tokens of death showed themselves. The body relaxed, and instantly grew stiff. The struggle was over. The insignificant little creature now knew death. As I looked at the dead moth, this minute wayside triumph of so great a force over so mean[3] an antagonist filled me with wonder. Just as life had been strange a few minutes before, so death was now as strange. The moth having righted himself now lay most decently and uncomplainingly composed. O yes, he seemed to say, death is stronger than I am.

[3]That is, lowly or insignificant.

WILLIAM BUTLER YEATS { *The Second Coming*

WILLIAM BUTLER YEATS (1865–1939), Irish dramatist and poet, was born to a prosperous Protestant family of artists and merchants. He immersed himself in the complex politics of his time as Irish nationalists struggled to free Ireland from British rule, and though he was ambivalent about its factionalism, he embraced Ireland's cultural identity and incorporated Irish legends, mythology, and history into his poems and plays. Late in life he served two terms in the Senate of the newly independent Irish Republic. Although mainstream Christianity never held much interest for Yeats, he was fascinated by spiritualism and the occult, and much of his writing reflects religious themes. In 1923 Yeats was awarded the Nobel Prize in Literature for what the Nobel committee called his "inspired poetry, which in a highly artistic form gives expression to the spirit of a whole nation."

In "The Second Coming," one of his most anthologized poems, Yeats evokes an apocalyptic vision in which the modern world's turmoil ushers in an era not of Christian redemption but of "anarchy" and "darkness." As you read, pay particular attention to the way Yeats paces the poem to create first a sense of almost panicky urgency and then a slowly dawning awareness of what cannot be stopped.

Turning and turning in the widening gyre[1]
The falcon cannot hear the falconer;
Things fall apart; the centre cannot hold;
Mere anarchy is loosed upon the world,

[1] A vast circle or spiral, Yeats's image in many of his poems for the turnings and patterns of history.

The blood-dimmed tide is loosed, and everywhere 5
The ceremony of innocence is drowned;
The best lack all conviction, while the worst
Are full of passionate intensity.

Surely some revelation is at hand;
Surely the Second Coming[2] is at hand. 10
The Second Coming! Hardly are those words out
When a vast image out of Spiritus Mundi[3]
Troubles my sight: a waste of desert sand;
A shape with lion body and the head of a man,
A gaze blank and pitiless as the sun, 15
Is moving its slow thighs, while all about it
Wind shadows of the indignant desert birds.

The darkness drops again but now I know
That twenty centuries of stony sleep
Were vexed to nightmare by a rocking cradle, 20
And what rough beast, its hour come round at last,
Slouches towards Bethlehem to be born?

[2]That is, of Jesus Christ.
[3]The spirit of the world (Latin).